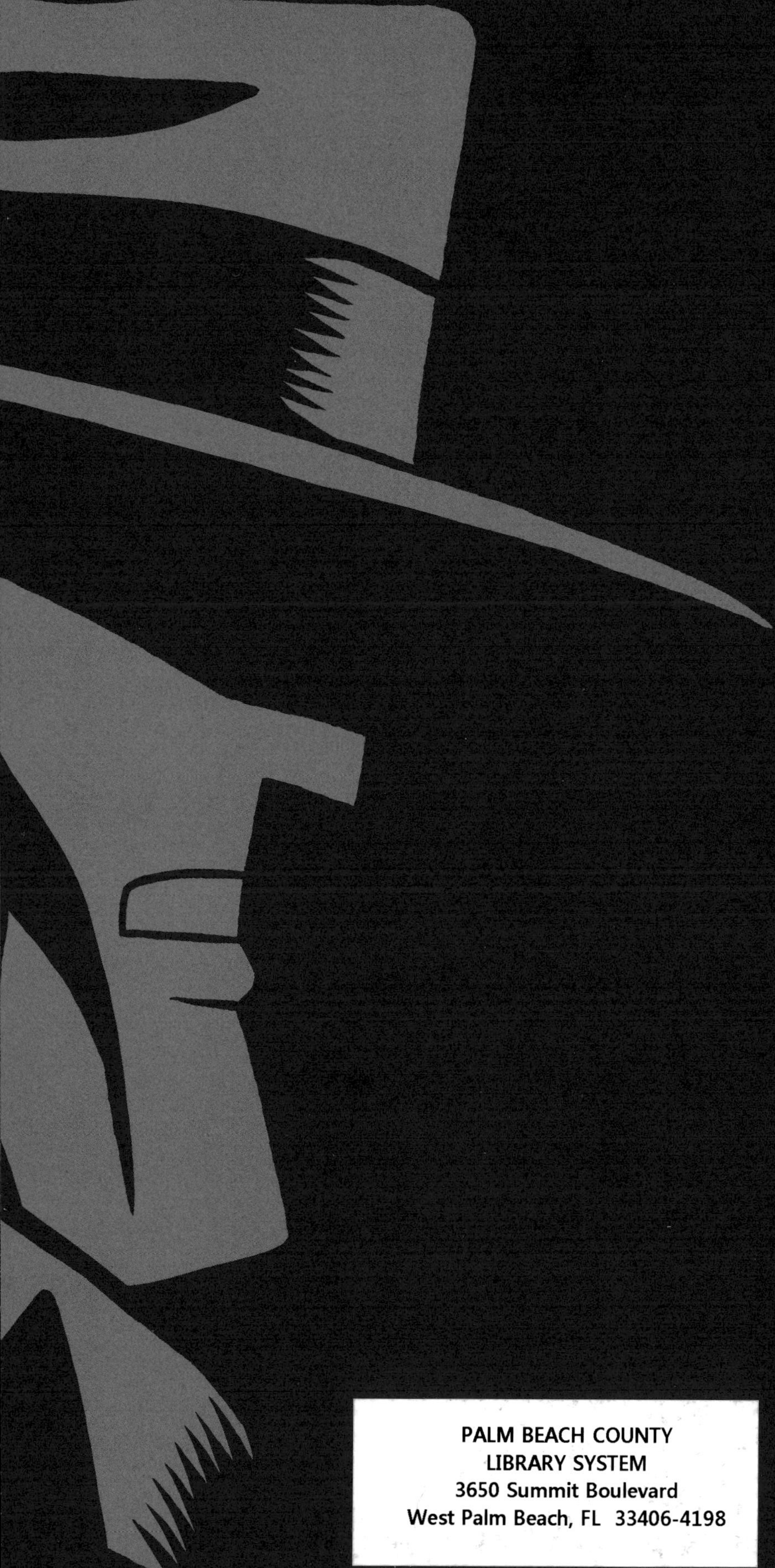

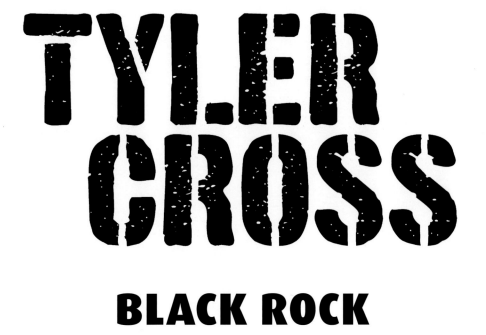

TYLER CROSS

BLACK ROCK

Titan® COMICS

ALSO FROM TITAN COMICS AND HARD CASE CRIME

GRAPHIC NOVELS

THE ASSIGNMENT

BABYLON BERLIN

MICKEY SPILLANE'S MIKE HAMMER

MILLENNIUM: THE GIRL WITH THE DRAGON TATTOO

MILLENNIUM: THE GIRL WHO PLAYED WITH FIRE

MILLENNIUM: THE GIRL WHO KICKED THE HORNET'S NEST

MILLENNIUM: THE GIRL WHO DANCED WITH DEATH

MINKY WOODCOCK: THE GIRL WHO HANDCUFFED HOUDINI

NORMANDY GOLD

PEEPLAND

THE PRAGUE COUP

QUARRY'S WAR

TRIGGERMAN

TYLER CROSS: BLACK ROCK

TYLER CROSS: ANGOLA

NOVELS

361

A DIET OF TREACLE

A TOUCH OF DEATH

A WALK AMONG THE TOMBSTONES

BABY MOLL

BINARY

BLACKMAILER

BLOOD ON THE MINK

BORDERLINE

BRAINQUAKE

BRANDED WOMAN

BUST

CASINO MOON

CHARLESGATE CONFIDENTIAL

CHOKE HOLD

THE COCKTAIL WAITRESS

THE COMEDY IS FINISHED

THE CONFESSION

THE CONSUMMATA

THE CORPSE WORE PASTIES

THE COUNT OF 9

CUT ME IN

THE CUTIE

THE DEAD MAN'S BROTHER

DEAD STREET

DEADLY BELOVED

DRUG OF CHOICE

DUTCH UNCLE

EASY DEATH

EASY GO

FADE TO BLONDE

FAKE I.D.

FALSE NEGATIVE

FIFTY-TO-ONE

FOREVER AND A DEATH

GETTING OFF: A NOVEL OF SEX AND VIOLENCE

THE GIRL WITH THE DEEP BLUE EYES

THE GIRL WITH THE LONG GREEN HEART

GRAVE DESCEND

GRIFTER'S GAME

GUN WORK

THE GUTTER AND THE GRAVE

HELP I AM BEING HELD PRISONER

HOME IS THE SAILOR

HONEY IN HIS MOUTH

HOUSE DICK

JOYLAND

KILL NOW PAY LATER

KILLING CASTRO

THE KNIFE SLIPPED

THE LAST MATCH

THE LAST STAND

LEMONS NEVER LIE

LITTLE GIRL LOST

LOSERS LIVE LONGER

LUCKY AT CARDS

THE MAX

MEMORY

MONEY SHOT

MURDER IS MY BUSINESS

THE NICE GUYS

NIGHT WALKER

NO HOUSE LIMIT

NOBODY'S ANGEL

ODDS ON

PASSPORT TO PERIL

PIMP

PLUNDER OF THE SUN

ROBBIE'S WIFE

SAY IT WITH BULLETS

SCRATCH ONE

THE SECRET LIVES OF MARRIED WOMEN

SEDUCTION OF THE INNOCENT

SINNER MAN

SLIDE

SNATCH

SO MANY DOORS

SO NUDE, SO DEAD

SOHO SINS

SOMEBODY OWES ME MONEY

SONGS OF INNOCENCE

STOP THIS MAN!

STRAIGHT CUT

THIEVES FALL OUT

TOP OF THE HEAP

TURN ON THE HEAT

THE TWENTY-YEAR DEATH

TWO FOR THE MONEY

UNDERSTUDY FOR DEATH

THE VALLEY OF FEAR

THE VENGEFUL VIRGIN

THE VENOM BUSINESS

WEB OF THE CITY

WITNESS TO MYSELF

THE WOUNDED AND THE SLAIN

ZERO COOL

QUARRY

THE FIRST QUARRY

THE LAST QUARRY

QUARRY

QUARRY'S CHOICE

QUARRY'S CLIMAX

QUARRY'S CUT

QUARRY'S DEAL

QUARRY'S EX

QUARRY'S LIST

QUARRY'S VOTE

QUARRY IN THE BLACK

QUARRY IN THE MIDDLE

THE WRONG QUARRY

ALSO FROM TITAN COMICS AND FABIEN NURY.

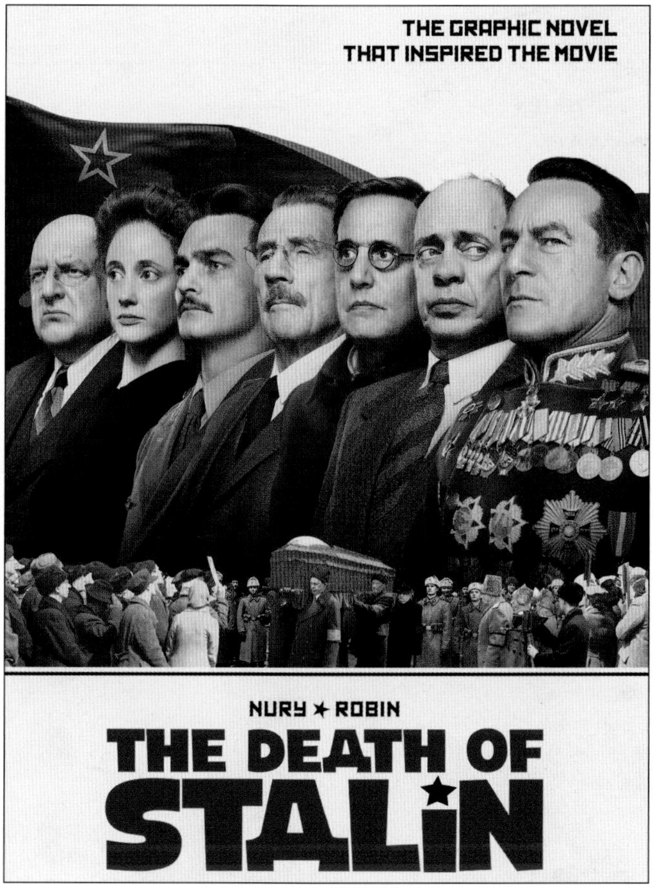
THE GRAPHIC NOVEL
THAT INSPIRED THE MOVIE
NURY ★ ROBIN
THE DEATH OF STALIN

THE DEATH OF STALIN

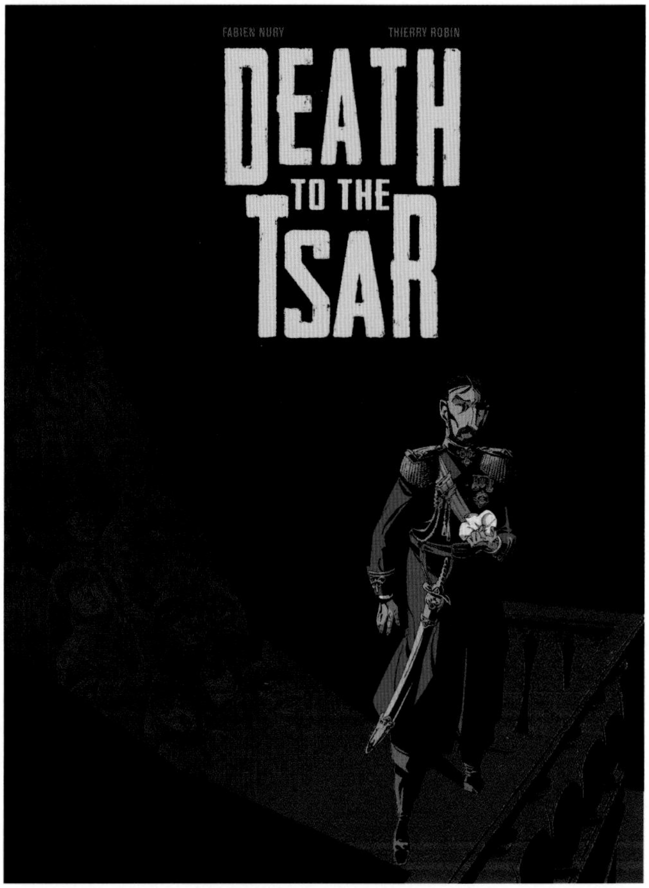
FABIEN NURY
THIERRY ROBIN
DEATH TO THE TSAR

DEATH TO THE TSAR

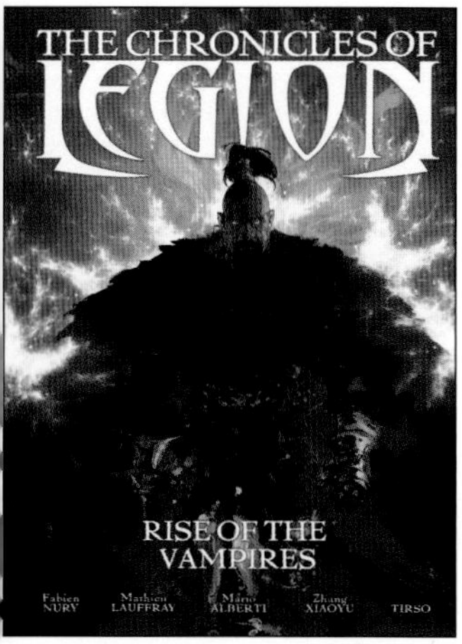
THE CHRONICLES OF LEGION
RISE OF THE VAMPIRES
Fabien NURY
Mathieu LAUFFRAY
Mario ALBERTI
Zhang XIAOYU
TIRSO

THE CHRONICLES OF LEGION - BOOK 1: RISE OF THE VAMPIRES

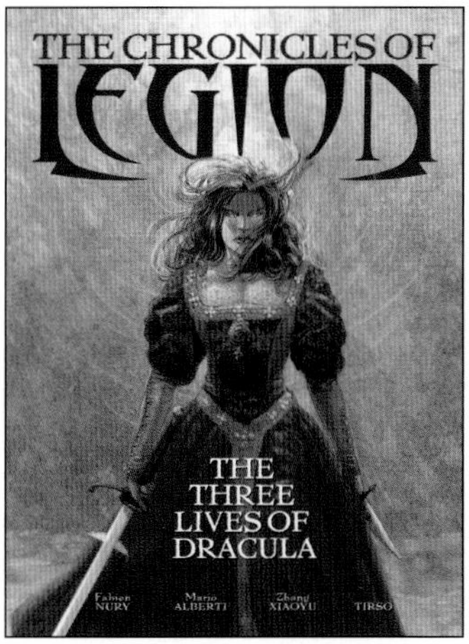
THE CHRONICLES OF LEGION
THE THREE LIVES OF DRACULA
Fabien NURY
Mario ALBERTI
Zhang XIAOYU
TIRSO

THE CHRONICLES OF LEGION - BOOK 2: THE THREE LIVES OF DRACULA

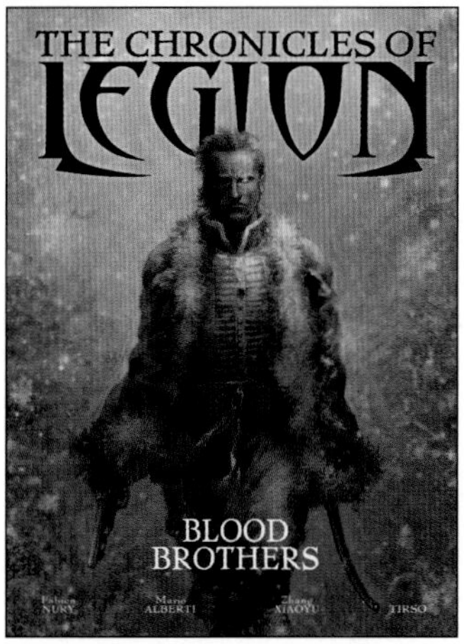
THE CHRONICLES OF LEGION
BLOOD BROTHERS

THE CHRONICLES OF LEGION - BOOK 3: THE BLOOD BROTHERS

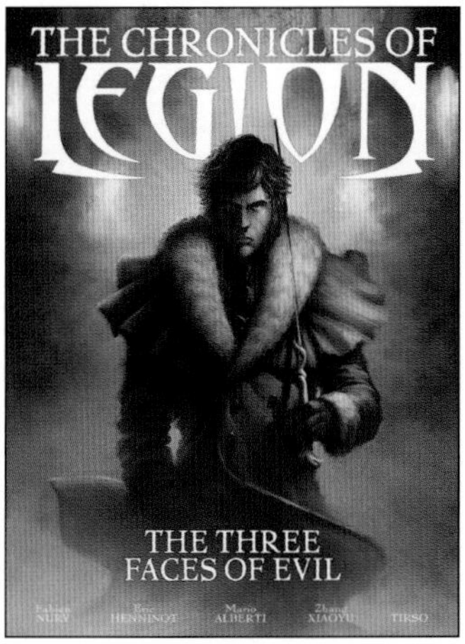
THE CHRONICLES OF LEGION
THE THREE FACES OF EVIL

THE CHRONICLES OF LEGION - BOOK 4: THE THREE FACES OF EVIL

WWW.TITAN-COMICS.COM

TYLER CROSS
BLACK ROCK

TITAN COMICS

COLLECTION EDITOR: **JONATHAN STEVENSON**
DESIGN: **WILFRIED TSHIKANA-EKUTSHU**
TRANSLATION: **N. COLMER**

Consulting Editor: **Charles Ardai**
Line Editor: **Tom Williams**

Managing & Launch Editor: **Andrew James**
Editorial Assistant: **Dan Boultwood**
Senior Production Controller: **Jackie Flook**
Production Supervisor: **Maria Pearson**
Production Controller: **Peter James**
Production Assistant: **Rhiannon Roy**
Art Director: **Oz Browne**
Senior Sales Manager: **Steve Tothill**
Circulation Executive: **Frances Hallam**
Press Officer: **Will O'Mullane**
Direct Sales & Marketing Manager: **Ricky Claydon**
Brand Manager: **Chris Thompson**
Commercial Manager: **Michelle Fairlamb**
Ads & Marketing Assistant: **Bella Hoy**
Publishing Manager: **Darryl Tothill**
Publishing Director: **Chris Teather**
Operations Director: **Leigh Baulch**
Executive Director: **Vivian Cheung**
Publisher: **Nick Landau**

TYLER CROSS: BLACK ROCK

9781785867309
Published by Titan Comics
A division of Titan Publishing Group Ltd.
144 Southwark St, London, SE1 0UP.
Titan Comics is a registered trademark of
Titan Publishing Group, Ltd. All rights reserved.

Originally published in French © 2015 DARGAUD - BRÜNO & NURY. All rights reserved.
The name *Hard Case Crime* and the Hard Case Crime logo are trademarks of Winterfall LLC. Hard Case Crime
Comics are produced with editorial guidance from Charles Ardai.

A CIP catalogue record for this title is available from the British Library

10 9 8 7 6 5 4 3 2 1
First Published September 2018
Printed in China.
Titan Comics.

WWW.TITAN-COMICS.COM
Follow us on Twitter @ComicsTitan
Visit us at facebook.com/comicstitan

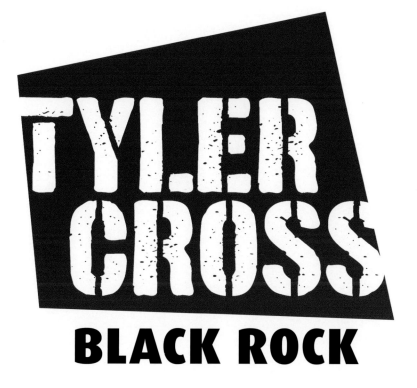

BLACK ROCK

WRITER
FABIEN NURY

ART
BRÜNO

COLORS
LAURENCE CROIX

1. HEIST

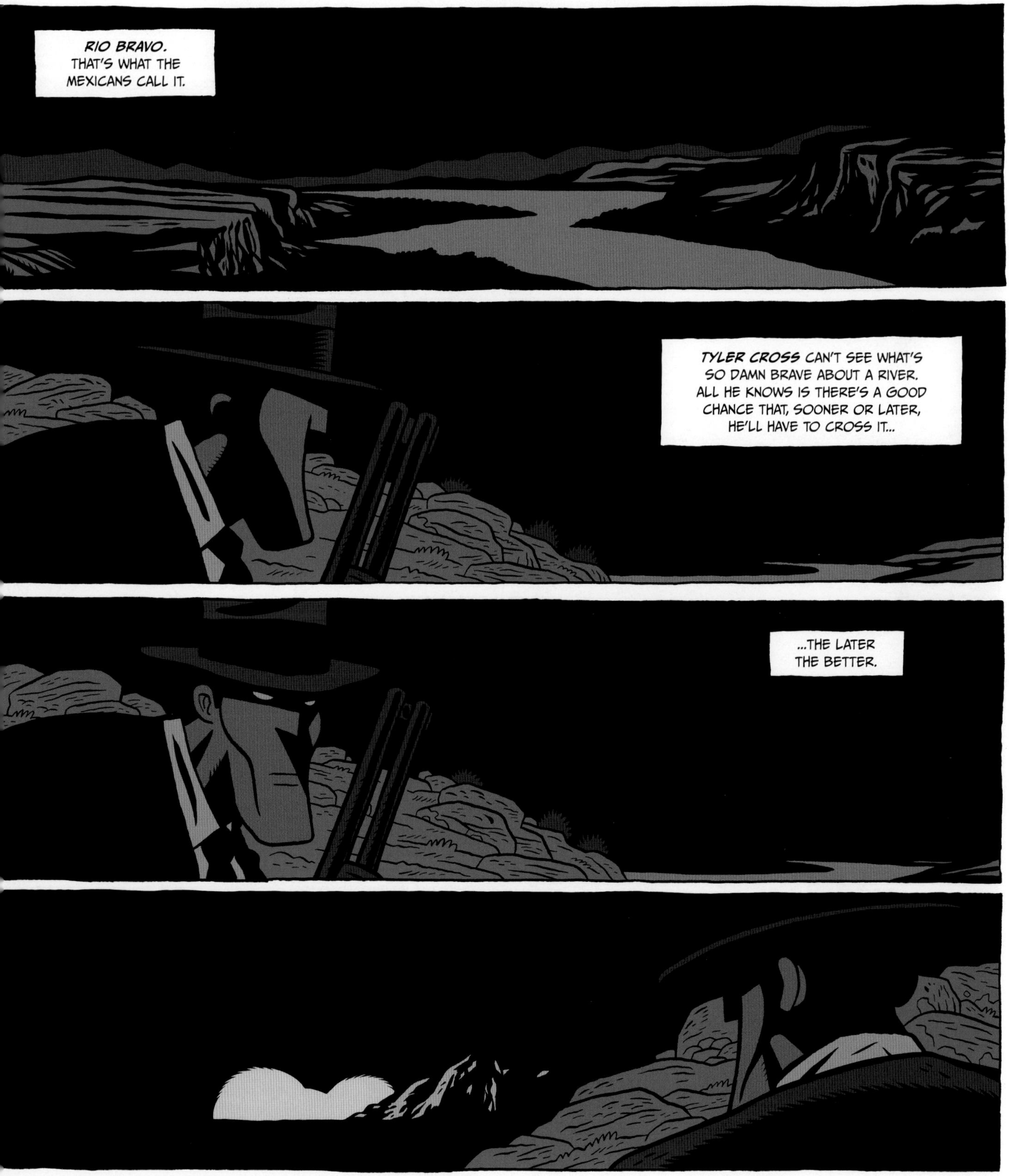
RIO BRAVO. THAT'S WHAT THE MEXICANS CALL IT.
TYLER CROSS CAN'T SEE WHAT'S SO DAMN BRAVE ABOUT A RIVER. ALL HE KNOWS IS THERE'S A GOOD CHANCE THAT, SOONER OR LATER, HE'LL HAVE TO CROSS IT...
...THE LATER THE BETTER.

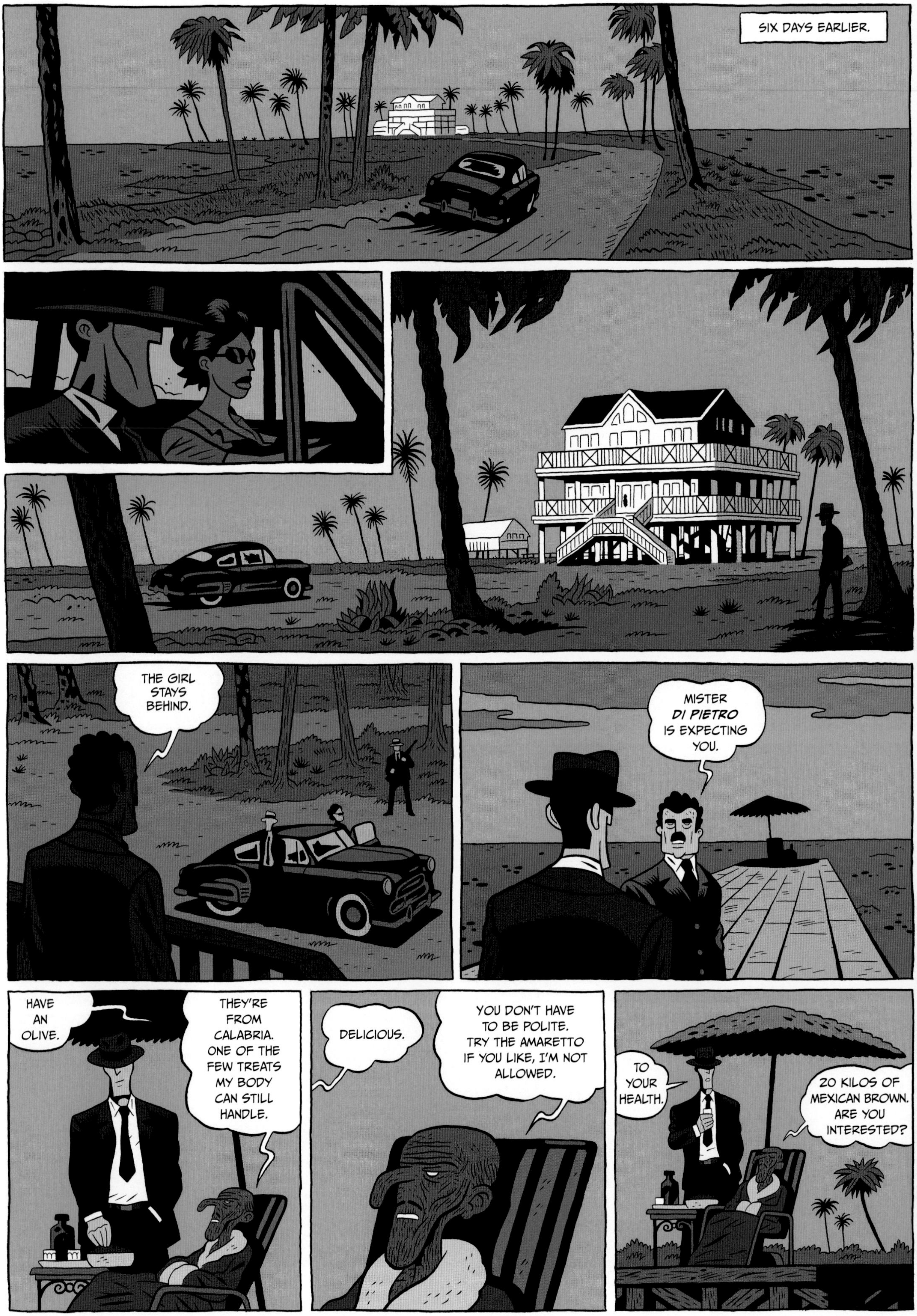
SIX DAYS EARLIER.
THE GIRL STAYS BEHIND.
MISTER DI PIETRO IS EXPECTING YOU.
HAVE AN OLIVE.
THEY'RE FROM CALABRIA. ONE OF THE FEW TREATS MY BODY CAN STILL HANDLE.
DELICIOUS.
YOU DON'T HAVE TO BE POLITE. TRY THE AMARETTO IF YOU LIKE, I'M NOT ALLOWED.
TO YOUR HEALTH.
20 KILOS OF MEXICAN BROWN. ARE YOU INTERESTED?

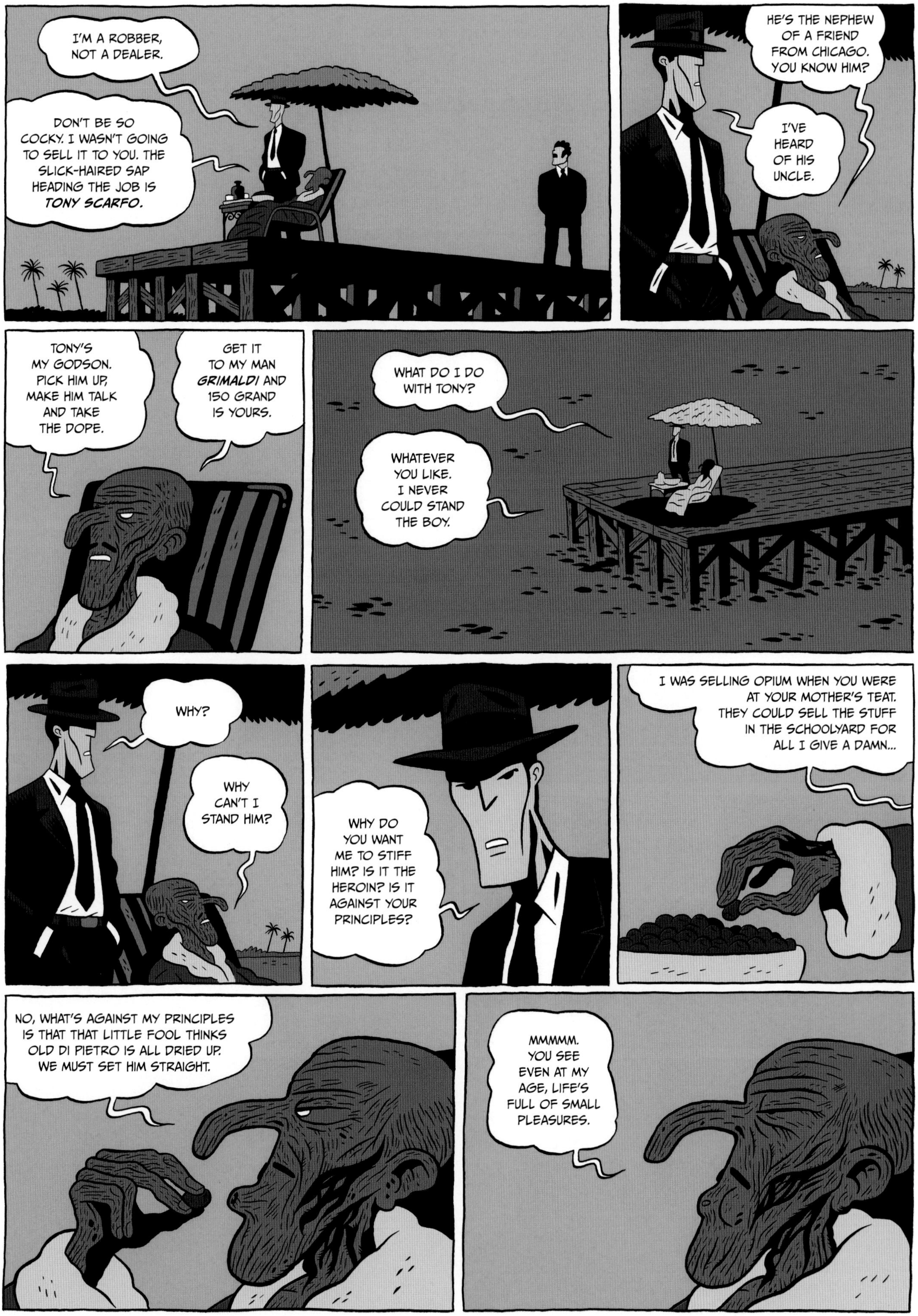

I'M A ROBBER, NOT A DEALER.
DON'T BE SO COCKY. I WASN'T GOING TO SELL IT TO YOU. THE SLICK-HAIRED SAP HEADING THE JOB IS *TONY SCARFO.*
HE'S THE NEPHEW OF A FRIEND FROM CHICAGO. YOU KNOW HIM?
I'VE HEARD OF HIS UNCLE.
TONY'S MY GODSON. PICK HIM UP, MAKE HIM TALK AND TAKE THE DOPE.
GET IT TO MY MAN *GRIMALDI* AND 150 GRAND IS YOURS.
WHAT DO I DO WITH TONY?
WHATEVER YOU LIKE. I NEVER COULD STAND THE BOY.
WHY?
WHY CAN'T I STAND HIM?
WHY DO YOU WANT ME TO STIFF HIM? IS IT THE HEROIN? IS IT AGAINST YOUR PRINCIPLES?
I WAS SELLING OPIUM WHEN YOU WERE AT YOUR MOTHER'S TEAT. THEY COULD SELL THE STUFF IN THE SCHOOLYARD FOR ALL I GIVE A DAMN...
NO, WHAT'S AGAINST MY PRINCIPLES IS THAT THAT LITTLE FOOL THINKS OLD DI PIETRO IS ALL DRIED UP. WE MUST SET HIM STRAIGHT.
MMMMM. YOU SEE EVEN AT MY AGE, LIFE'S FULL OF SMALL PLEASURES.

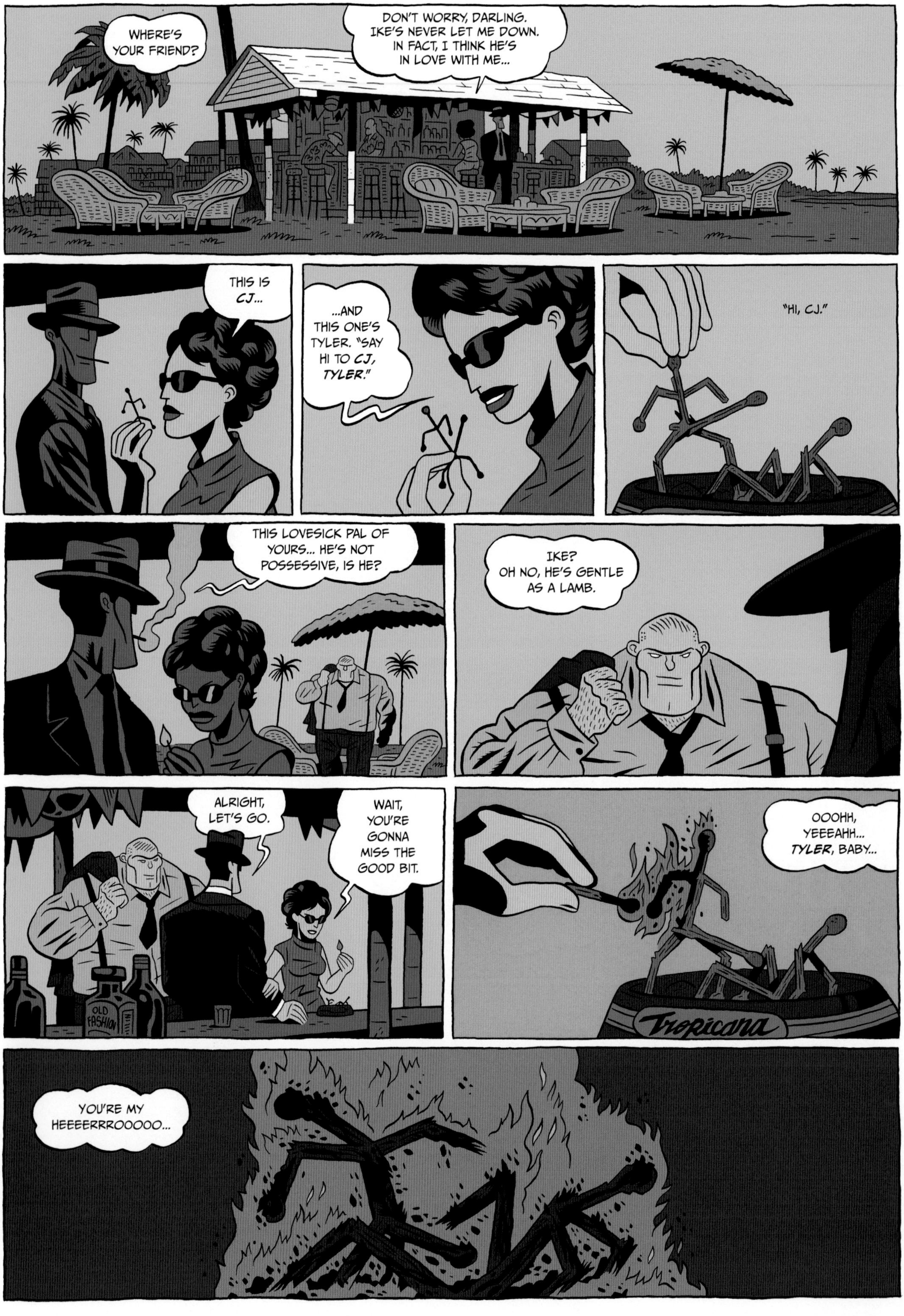
WHERE'S YOUR FRIEND?
DON'T WORRY, DARLING. IKE'S NEVER LET ME DOWN. IN FACT, I THINK HE'S IN LOVE WITH ME...
THIS IS CJ...
...AND THIS ONE'S TYLER. "SAY HI TO CJ, TYLER."
"HI, CJ."
THIS LOVESICK PAL OF YOURS... HE'S NOT POSSESSIVE, IS HE?
IKE? OH NO, HE'S GENTLE AS A LAMB.
ALRIGHT, LET'S GO.
WAIT, YOU'RE GONNA MISS THE GOOD BIT.
OLD FASHION
OOOHH, YEEEAHH... TYLER, BABY...
Tropicana
YOU'RE MY HEEEERRROOOOO...

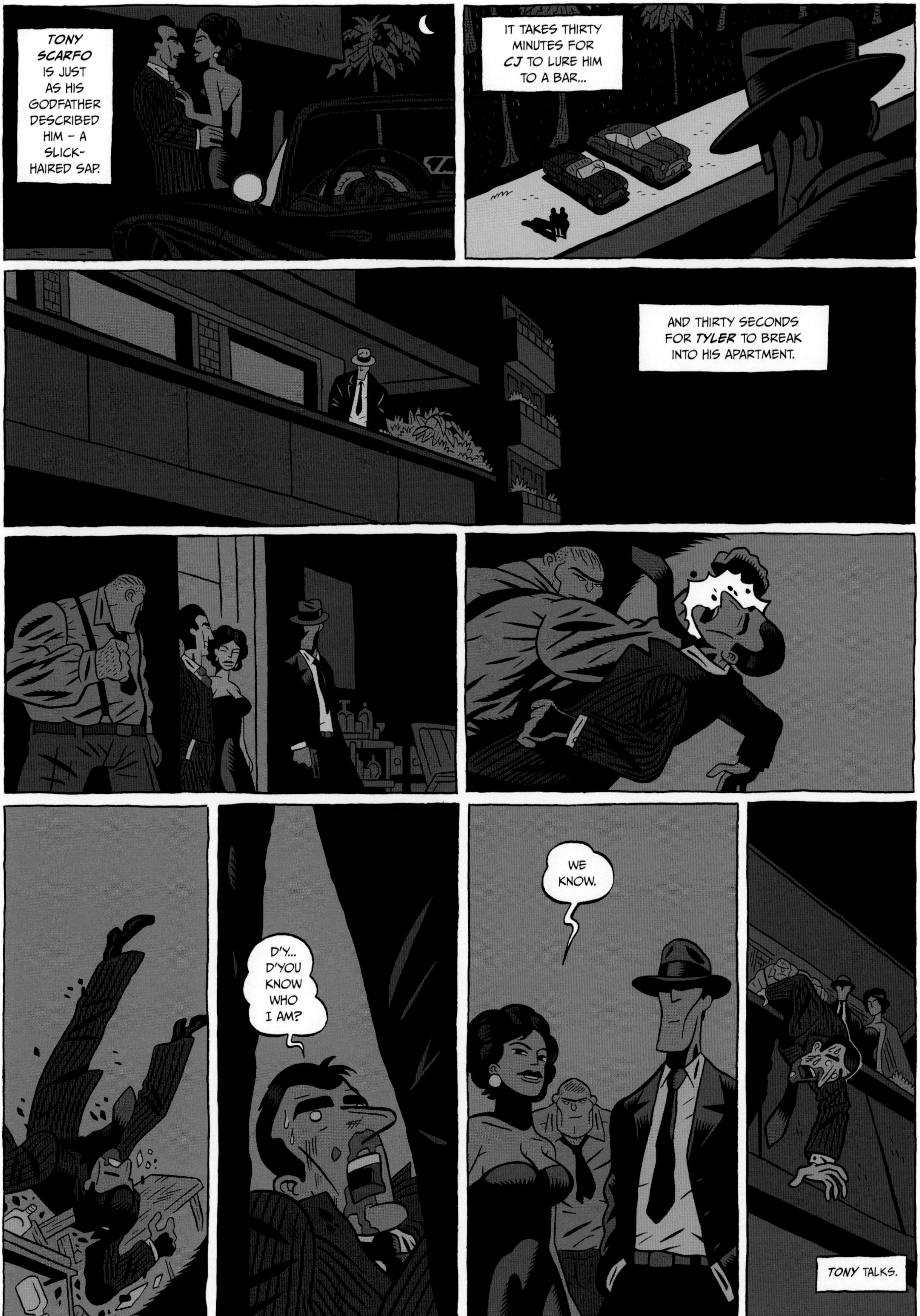

TONY SCARFO IS JUST AS HIS GODFATHER DESCRIBED HIM – A SLICK-HAIRED SAP.
IT TAKES THIRTY MINUTES FOR CJ TO LURE HIM TO A BAR...
AND THIRTY SECONDS FOR TYLER TO BREAK INTO HIS APARTMENT.
D'Y... D'YOU KNOW WHO I AM?
WE KNOW.
TONY TALKS.

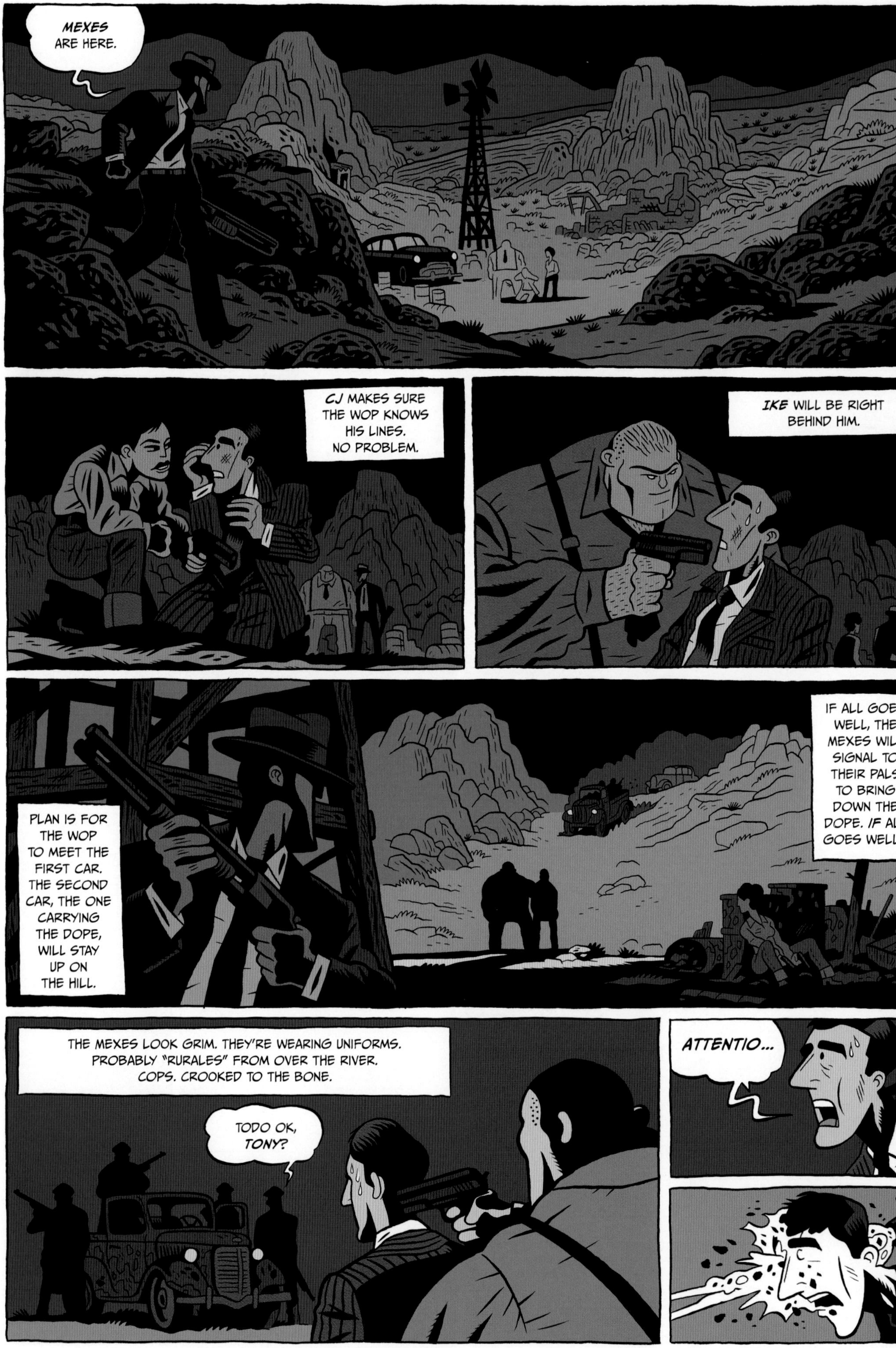
MEXES ARE HERE.
CJ MAKES SURE THE WOP KNOWS HIS LINES. NO PROBLEM.
IKE WILL BE RIGHT BEHIND HIM.
PLAN IS FOR THE WOP TO MEET THE FIRST CAR. THE SECOND CAR, THE ONE CARRYING THE DOPE, WILL STAY UP ON THE HILL.
IF ALL GOES WELL, THE MEXES WILL SIGNAL TO THEIR PALS TO BRING DOWN THE DOPE. IF ALL GOES WELL...
THE MEXES LOOK GRIM. THEY'RE WEARING UNIFORMS. PROBABLY "RURALES" FROM OVER THE RIVER. COPS. CROOKED TO THE BONE.
TODO OK, TONY?
ATTENTIO...

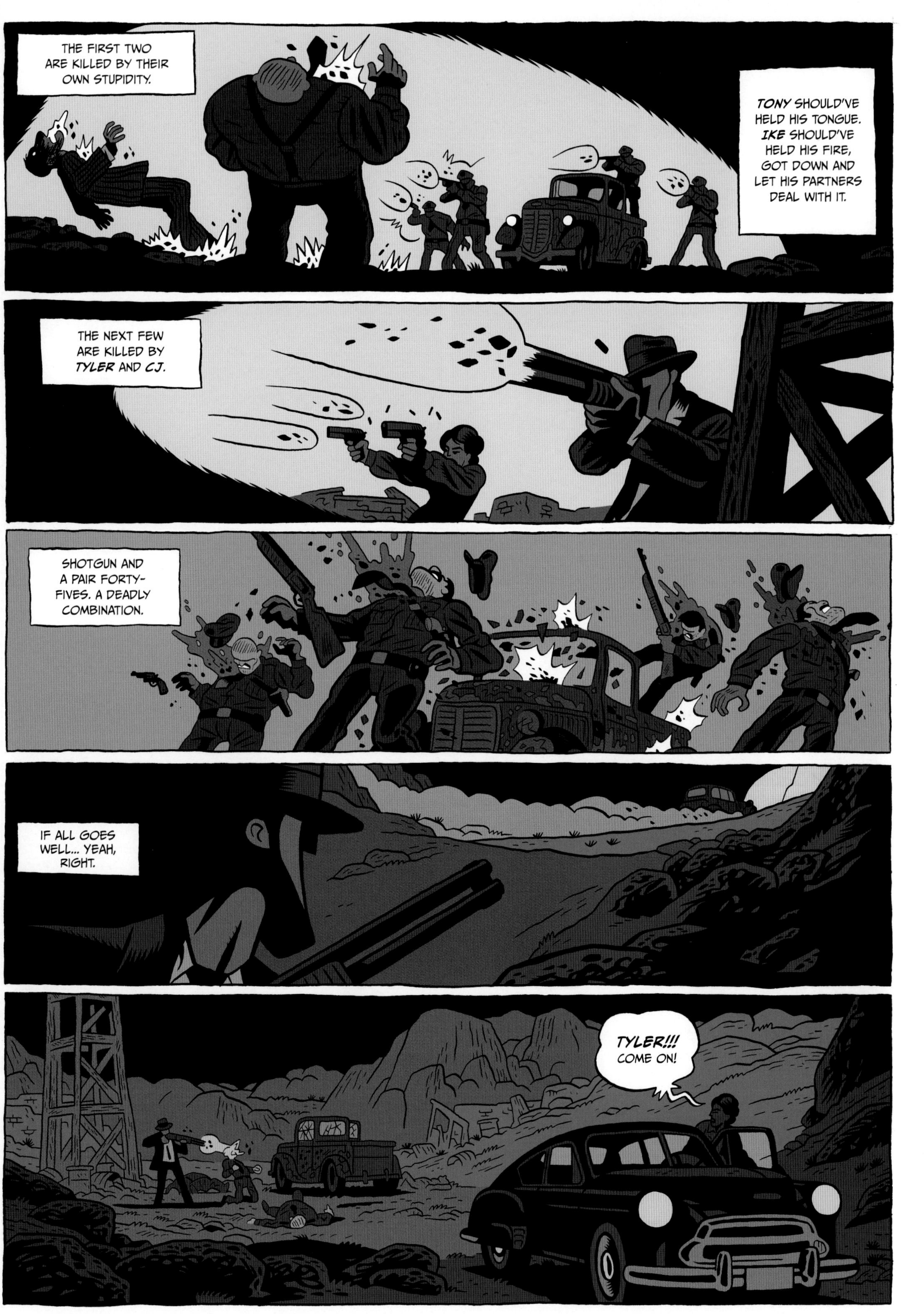
THE FIRST TWO ARE KILLED BY THEIR OWN STUPIDITY.
TONY SHOULD'VE HELD HIS TONGUE. IKE SHOULD'VE HELD HIS FIRE, GOT DOWN AND LET HIS PARTNERS DEAL WITH IT.
THE NEXT FEW ARE KILLED BY TYLER AND CJ.
SHOTGUN AND A PAIR FORTY-FIVES. A DEADLY COMBINATION.
IF ALL GOES WELL... YEAH, RIGHT.
TYLER!!! COME ON!

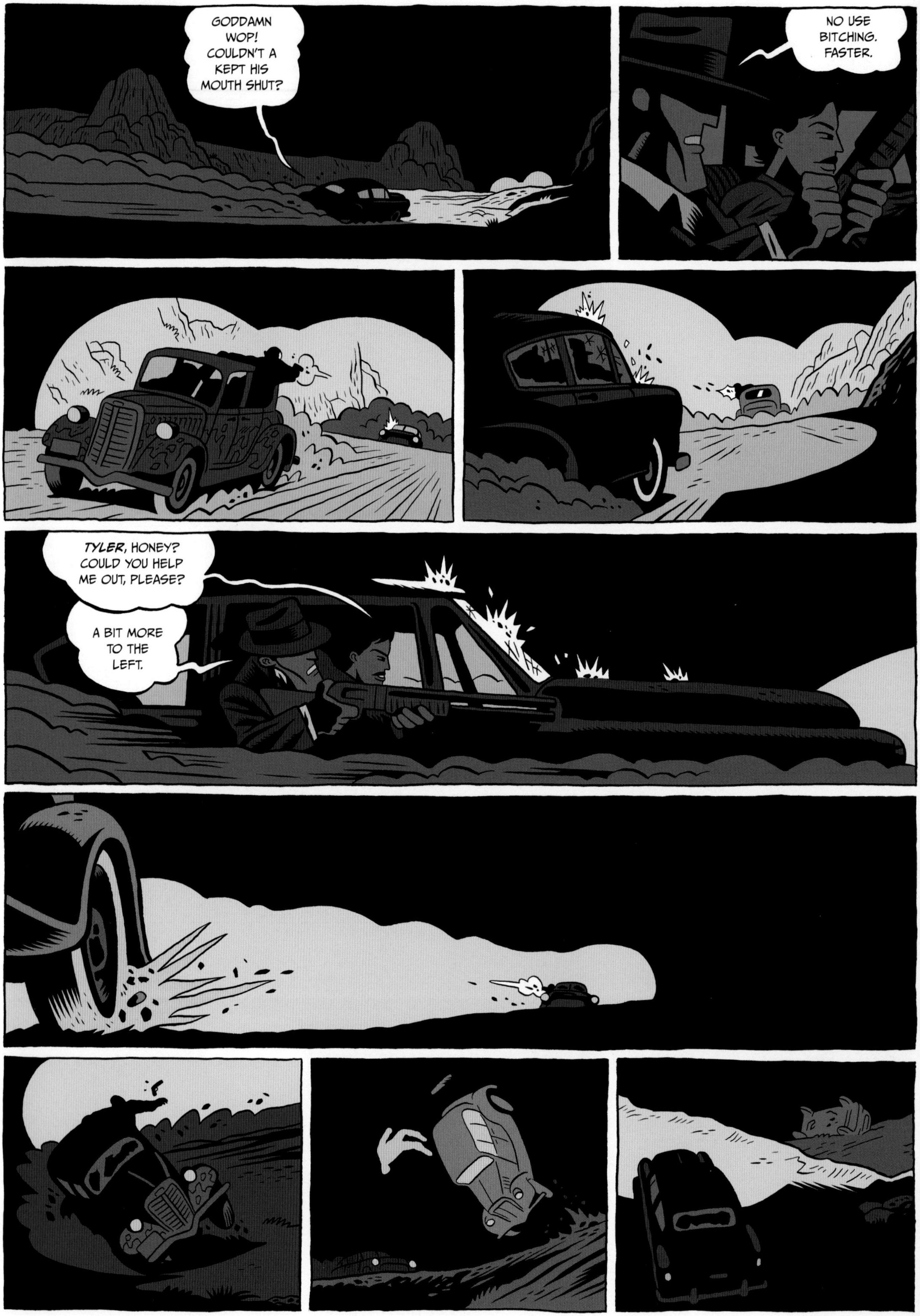
GODDAMN WOP! COULDN'T A KEPT HIS MOUTH SHUT?
NO USE BITCHING. FASTER.
TYLER, HONEY? COULD YOU HELP ME OUT, PLEASE?
A BIT MORE TO THE LEFT.

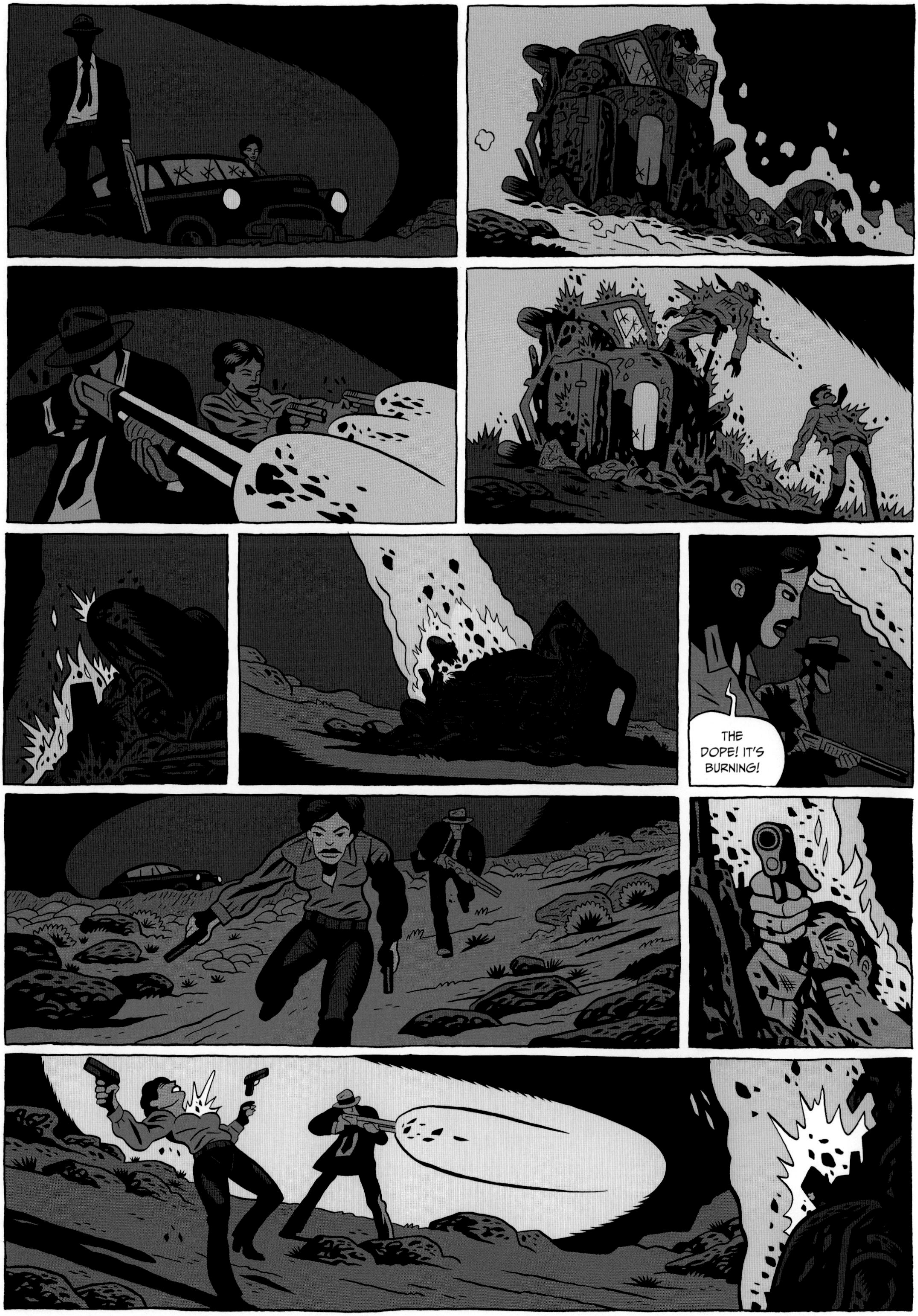
THE DOPE! IT'S BURNING!

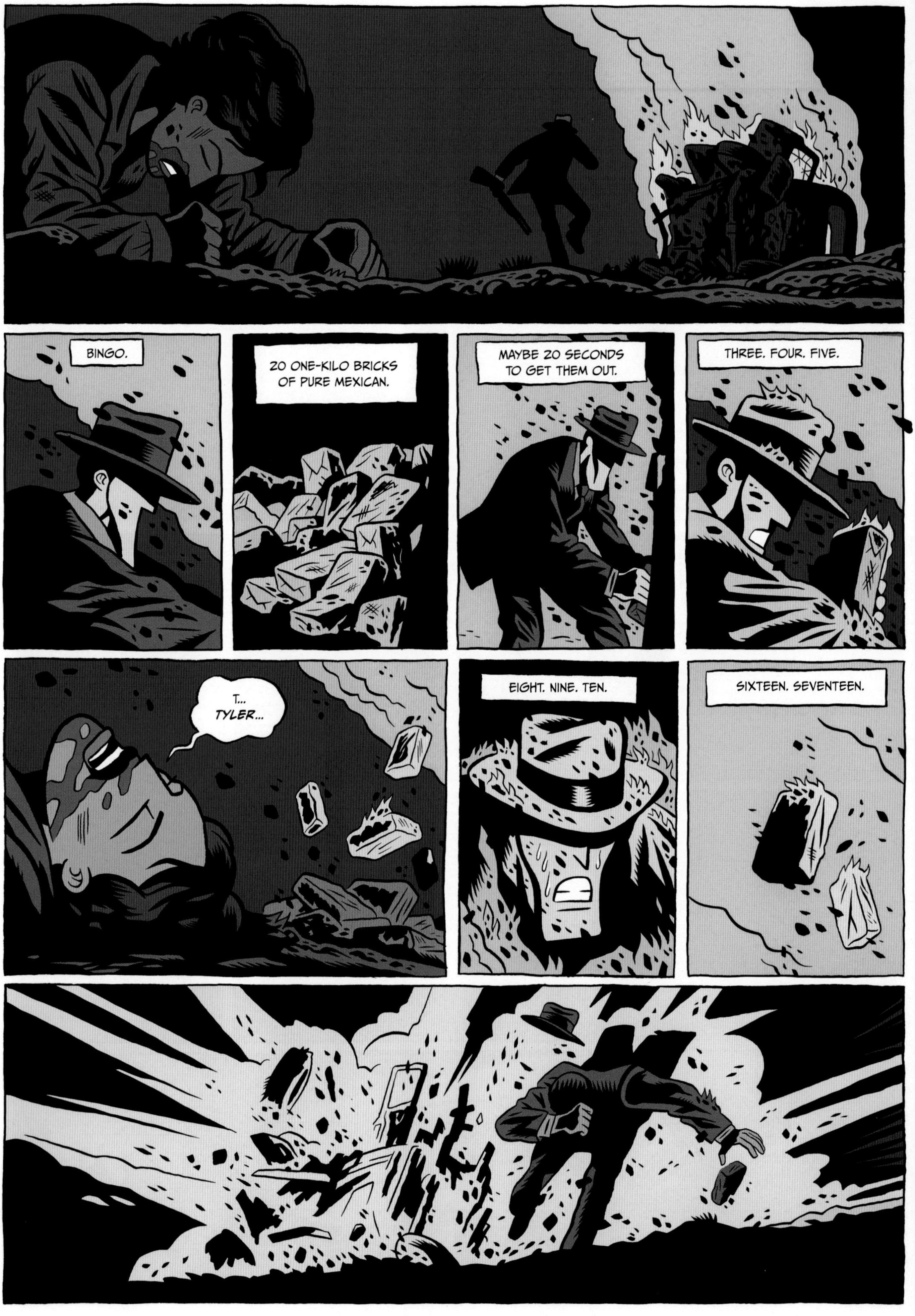
BINGO.
20 ONE-KILO BRICKS OF PURE MEXICAN.
MAYBE 20 SECONDS TO GET THEM OUT.
THREE. FOUR. FIVE.
T... TYLER...
EIGHT. NINE. TEN.
SIXTEEN. SEVENTEEN.

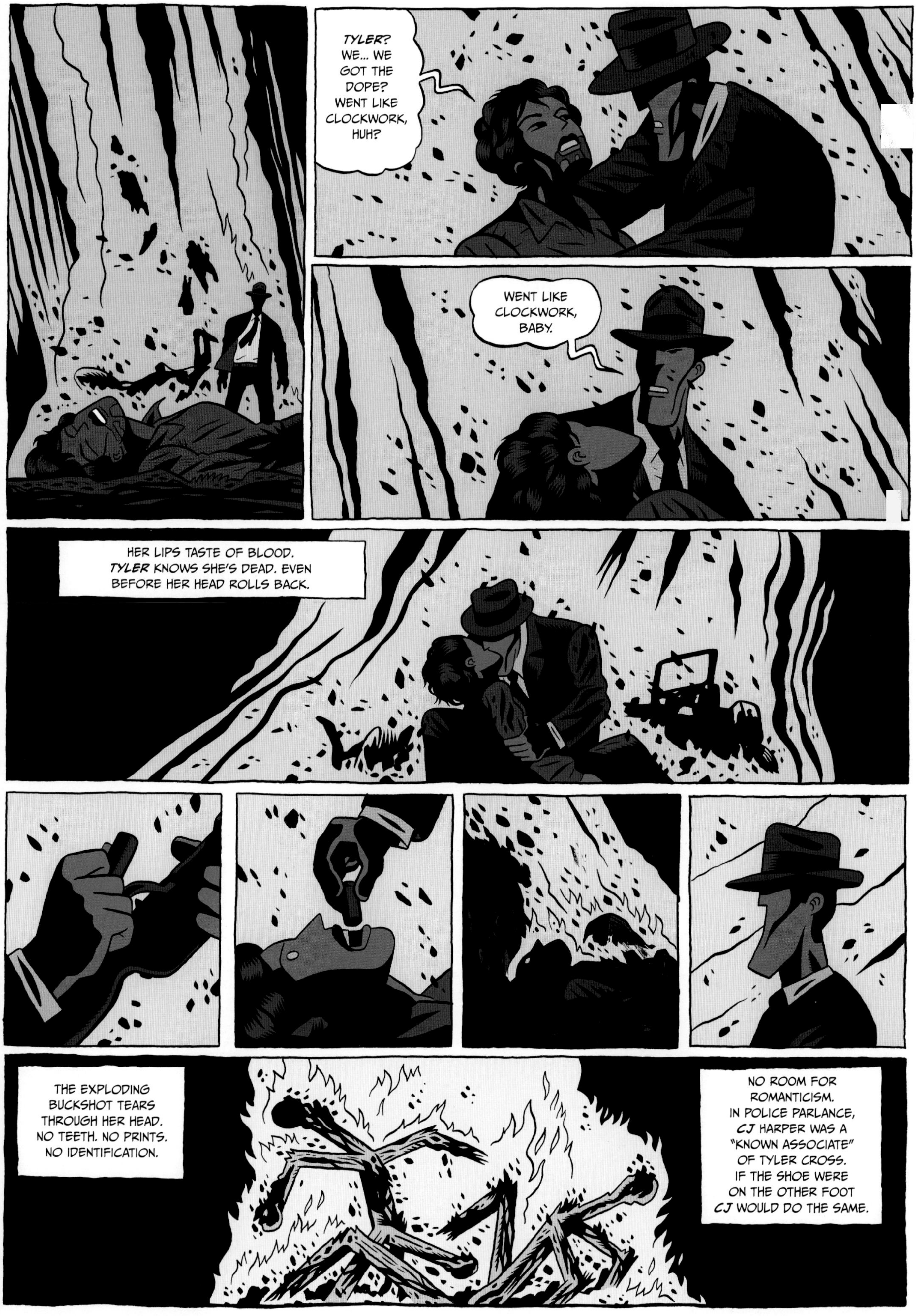
TYLER? WE... WE GOT THE DOPE? WENT LIKE CLOCKWORK, HUH?
WENT LIKE CLOCKWORK, BABY.
HER LIPS TASTE OF BLOOD. TYLER KNOWS SHE'S DEAD. EVEN BEFORE HER HEAD ROLLS BACK.
THE EXPLODING BUCKSHOT TEARS THROUGH HER HEAD. NO TEETH. NO PRINTS. NO IDENTIFICATION.
NO ROOM FOR ROMANTICISM. IN POLICE PARLANCE, CJ HARPER WAS A "KNOWN ASSOCIATE" OF TYLER CROSS. IF THE SHOE WERE ON THE OTHER FOOT CJ WOULD DO THE SAME.

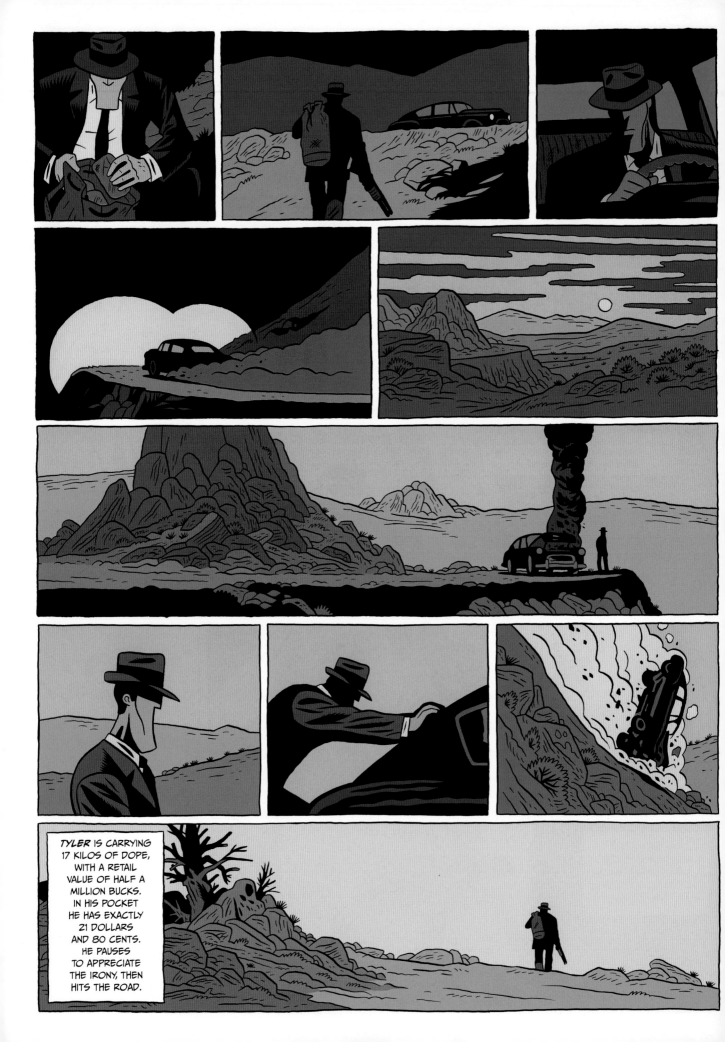

TYLER IS CARRYING
17 KILOS OF DOPE,
WITH A RETAIL
VALUE OF HALF A
MILLION BUCKS.
IN HIS POCKET
HE HAS EXACTLY
21 DOLLARS
AND 80 CENTS.
HE PAUSES
TO APPRECIATE
THE IRONY, THEN
HITS THE ROAD.

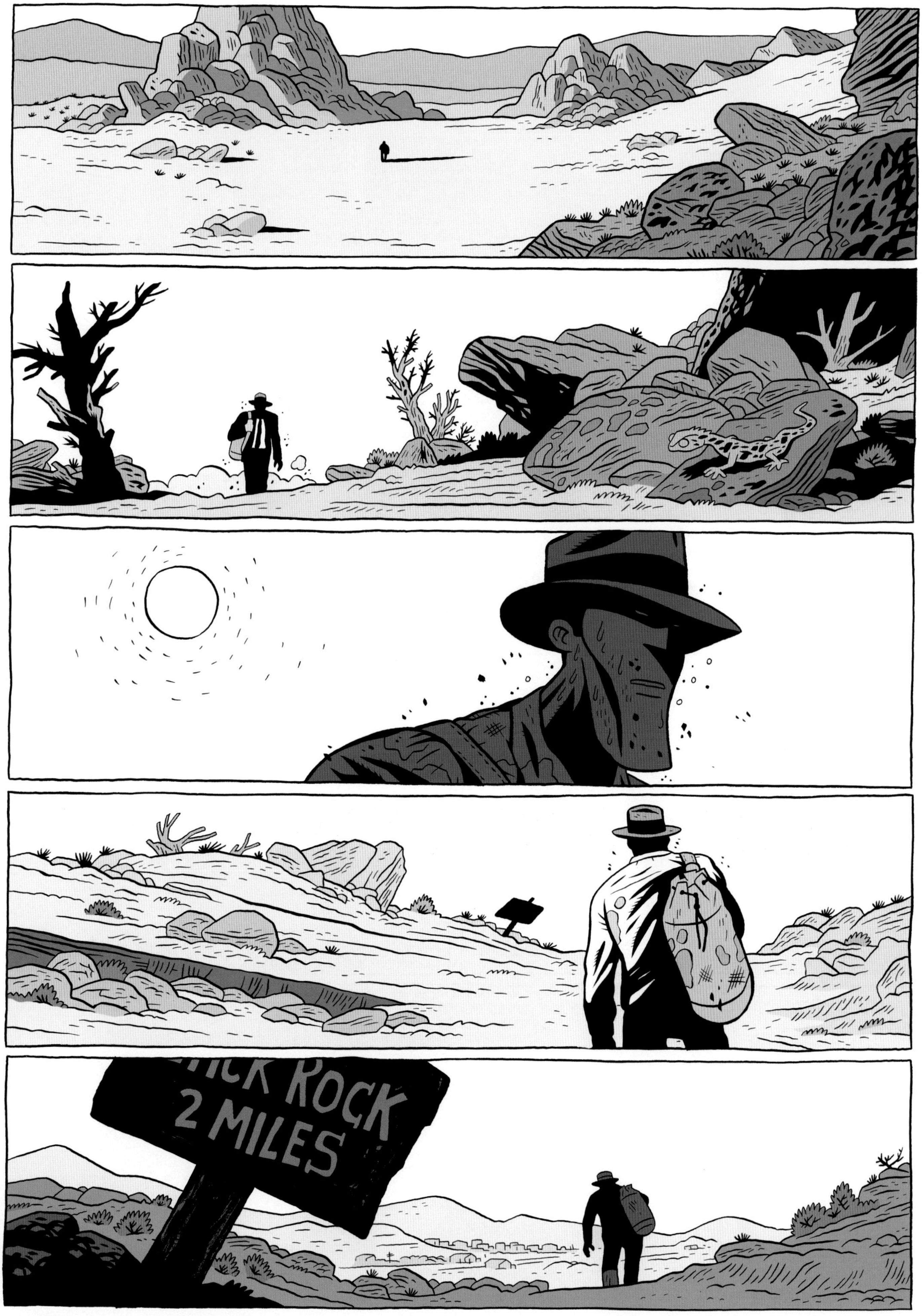
ROCK
2 MILES

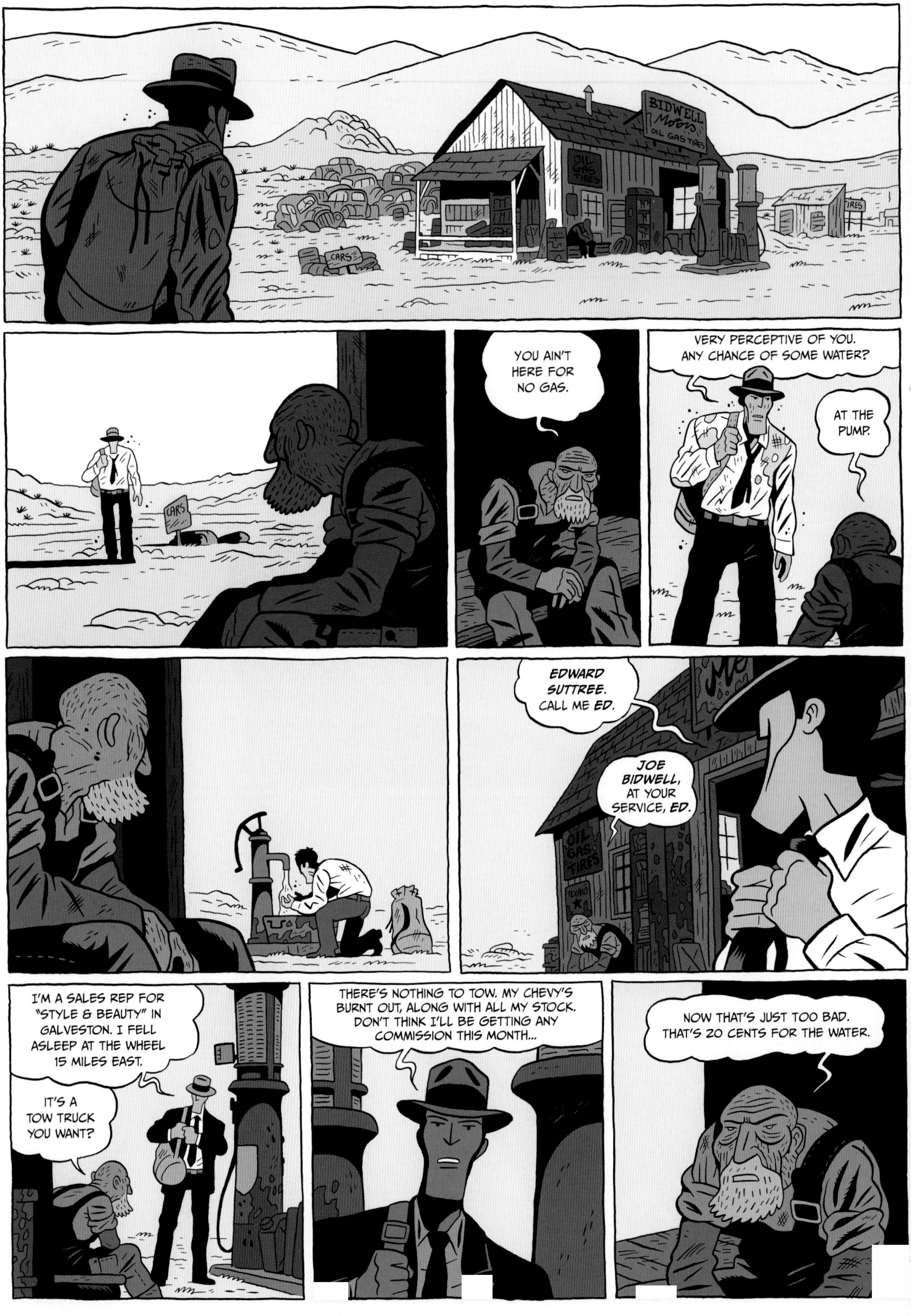
BIDWELL Motors OIL GAS TIRES
OIL GAS TIRES
CARS
TIRES
CARS
YOU AIN'T HERE FOR NO GAS.
VERY PERCEPTIVE OF YOU. ANY CHANCE OF SOME WATER?
AT THE PUMP.
EDWARD SUTTREE. CALL ME ED.
JOE BIDWELL, AT YOUR SERVICE, ED.
OIL GAS TIRES
TEXACO
I'M A SALES REP FOR "STYLE & BEAUTY" IN GALVESTON. I FELL ASLEEP AT THE WHEEL 15 MILES EAST.
IT'S A TOW TRUCK YOU WANT?
THERE'S NOTHING TO TOW. MY CHEVY'S BURNT OUT, ALONG WITH ALL MY STOCK. DON'T THINK I'LL BE GETTING ANY COMMISSION THIS MONTH...
NOW THAT'S JUST TOO BAD. THAT'S 20 CENTS FOR THE WATER.

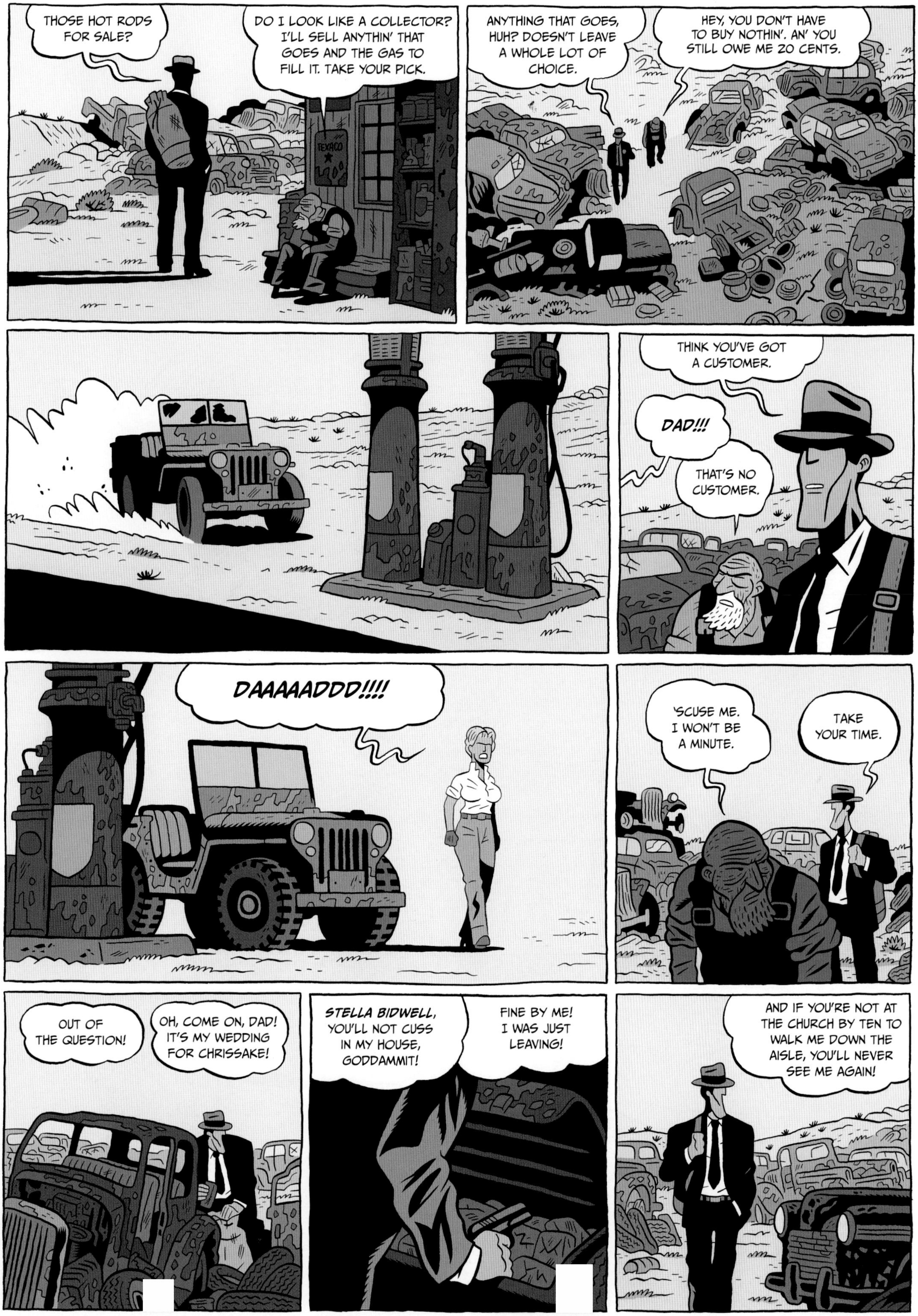
THOSE HOT RODS FOR SALE?
DO I LOOK LIKE A COLLECTOR? I'LL SELL ANYTHIN' THAT GOES AND THE GAS TO FILL IT. TAKE YOUR PICK.
TEXACO
ANYTHING THAT GOES, HUH? DOESN'T LEAVE A WHOLE LOT OF CHOICE.
HEY, YOU DON'T HAVE TO BUY NOTHIN'. AN' YOU STILL OWE ME 20 CENTS.
THINK YOU'VE GOT A CUSTOMER.
DAD!!!
THAT'S NO CUSTOMER.
DAAAAADDD!!!!
'SCUSE ME. I WON'T BE A MINUTE.
TAKE YOUR TIME.
OUT OF THE QUESTION!
OH, COME ON, DAD! IT'S MY WEDDING FOR CHRISSAKE!
STELLA BIDWELL, YOU'LL NOT CUSS IN MY HOUSE, GODDAMMIT!
FINE BY ME! I WAS JUST LEAVING!
AND IF YOU'RE NOT AT THE CHURCH BY TEN TO WALK ME DOWN THE AISLE, YOU'LL NEVER SEE ME AGAIN!

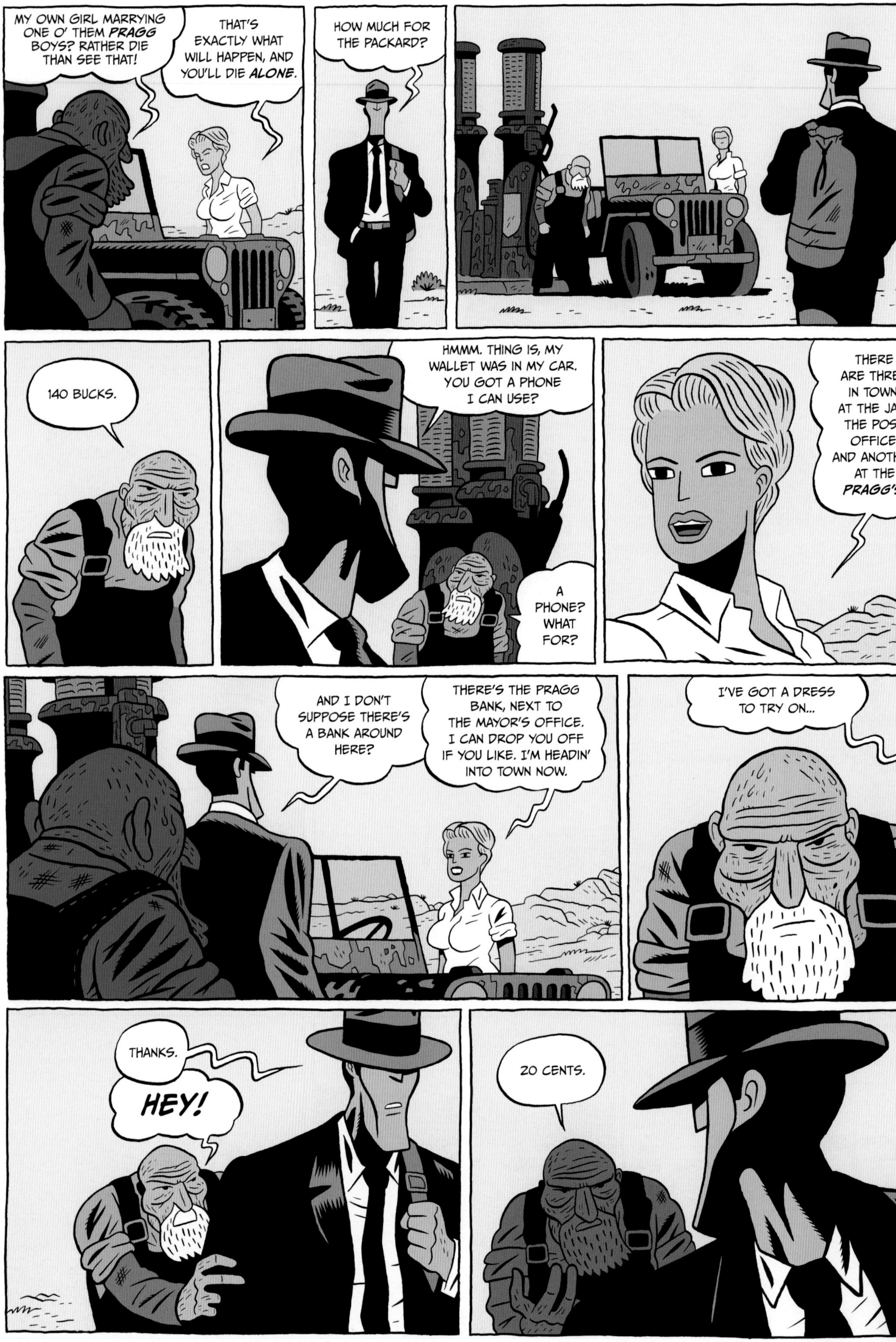
MY OWN GIRL MARRYING ONE O' THEM PRAGG BOYS? RATHER DIE THAN SEE THAT!
THAT'S EXACTLY WHAT WILL HAPPEN, AND YOU'LL DIE ALONE.
HOW MUCH FOR THE PACKARD?
140 BUCKS.
HMMM. THING IS, MY WALLET WAS IN MY CAR. YOU GOT A PHONE I CAN USE?
A PHONE? WHAT FOR?
THERE ARE THREE IN TOWN. AT THE JAIL, THE POST OFFICE, AND ANOTHER AT THE PRAGG'S.
AND I DON'T SUPPOSE THERE'S A BANK AROUND HERE?
THERE'S THE PRAGG BANK, NEXT TO THE MAYOR'S OFFICE. I CAN DROP YOU OFF IF YOU LIKE. I'M HEADIN' INTO TOWN NOW.
I'VE GOT A DRESS TO TRY ON...
THANKS.
HEY!
20 CENTS.

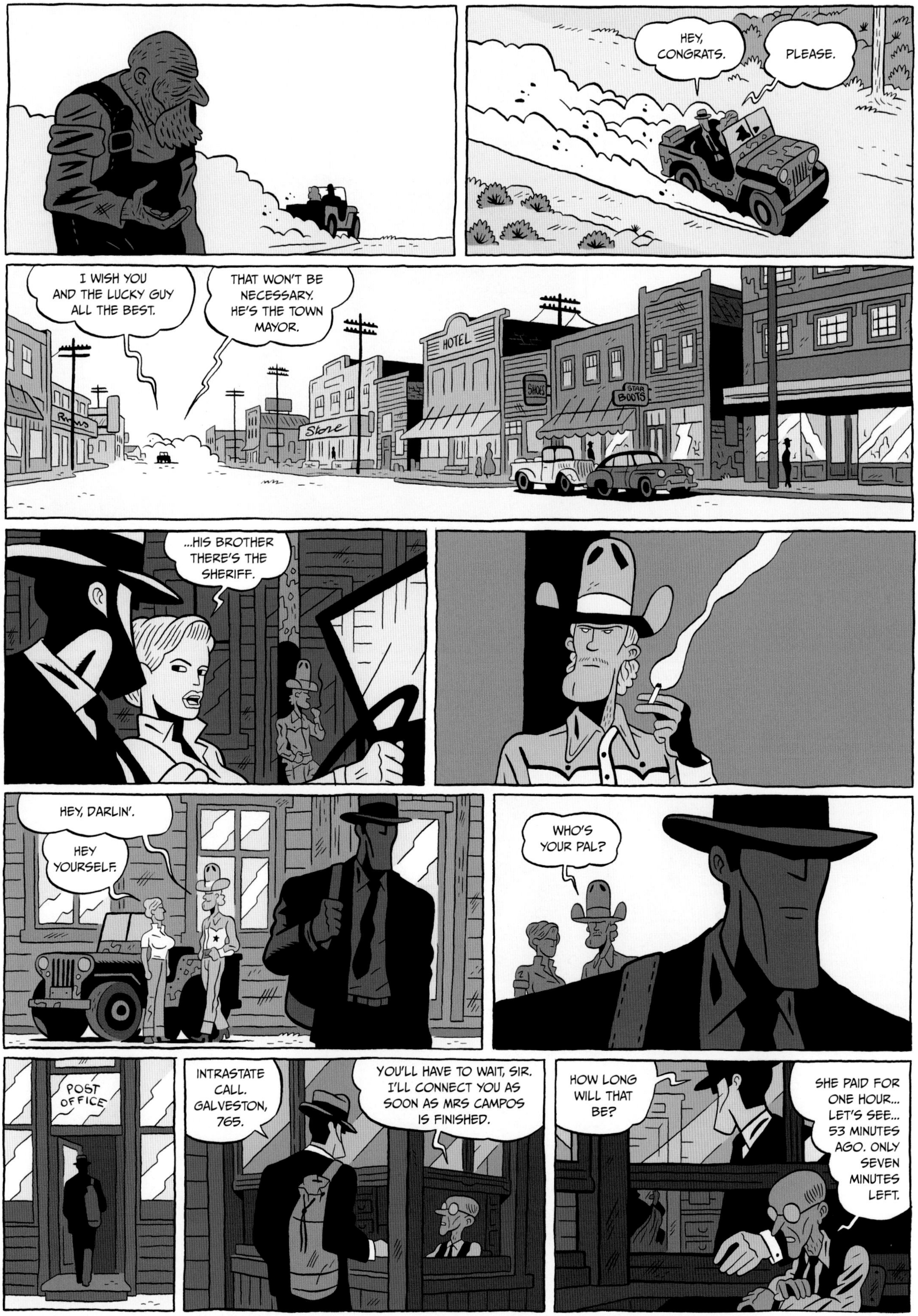

HEY, CONGRATS.
PLEASE.
I WISH YOU AND THE LUCKY GUY ALL THE BEST.
THAT WON'T BE NECESSARY. HE'S THE TOWN MAYOR.
HOTEL
SHOES
STAR BOOTS
Store
...HIS BROTHER THERE'S THE SHERIFF.
HEY, DARLIN'.
HEY YOURSELF.
WHO'S YOUR PAL?
POST OFFICE
INTRASTATE CALL. GALVESTON, 765.
YOU'LL HAVE TO WAIT, SIR. I'LL CONNECT YOU AS SOON AS MRS CAMPOS IS FINISHED.
HOW LONG WILL THAT BE?
SHE PAID FOR ONE HOUR... LET'S SEE... 53 MINUTES AGO. ONLY SEVEN MINUTES LEFT.

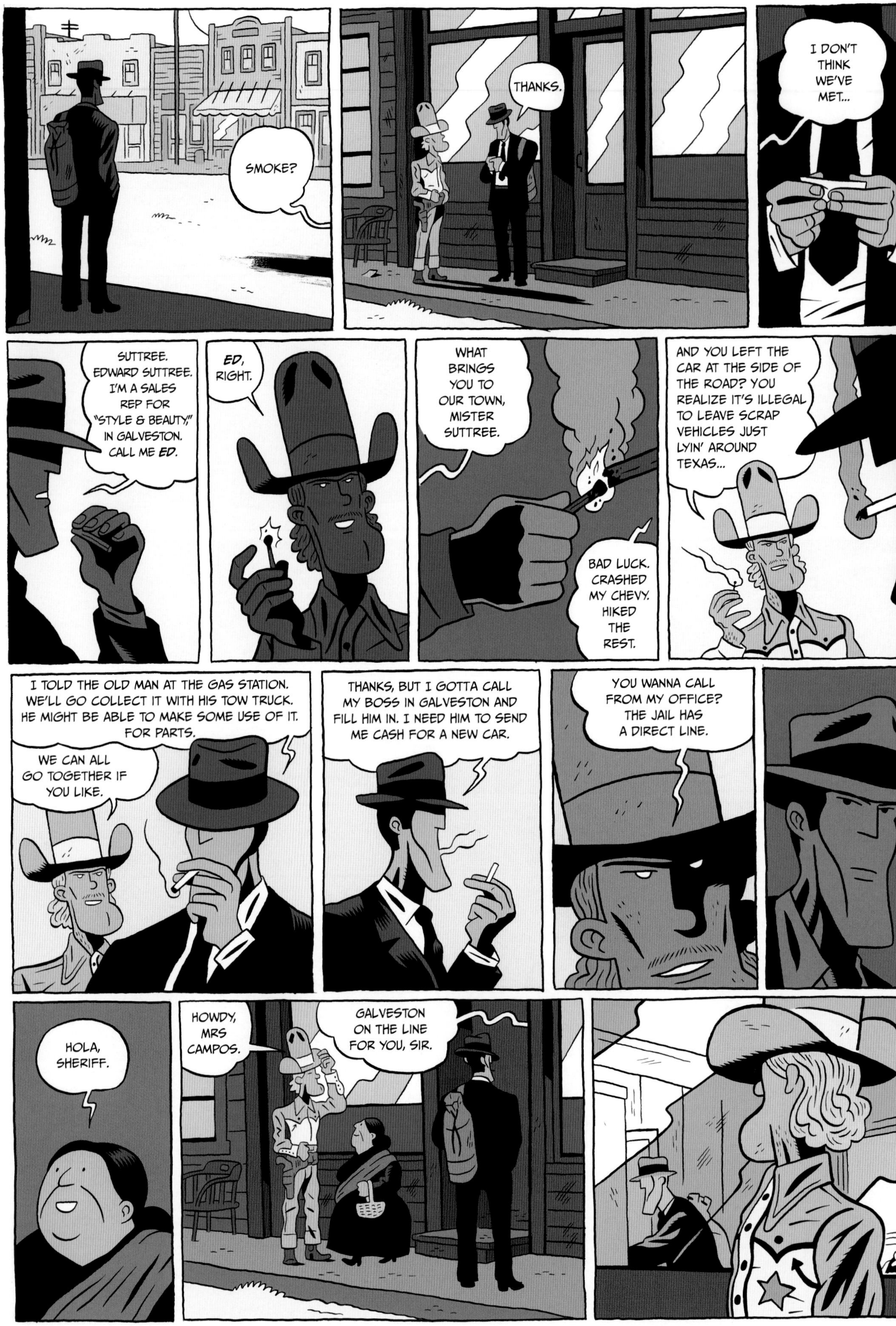
SMOKE?
THANKS.
I DON'T THINK WE'VE MET...
SUTTREE. EDWARD SUTTREE. I'M A SALES REP FOR "STYLE & BEAUTY," IN GALVESTON. CALL ME ED.
ED, RIGHT.
WHAT BRINGS YOU TO OUR TOWN, MISTER SUTTREE.
BAD LUCK. CRASHED MY CHEVY. HIKED THE REST.
AND YOU LEFT THE CAR AT THE SIDE OF THE ROAD? YOU REALIZE IT'S ILLEGAL TO LEAVE SCRAP VEHICLES JUST LYIN' AROUND TEXAS...
I TOLD THE OLD MAN AT THE GAS STATION. WE'LL GO COLLECT IT WITH HIS TOW TRUCK. HE MIGHT BE ABLE TO MAKE SOME USE OF IT. FOR PARTS.
WE CAN ALL GO TOGETHER IF YOU LIKE.
THANKS, BUT I GOTTA CALL MY BOSS IN GALVESTON AND FILL HIM IN. I NEED HIM TO SEND ME CASH FOR A NEW CAR.
YOU WANNA CALL FROM MY OFFICE? THE JAIL HAS A DIRECT LINE.
HOLA, SHERIFF.
HOWDY, MRS CAMPOS.
GALVESTON ON THE LINE FOR YOU, SIR.

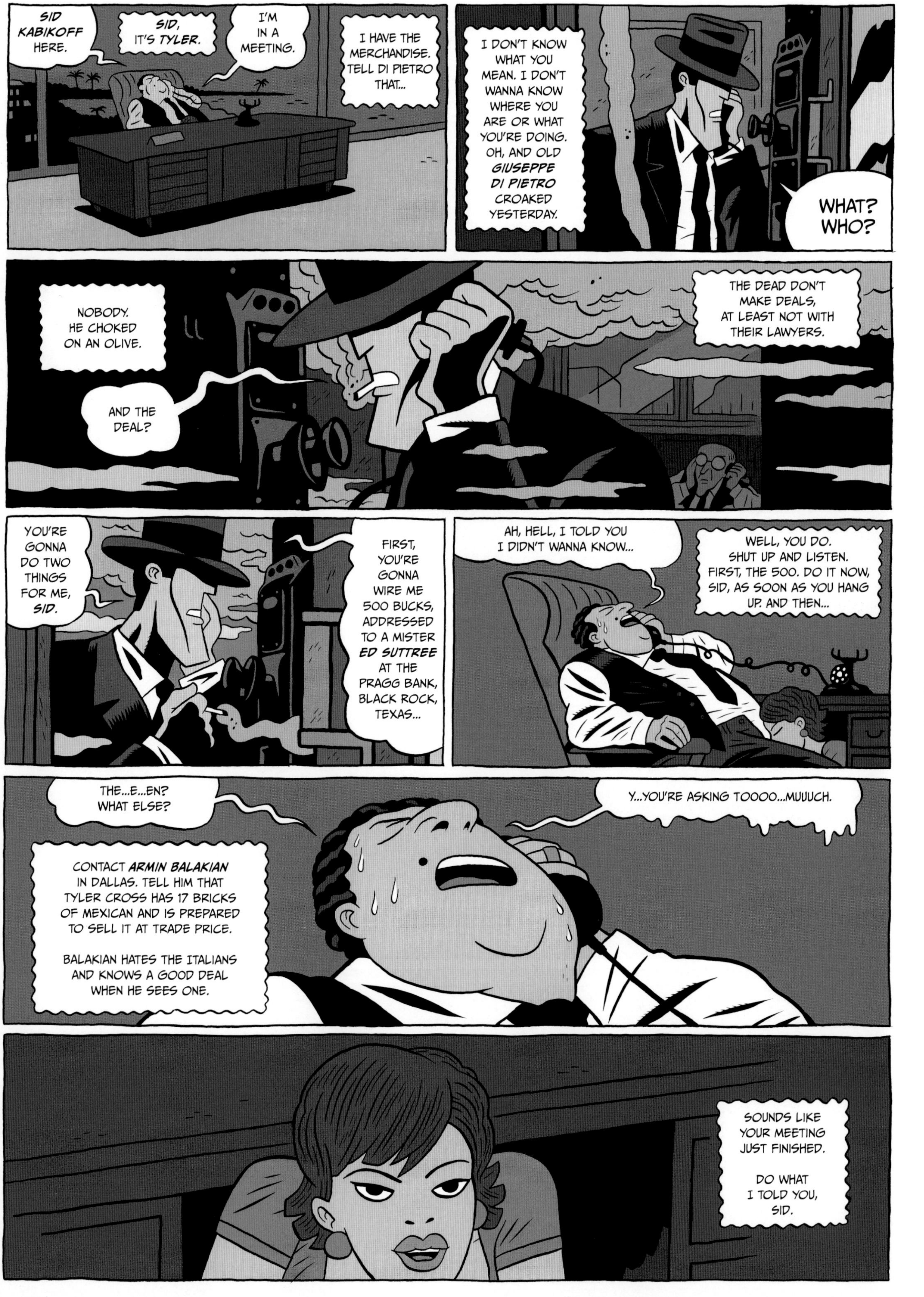
SID KABIKOFF HERE.
SID, IT'S TYLER.
I'M IN A MEETING.
I HAVE THE MERCHANDISE. TELL DI PIETRO THAT...
I DON'T KNOW WHAT YOU MEAN. I DON'T WANNA KNOW WHERE YOU ARE OR WHAT YOU'RE DOING. OH, AND OLD GIUSEPPE DI PIETRO CROAKED YESTERDAY.
WHAT? WHO?
NOBODY. HE CHOKED ON AN OLIVE.
AND THE DEAL?
THE DEAD DON'T MAKE DEALS, AT LEAST NOT WITH THEIR LAWYERS.
YOU'RE GONNA DO TWO THINGS FOR ME, SID.
FIRST, YOU'RE GONNA WIRE ME 500 BUCKS, ADDRESSED TO A MISTER ED SUTTREE AT THE PRAGG BANK, BLACK ROCK, TEXAS...
AH, HELL, I TOLD YOU I DIDN'T WANNA KNOW...
WELL, YOU DO. SHUT UP AND LISTEN. FIRST, THE 500. DO IT NOW, SID, AS SOON AS YOU HANG UP. AND THEN...
THE...E...EN? WHAT ELSE?
Y...YOU'RE ASKING TOOOO...MUUUCH.
CONTACT ARMIN BALAKIAN IN DALLAS. TELL HIM THAT TYLER CROSS HAS 17 BRICKS OF MEXICAN AND IS PREPARED TO SELL IT AT TRADE PRICE.
BALAKIAN HATES THE ITALIANS AND KNOWS A GOOD DEAL WHEN HE SEES ONE.
SOUNDS LIKE YOUR MEETING JUST FINISHED.
DO WHAT I TOLD YOU, SID.

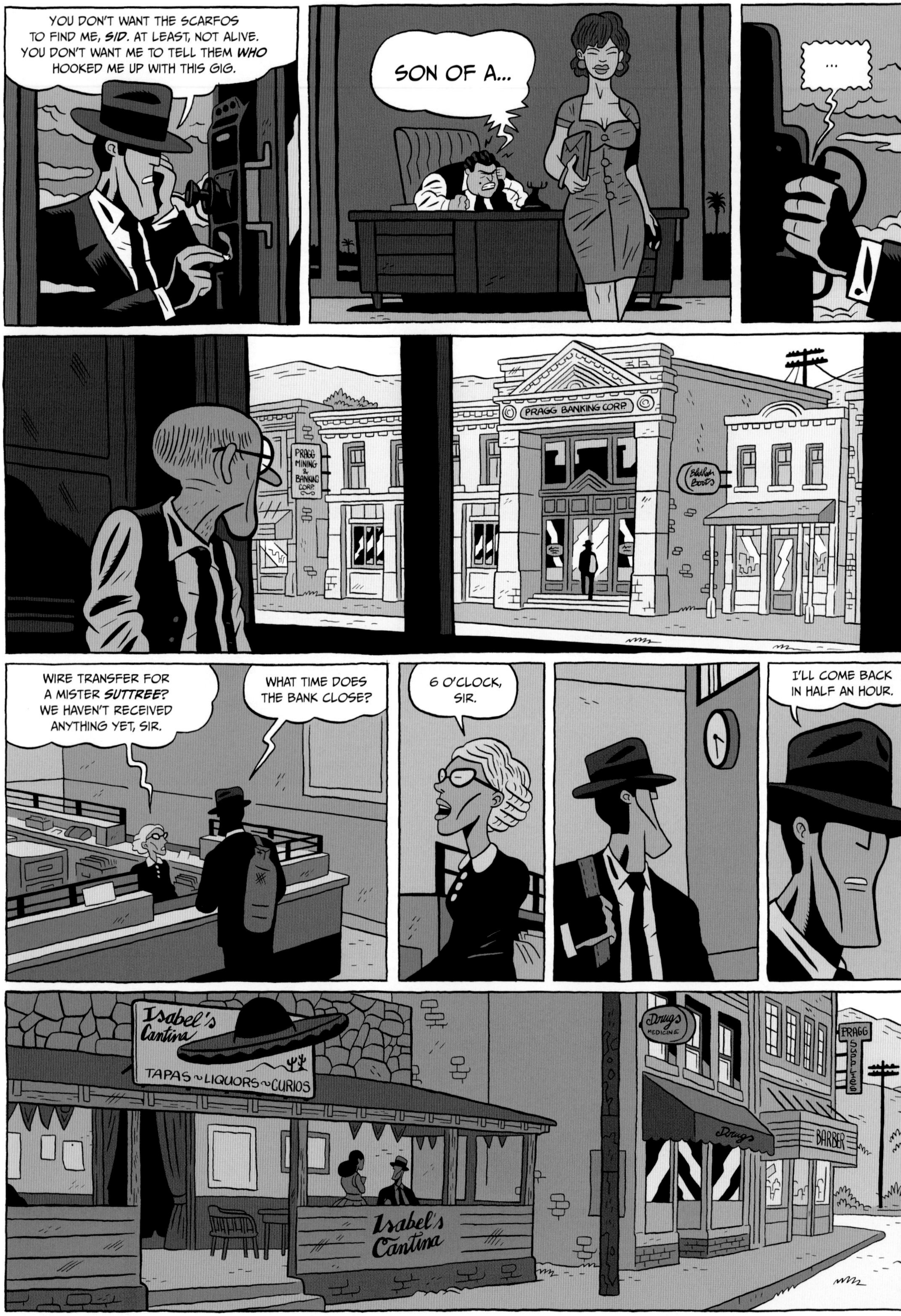

YOU DON'T WANT THE SCARFOS TO FIND ME, *SID*. AT LEAST, NOT ALIVE. YOU DON'T WANT ME TO TELL THEM *WHO* HOOKED ME UP WITH THIS GIG.
SON OF A...
...
PRAGG MINING & BANKING CORP
PRAGG BANKING CORP.
WIRE TRANSFER FOR A MISTER *SUTTREE*? WE HAVEN'T RECEIVED ANYTHING YET, SIR.
WHAT TIME DOES THE BANK CLOSE?
6 O'CLOCK, SIR.
I'LL COME BACK IN HALF AN HOUR.
Isabel's Cantina
TAPAS ~ LIQUORS ~ CURIOS
Drugs
MEDICINE
Isabel's Cantina
Drugs
BARBER

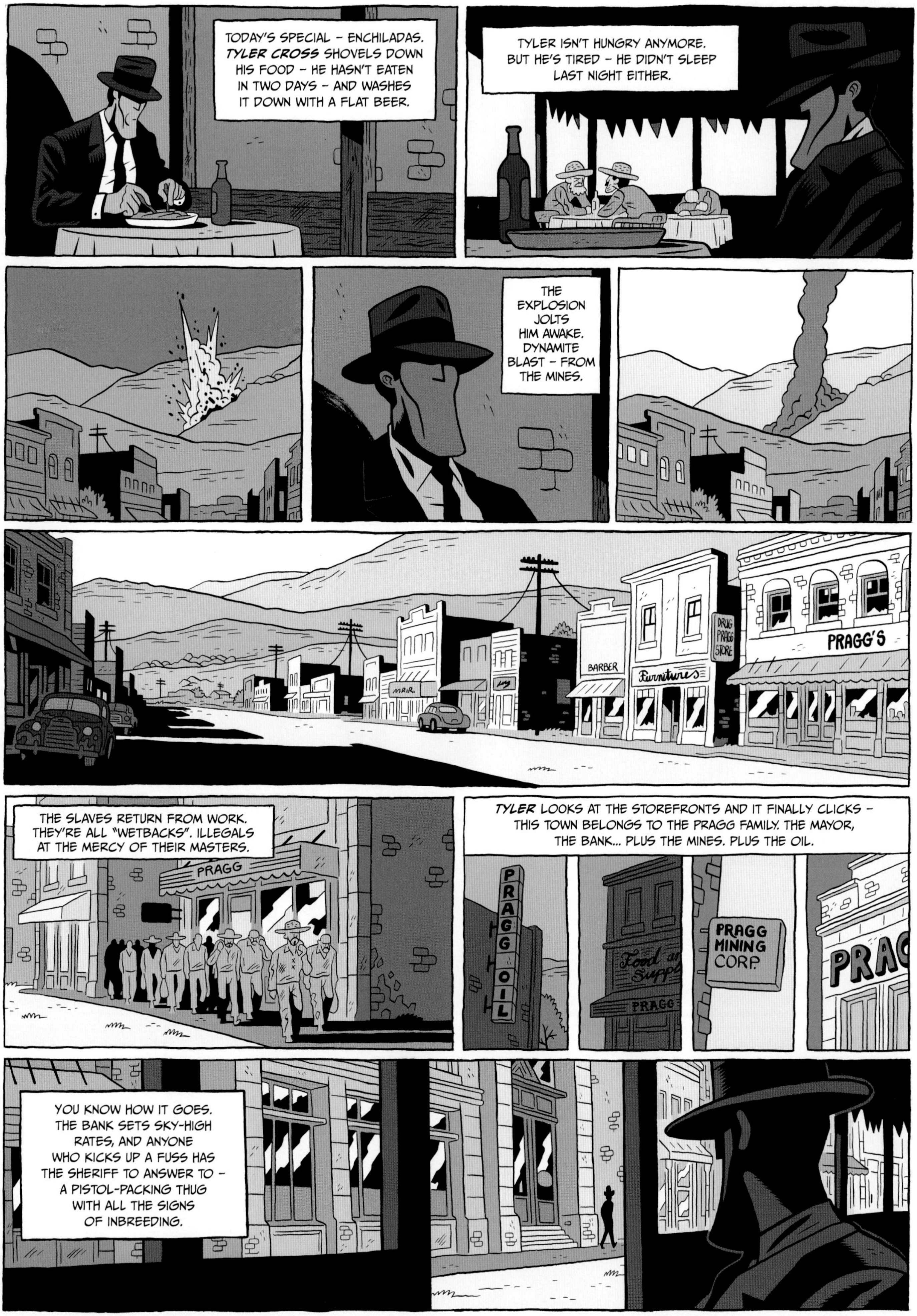
TODAY'S SPECIAL – ENCHILADAS. *TYLER CROSS* SHOVELS DOWN HIS FOOD – HE HASN'T EATEN IN TWO DAYS – AND WASHES IT DOWN WITH A FLAT BEER.
TYLER ISN'T HUNGRY ANYMORE. BUT HE'S TIRED – HE DIDN'T SLEEP LAST NIGHT EITHER.
THE EXPLOSION JOLTS HIM AWAKE. DYNAMITE BLAST – FROM THE MINES.
BARBER
Furniture
DRUG PRAGG STORE
PRAGG'S
THE SLAVES RETURN FROM WORK. THEY'RE ALL "WETBACKS". ILLEGALS AT THE MERCY OF THEIR MASTERS.
PRAGG
TYLER LOOKS AT THE STOREFRONTS AND IT FINALLY CLICKS – THIS TOWN BELONGS TO THE PRAGG FAMILY. THE MAYOR, THE BANK... PLUS THE MINES. PLUS THE OIL.
PRAGG OIL
PRAGG MINING CORP.
PRAGG
YOU KNOW HOW IT GOES. THE BANK SETS SKY-HIGH RATES, AND ANYONE WHO KICKS UP A FUSS HAS THE SHERIFF TO ANSWER TO – A PISTOL-PACKING THUG WITH ALL THE SIGNS OF INBREEDING.

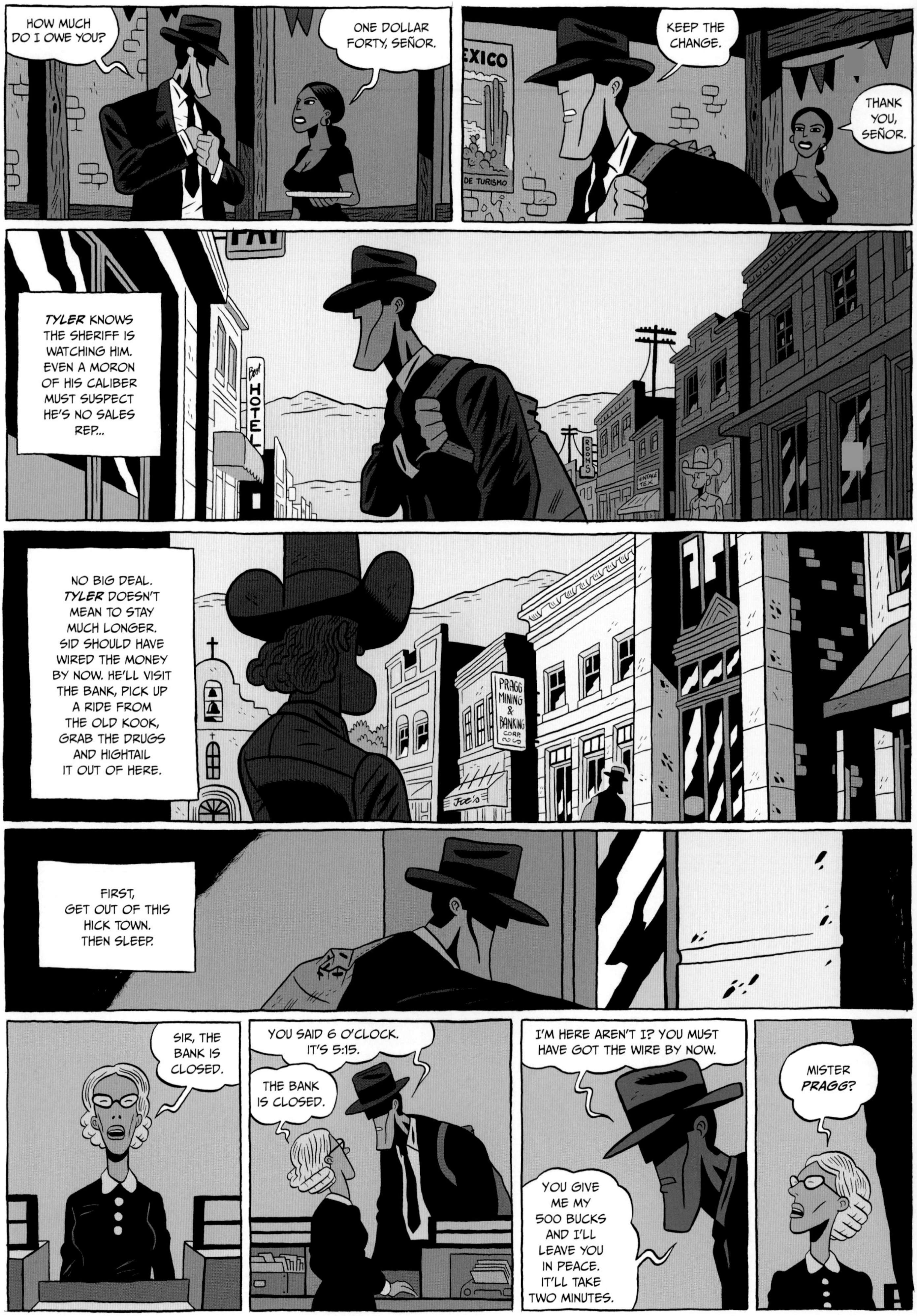
HOW MUCH DO I OWE YOU?
ONE DOLLAR FORTY, SEÑOR.
KEEP THE CHANGE.
THANK YOU, SEÑOR.
MEXICO
DE TURISMO
TYLER KNOWS THE SHERIFF IS WATCHING HIM. EVEN A MORON OF HIS CALIBER MUST SUSPECT HE'S NO SALES REP...
HOTEL
ROOMS
NO BIG DEAL. TYLER DOESN'T MEAN TO STAY MUCH LONGER. SID SHOULD HAVE WIRED THE MONEY BY NOW. HE'LL VISIT THE BANK, PICK UP A RIDE FROM THE OLD KOOK, GRAB THE DRUGS AND HIGHTAIL IT OUT OF HERE.
PRAGG MINING & BANKING CORP.
JOE'S
FIRST, GET OUT OF THIS HICK TOWN. THEN SLEEP.
SIR, THE BANK IS CLOSED.
YOU SAID 6 O'CLOCK. IT'S 5:15.
THE BANK IS CLOSED.
I'M HERE AREN'T I? YOU MUST HAVE GOT THE WIRE BY NOW.
YOU GIVE ME MY 500 BUCKS AND I'LL LEAVE YOU IN PEACE. IT'LL TAKE TWO MINUTES.
MISTER PRAGG?

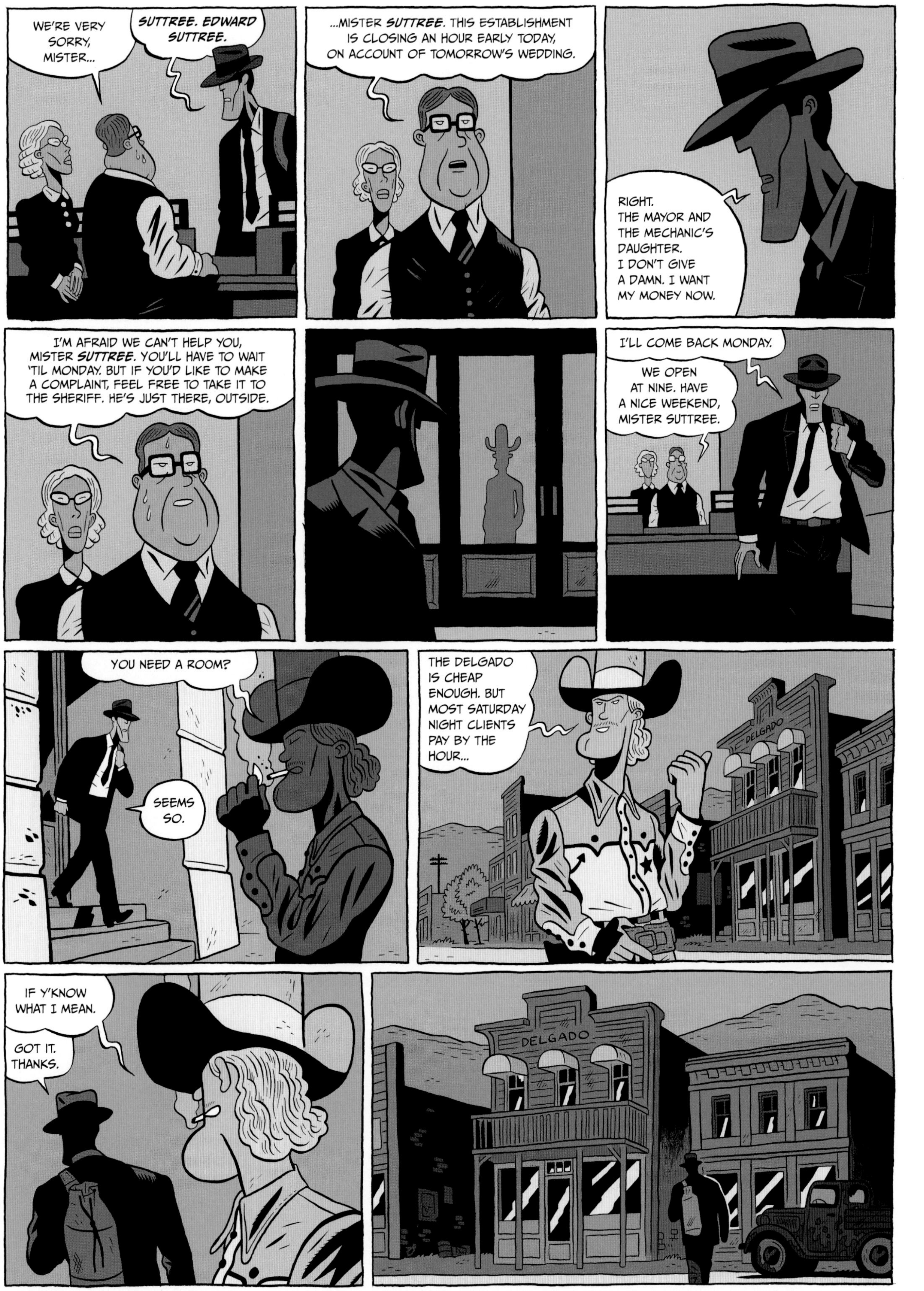
WE'RE VERY SORRY, MISTER...
SUTTREE. EDWARD SUTTREE.
...MISTER SUTTREE. THIS ESTABLISHMENT IS CLOSING AN HOUR EARLY TODAY, ON ACCOUNT OF TOMORROW'S WEDDING.
RIGHT. THE MAYOR AND THE MECHANIC'S DAUGHTER. I DON'T GIVE A DAMN. I WANT MY MONEY NOW.
I'M AFRAID WE CAN'T HELP YOU, MISTER SUTTREE. YOU'LL HAVE TO WAIT 'TIL MONDAY. BUT IF YOU'D LIKE TO MAKE A COMPLAINT, FEEL FREE TO TAKE IT TO THE SHERIFF. HE'S JUST THERE, OUTSIDE.
I'LL COME BACK MONDAY.
WE OPEN AT NINE. HAVE A NICE WEEKEND, MISTER SUTTREE.
YOU NEED A ROOM?
SEEMS SO.
THE DELGADO IS CHEAP ENOUGH. BUT MOST SATURDAY NIGHT CLIENTS PAY BY THE HOUR...
DELGADO
IF Y'KNOW WHAT I MEAN.
GOT IT. THANKS.
DELGADO

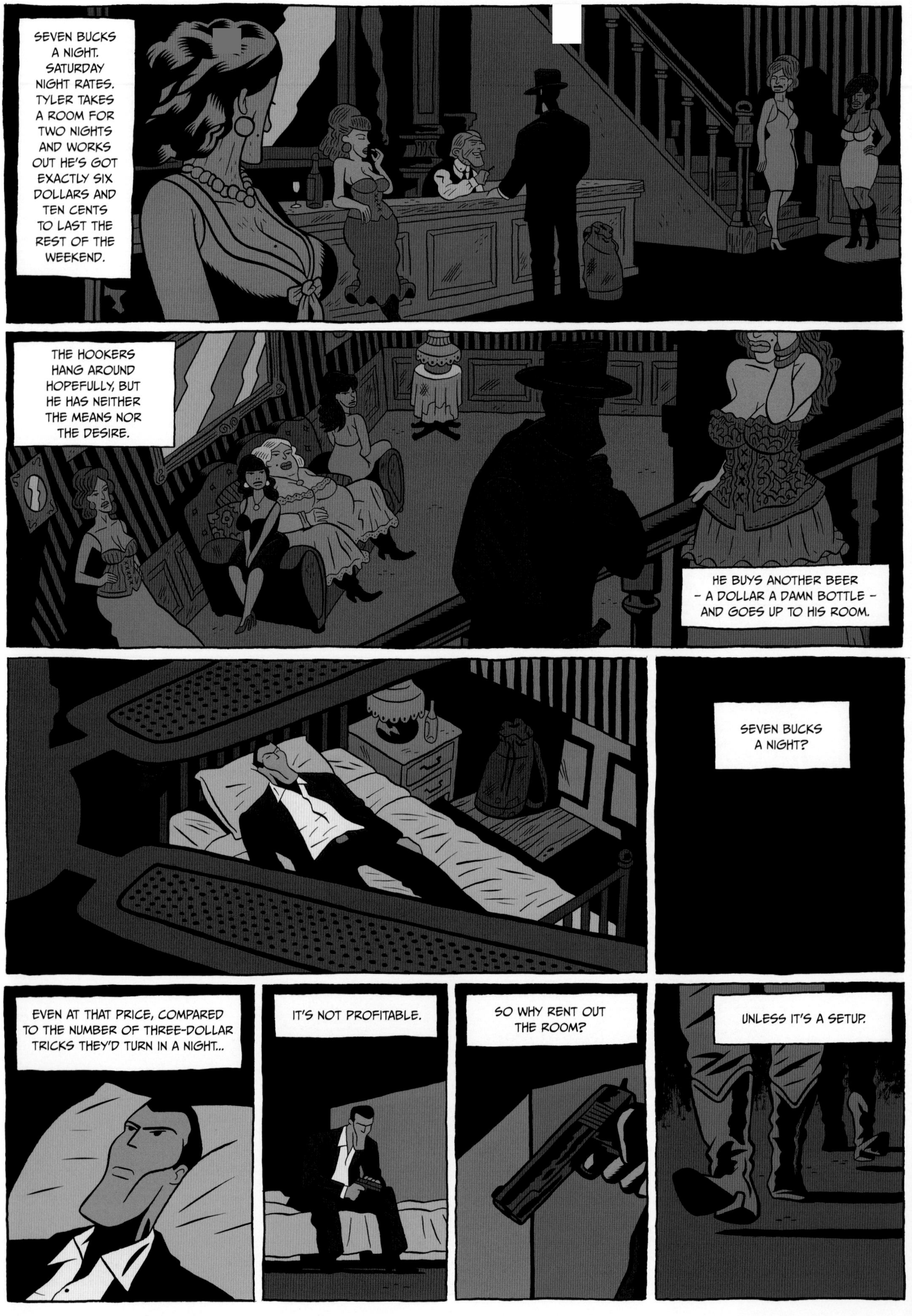
SEVEN BUCKS A NIGHT. SATURDAY NIGHT RATES. TYLER TAKES A ROOM FOR TWO NIGHTS AND WORKS OUT HE'S GOT EXACTLY SIX DOLLARS AND TEN CENTS TO LAST THE REST OF THE WEEKEND.
THE HOOKERS HANG AROUND HOPEFULLY, BUT HE HAS NEITHER THE MEANS NOR THE DESIRE.
HE BUYS ANOTHER BEER – A DOLLAR A DAMN BOTTLE – AND GOES UP TO HIS ROOM.
SEVEN BUCKS A NIGHT?
EVEN AT THAT PRICE, COMPARED TO THE NUMBER OF THREE-DOLLAR TRICKS THEY'D TURN IN A NIGHT...
IT'S NOT PROFITABLE.
SO WHY RENT OUT THE ROOM?
UNLESS IT'S A SETUP.

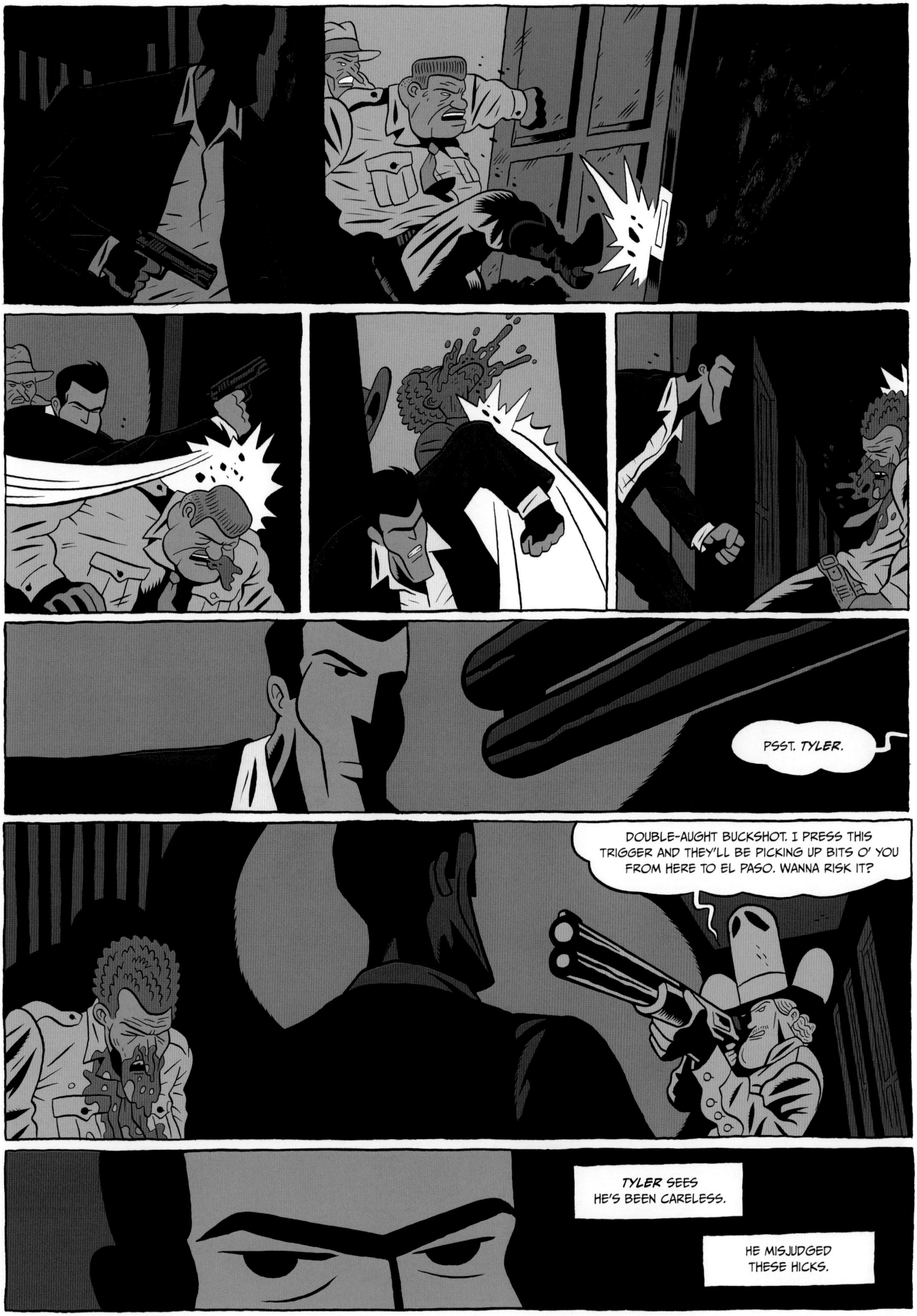
PSST. *TYLER.*
DOUBLE-AUGHT BUCKSHOT. I PRESS THIS TRIGGER AND THEY'LL BE PICKING UP BITS O' YOU FROM HERE TO EL PASO. WANNA RISK IT?
TYLER SEES HE'S BEEN CARELESS.
HE MISJUDGED THESE HICKS.

2. WEDDING

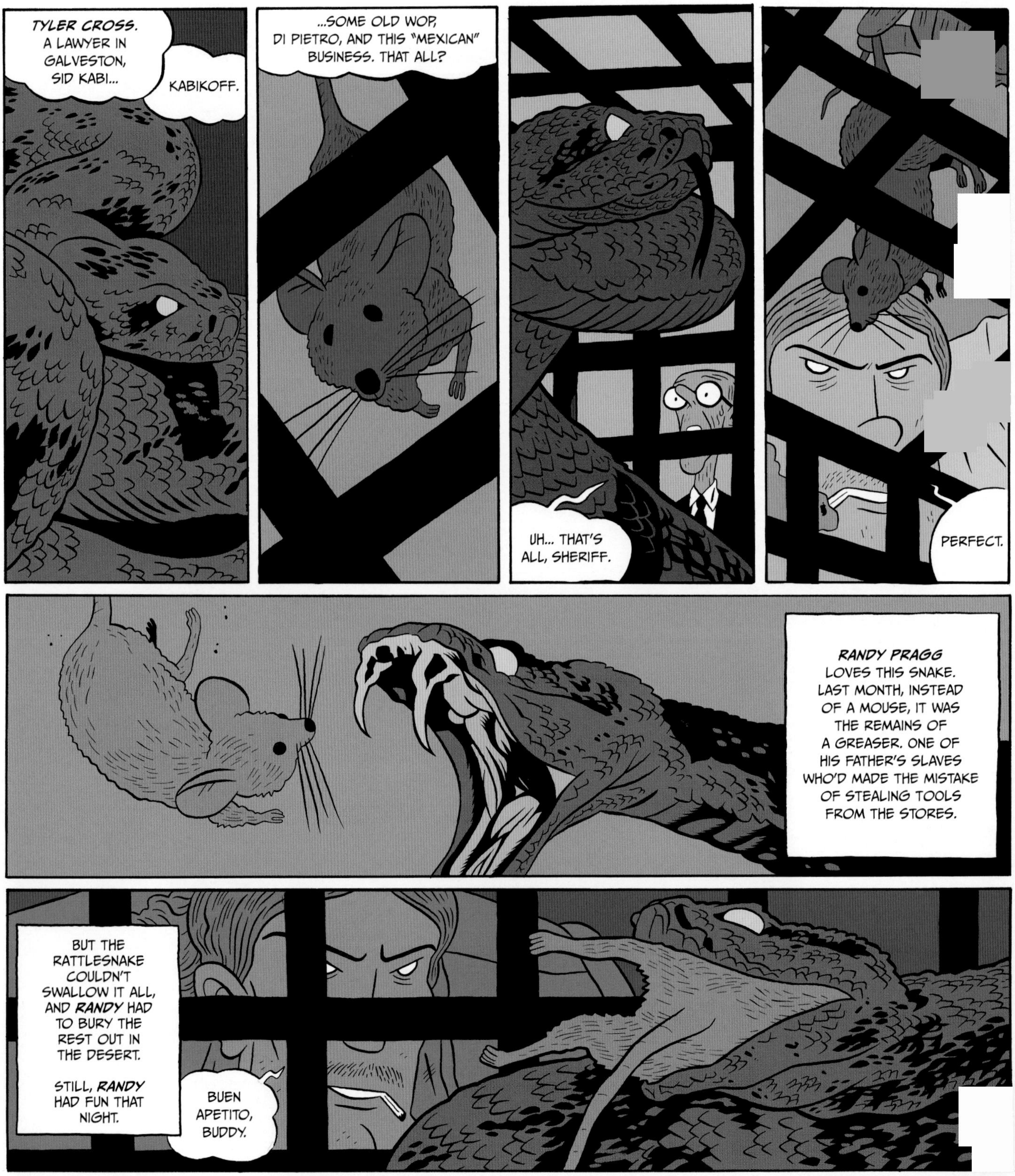
TYLER CROSS. A LAWYER IN GALVESTON, SID KABI...
KABIKOFF.
...SOME OLD WOP, DI PIETRO, AND THIS "MEXICAN" BUSINESS. THAT ALL?
UH... THAT'S ALL, SHERIFF.
PERFECT.
RANDY PRAGG LOVES THIS SNAKE. LAST MONTH, INSTEAD OF A MOUSE, IT WAS THE REMAINS OF A GREASER. ONE OF HIS FATHER'S SLAVES WHO'D MADE THE MISTAKE OF STEALING TOOLS FROM THE STORES.
BUT THE RATTLESNAKE COULDN'T SWALLOW IT ALL, AND *RANDY* HAD TO BURY THE REST OUT IN THE DESERT.
STILL, *RANDY* HAD FUN THAT NIGHT.
BUEN APETITO, BUDDY.

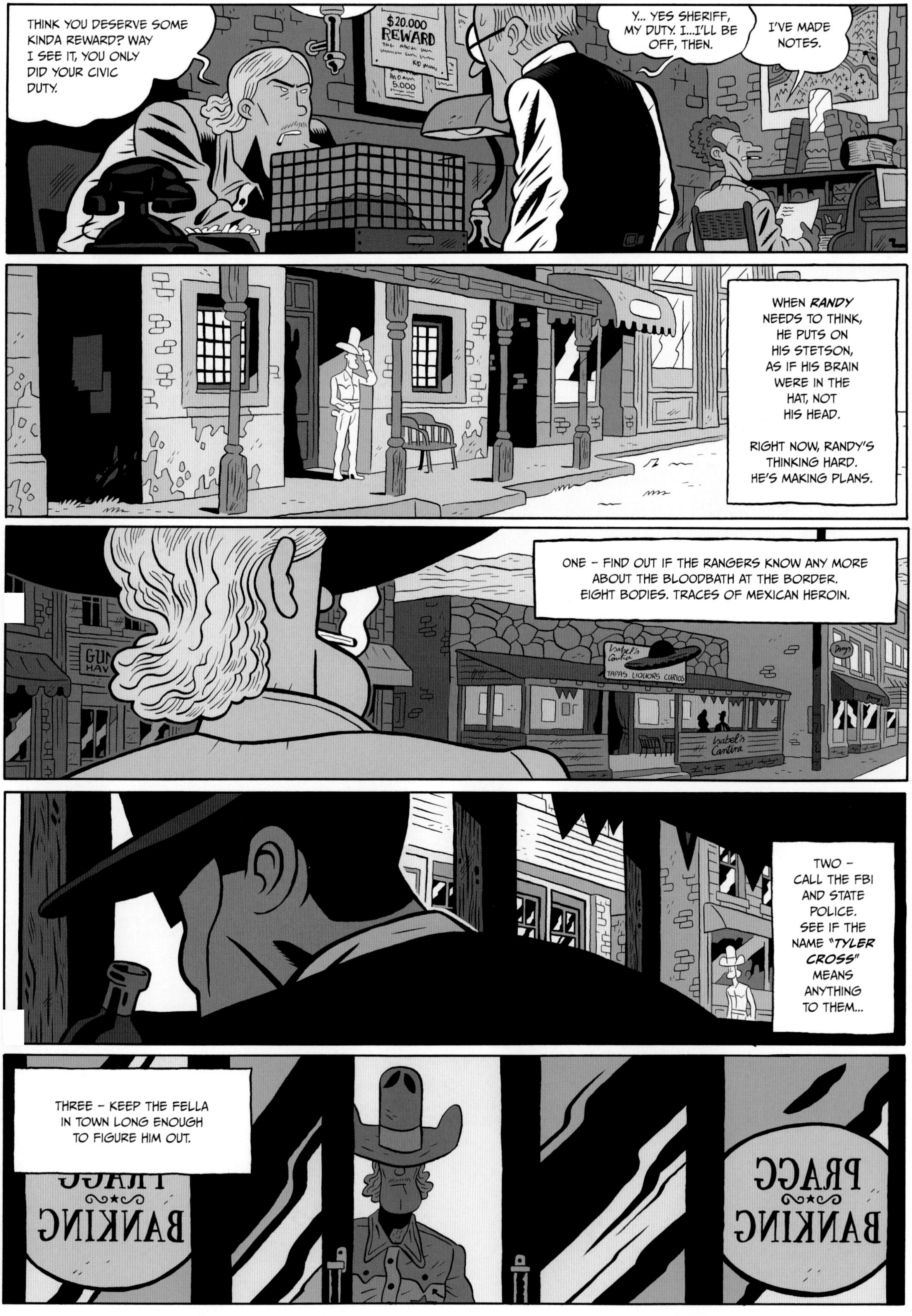
THINK YOU DESERVE SOME KINDA REWARD? WAY I SEE IT, YOU ONLY DID YOUR CIVIC DUTY.
$20.000 REWARD
5.000
Y... YES SHERIFF, MY DUTY. I...I'LL BE OFF, THEN.
I'VE MADE NOTES.
WHEN RANDY NEEDS TO THINK, HE PUTS ON HIS STETSON, AS IF HIS BRAIN WERE IN THE HAT, NOT HIS HEAD.
RIGHT NOW, RANDY'S THINKING HARD. HE'S MAKING PLANS.
ONE – FIND OUT IF THE RANGERS KNOW ANY MORE ABOUT THE BLOODBATH AT THE BORDER. EIGHT BODIES. TRACES OF MEXICAN HEROIN.
Isabel's Cantina
TAPAS LIQUORS CURIOS
Isabel's Cantina
TWO – CALL THE FBI AND STATE POLICE. SEE IF THE NAME "TYLER CROSS" MEANS ANYTHING TO THEM...
THREE – KEEP THE FELLA IN TOWN LONG ENOUGH TO FIGURE HIM OUT.

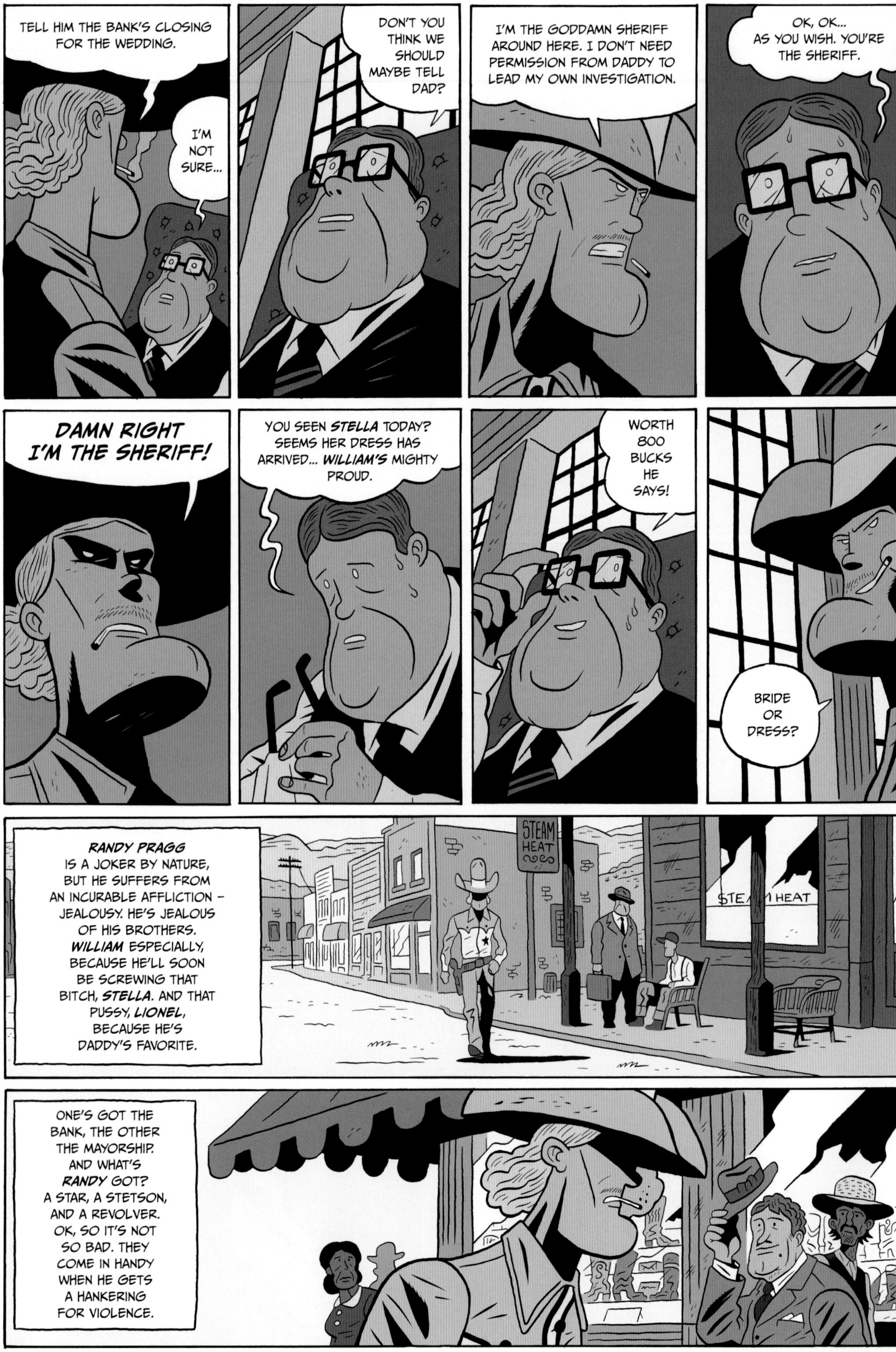
TELL HIM THE BANK'S CLOSING FOR THE WEDDING.
I'M NOT SURE...
DON'T YOU THINK WE SHOULD MAYBE TELL DAD?
I'M THE GODDAMN SHERIFF AROUND HERE. I DON'T NEED PERMISSION FROM DADDY TO LEAD MY OWN INVESTIGATION.
OK, OK... AS YOU WISH. YOU'RE THE SHERIFF.
DAMN RIGHT I'M THE SHERIFF!
YOU SEEN STELLA TODAY? SEEMS HER DRESS HAS ARRIVED... WILLIAM'S MIGHTY PROUD.
WORTH 800 BUCKS HE SAYS!
BRIDE OR DRESS?
RANDY PRAGG IS A JOKER BY NATURE, BUT HE SUFFERS FROM AN INCURABLE AFFLICTION – JEALOUSY. HE'S JEALOUS OF HIS BROTHERS. WILLIAM ESPECIALLY, BECAUSE HE'LL SOON BE SCREWING THAT BITCH, STELLA. AND THAT PUSSY, LIONEL, BECAUSE HE'S DADDY'S FAVORITE.
STEAM HEAT
STEAM HEAT
ONE'S GOT THE BANK, THE OTHER THE MAYORSHIP. AND WHAT'S RANDY GOT? A STAR, A STETSON, AND A REVOLVER. OK, SO IT'S NOT SO BAD. THEY COME IN HANDY WHEN HE GETS A HANKERING FOR VIOLENCE.

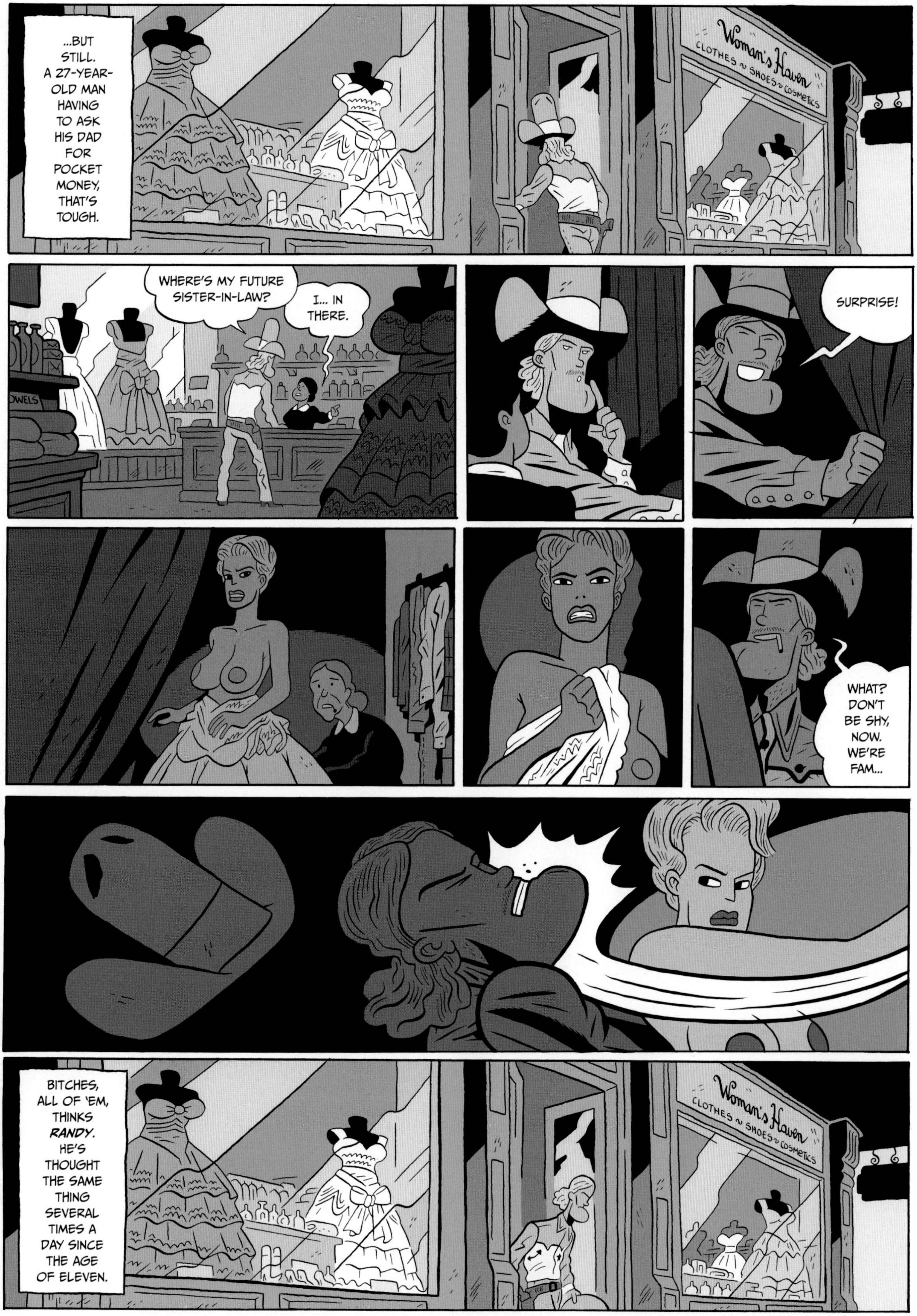
...BUT STILL. A 27-YEAR-OLD MAN HAVING TO ASK HIS DAD FOR POCKET MONEY, THAT'S TOUGH.
Woman's Haven
CLOTHES ~ SHOES ~ COSMETICS
WHERE'S MY FUTURE SISTER-IN-LAW?
I... IN THERE.
SURPRISE!
WHAT? DON'T BE SHY, NOW. WE'RE FAM...
BITCHES, ALL OF 'EM, THINKS *RANDY*. HE'S THOUGHT THE SAME THING SEVERAL TIMES A DAY SINCE THE AGE OF ELEVEN.
Woman's Haven
CLOTHES ~ SHOES ~ COSMETICS

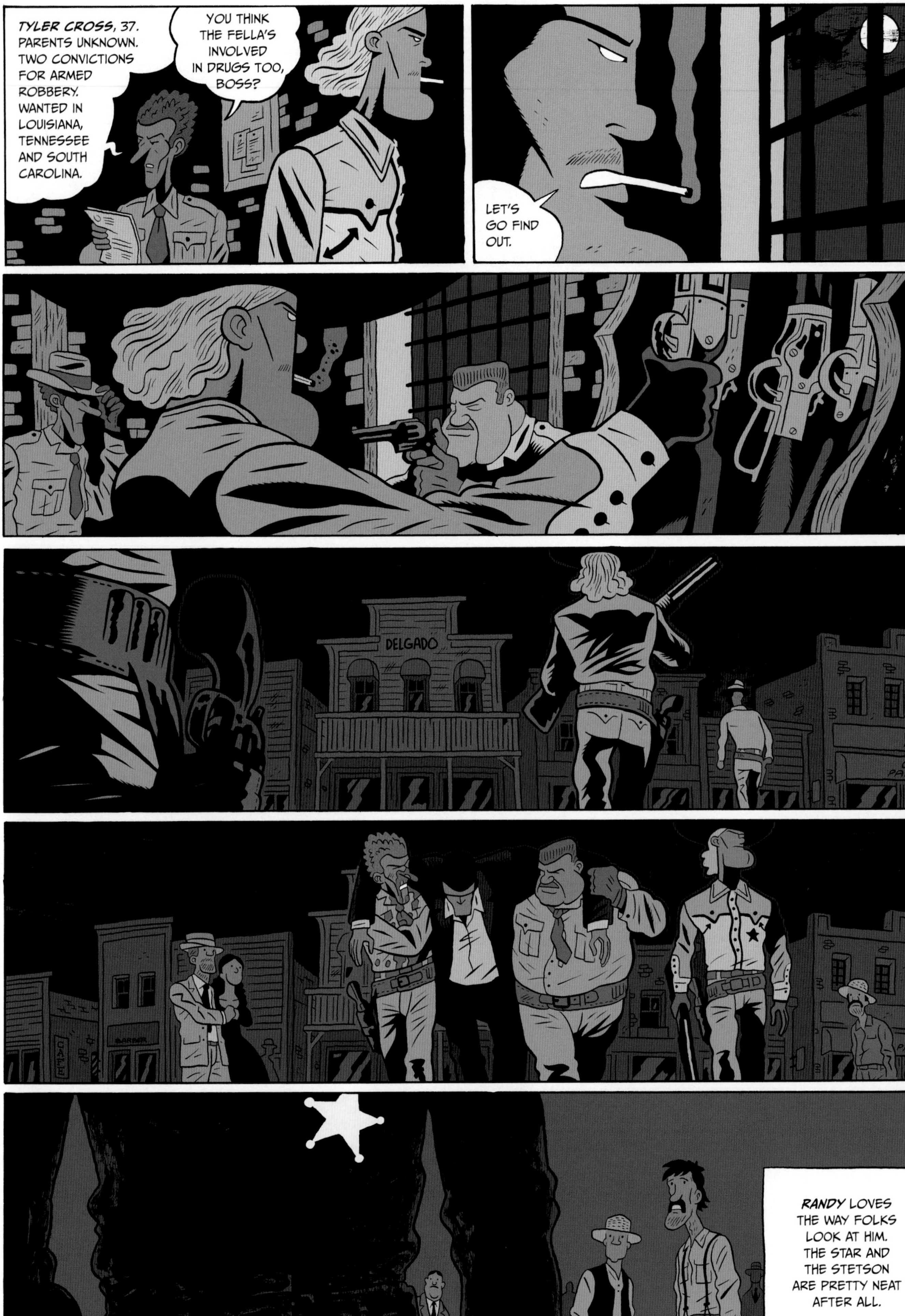
TYLER CROSS, 37. PARENTS UNKNOWN. TWO CONVICTIONS FOR ARMED ROBBERY. WANTED IN LOUISIANA, TENNESSEE AND SOUTH CAROLINA.
YOU THINK THE FELLA'S INVOLVED IN DRUGS TOO, BOSS?
LET'S GO FIND OUT.
DELGADO
RANDY LOVES THE WAY FOLKS LOOK AT HIM. THE STAR AND THE STETSON ARE PRETTY NEAT AFTER ALL.

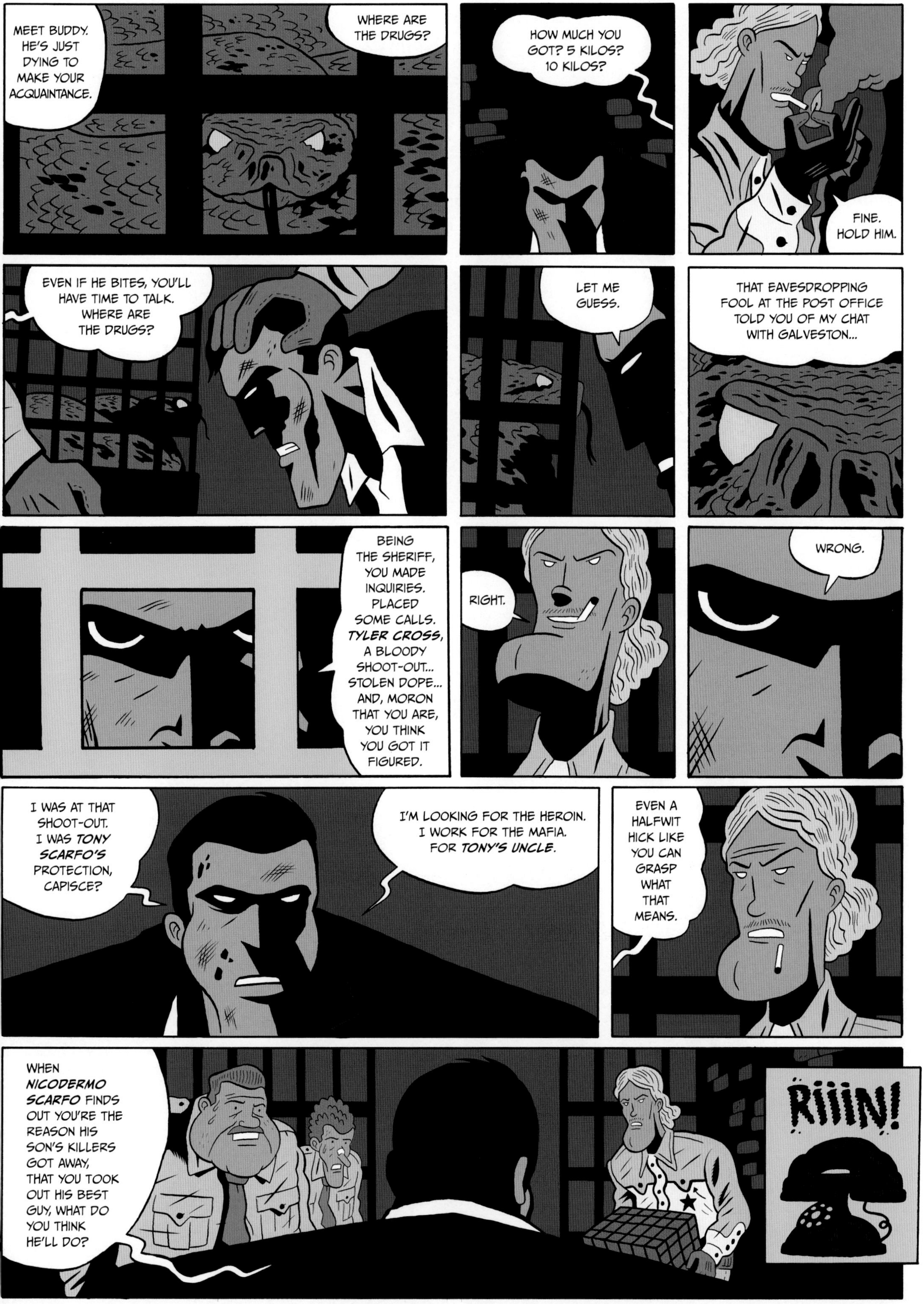
MEET BUDDY. HE'S JUST DYING TO MAKE YOUR ACQUAINTANCE.
WHERE ARE THE DRUGS?
HOW MUCH YOU GOT? 5 KILOS? 10 KILOS?
FINE. HOLD HIM.
EVEN IF HE BITES, YOU'LL HAVE TIME TO TALK. WHERE ARE THE DRUGS?
LET ME GUESS.
THAT EAVESDROPPING FOOL AT THE POST OFFICE TOLD YOU OF MY CHAT WITH GALVESTON...
BEING THE SHERIFF, YOU MADE INQUIRIES. PLACED SOME CALLS. *TYLER CROSS*, A BLOODY SHOOT-OUT... STOLEN DOPE... AND, MORON THAT YOU ARE, YOU THINK YOU GOT IT FIGURED.
RIGHT.
WRONG.
I WAS AT THAT SHOOT-OUT. I WAS *TONY SCARFO'S* PROTECTION, CAPISCE?
I'M LOOKING FOR THE HEROIN. I WORK FOR THE MAFIA. FOR *TONY'S UNCLE*.
EVEN A HALFWIT HICK LIKE YOU CAN GRASP WHAT THAT MEANS.
WHEN *NICODERMO SCARFO* FINDS OUT YOU'RE THE REASON HIS SON'S KILLERS GOT AWAY, THAT YOU TOOK OUT HIS BEST GUY, WHAT DO YOU THINK HE'LL DO?
RIIIN!

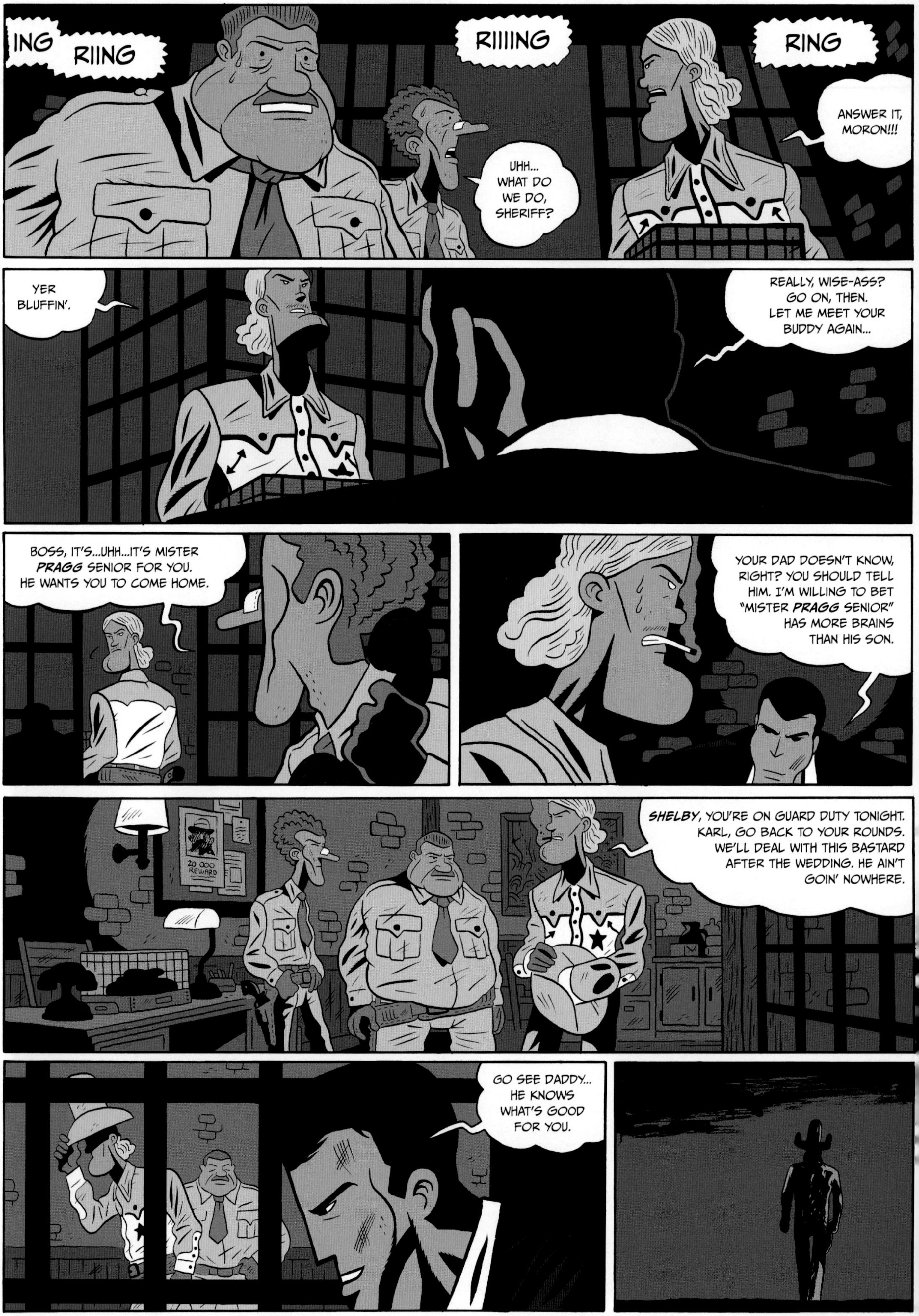
ING
RIING
RIIIING
RING
UHH... WHAT DO WE DO, SHERIFF?
ANSWER IT, MORON!!!
YER BLUFFIN'.
REALLY, WISE-ASS? GO ON, THEN. LET ME MEET YOUR BUDDY AGAIN...
BOSS, IT'S...UHH...IT'S MISTER PRAGG SENIOR FOR YOU. HE WANTS YOU TO COME HOME.
YOUR DAD DOESN'T KNOW, RIGHT? YOU SHOULD TELL HIM. I'M WILLING TO BET "MISTER PRAGG SENIOR" HAS MORE BRAINS THAN HIS SON.
20 000 REWARD
SHELBY, YOU'RE ON GUARD DUTY TONIGHT. KARL, GO BACK TO YOUR ROUNDS. WE'LL DEAL WITH THIS BASTARD AFTER THE WEDDING. HE AIN'T GOIN' NOWHERE.
GO SEE DADDY... HE KNOWS WHAT'S GOOD FOR YOU.

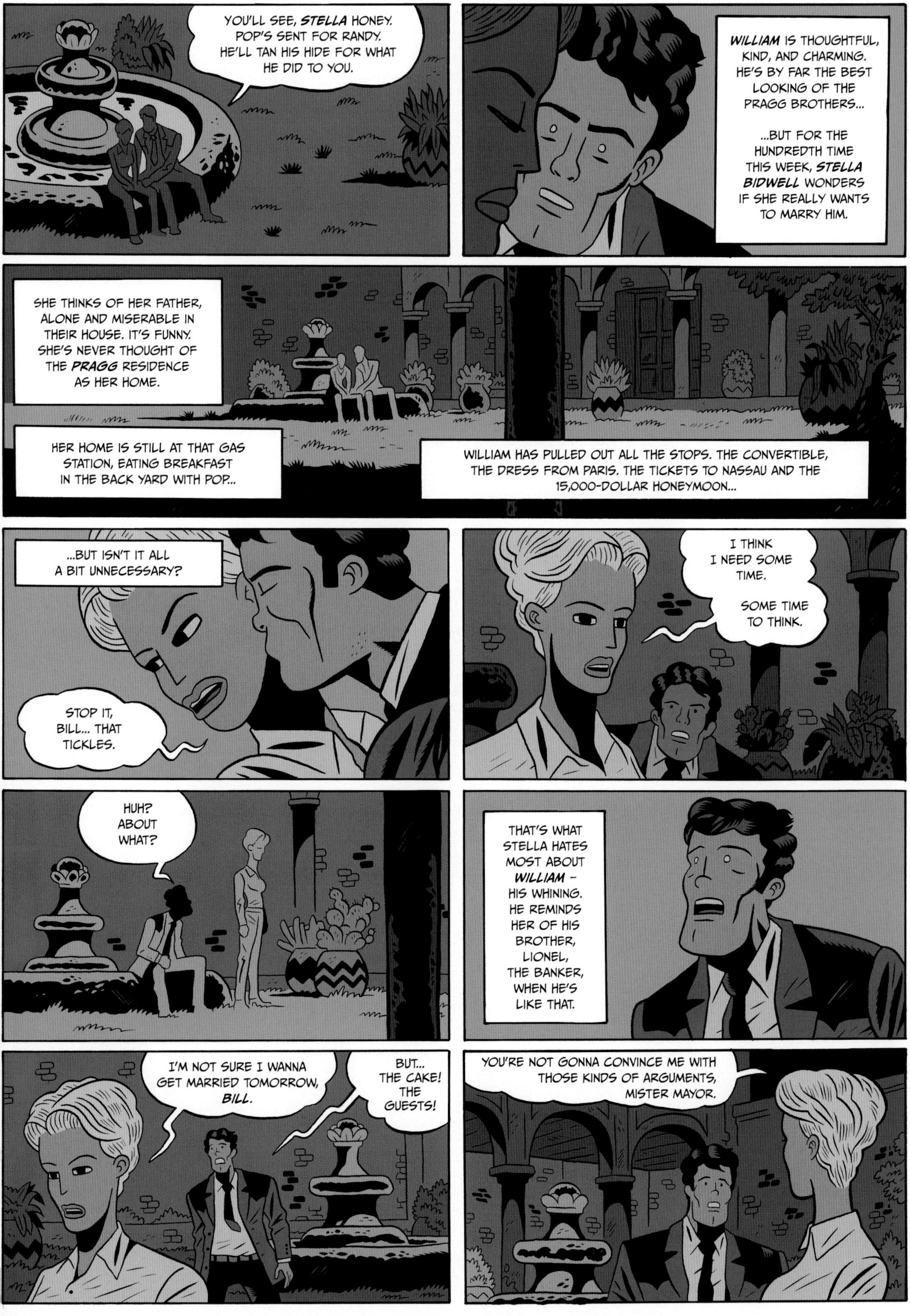
YOU'LL SEE, STELLA HONEY. POP'S SENT FOR RANDY. HE'LL TAN HIS HIDE FOR WHAT HE DID TO YOU.
WILLIAM IS THOUGHTFUL, KIND, AND CHARMING. HE'S BY FAR THE BEST LOOKING OF THE PRAGG BROTHERS...
...BUT FOR THE HUNDREDTH TIME THIS WEEK, STELLA BIDWELL WONDERS IF SHE REALLY WANTS TO MARRY HIM.
SHE THINKS OF HER FATHER, ALONE AND MISERABLE IN THEIR HOUSE. IT'S FUNNY. SHE'S NEVER THOUGHT OF THE PRAGG RESIDENCE AS HER HOME.
HER HOME IS STILL AT THAT GAS STATION, EATING BREAKFAST IN THE BACK YARD WITH POP...
WILLIAM HAS PULLED OUT ALL THE STOPS. THE CONVERTIBLE, THE DRESS FROM PARIS. THE TICKETS TO NASSAU AND THE 15,000-DOLLAR HONEYMOON...
...BUT ISN'T IT ALL A BIT UNNECESSARY?
STOP IT, BILL... THAT TICKLES.
I THINK I NEED SOME TIME.
SOME TIME TO THINK.
HUH? ABOUT WHAT?
THAT'S WHAT STELLA HATES MOST ABOUT WILLIAM – HIS WHINING. HE REMINDS HER OF HIS BROTHER, LIONEL, THE BANKER, WHEN HE'S LIKE THAT.
I'M NOT SURE I WANNA GET MARRIED TOMORROW, BILL.
BUT... THE CAKE! THE GUESTS!
YOU'RE NOT GONNA CONVINCE ME WITH THOSE KINDS OF ARGUMENTS, MISTER MAYOR.

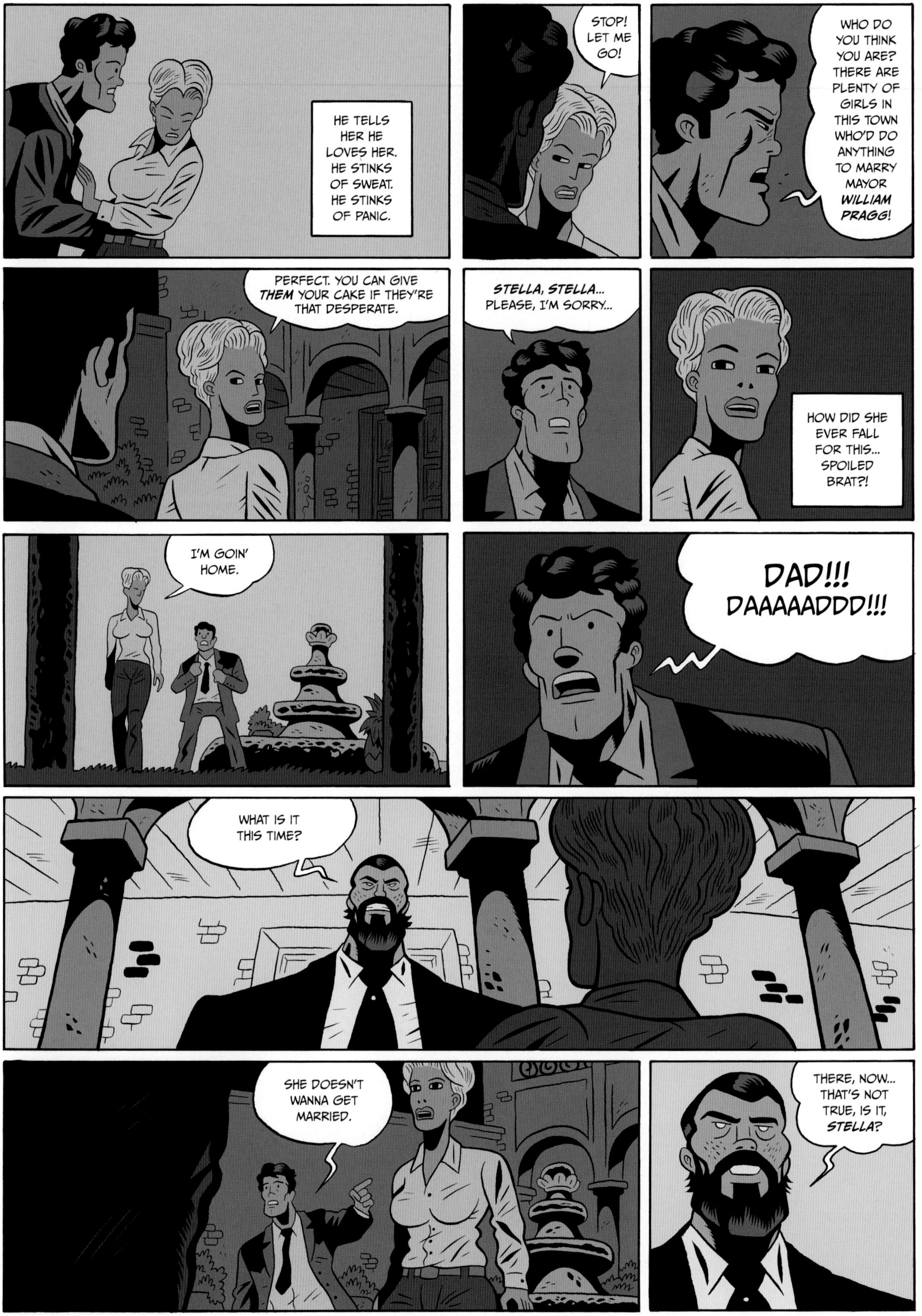
HE TELLS HER HE LOVES HER. HE STINKS OF SWEAT. HE STINKS OF PANIC.
STOP! LET ME GO!
WHO DO YOU THINK YOU ARE? THERE ARE PLENTY OF GIRLS IN THIS TOWN WHO'D DO ANYTHING TO MARRY MAYOR WILLIAM PRAGG!
PERFECT. YOU CAN GIVE THEM YOUR CAKE IF THEY'RE THAT DESPERATE.
STELLA, STELLA... PLEASE, I'M SORRY...
HOW DID SHE EVER FALL FOR THIS... SPOILED BRAT?!
I'M GOIN' HOME.
DAD!!! DAAAAADDD!!!
WHAT IS IT THIS TIME?
SHE DOESN'T WANNA GET MARRIED.
THERE, NOW... THAT'S NOT TRUE, IS IT, STELLA?

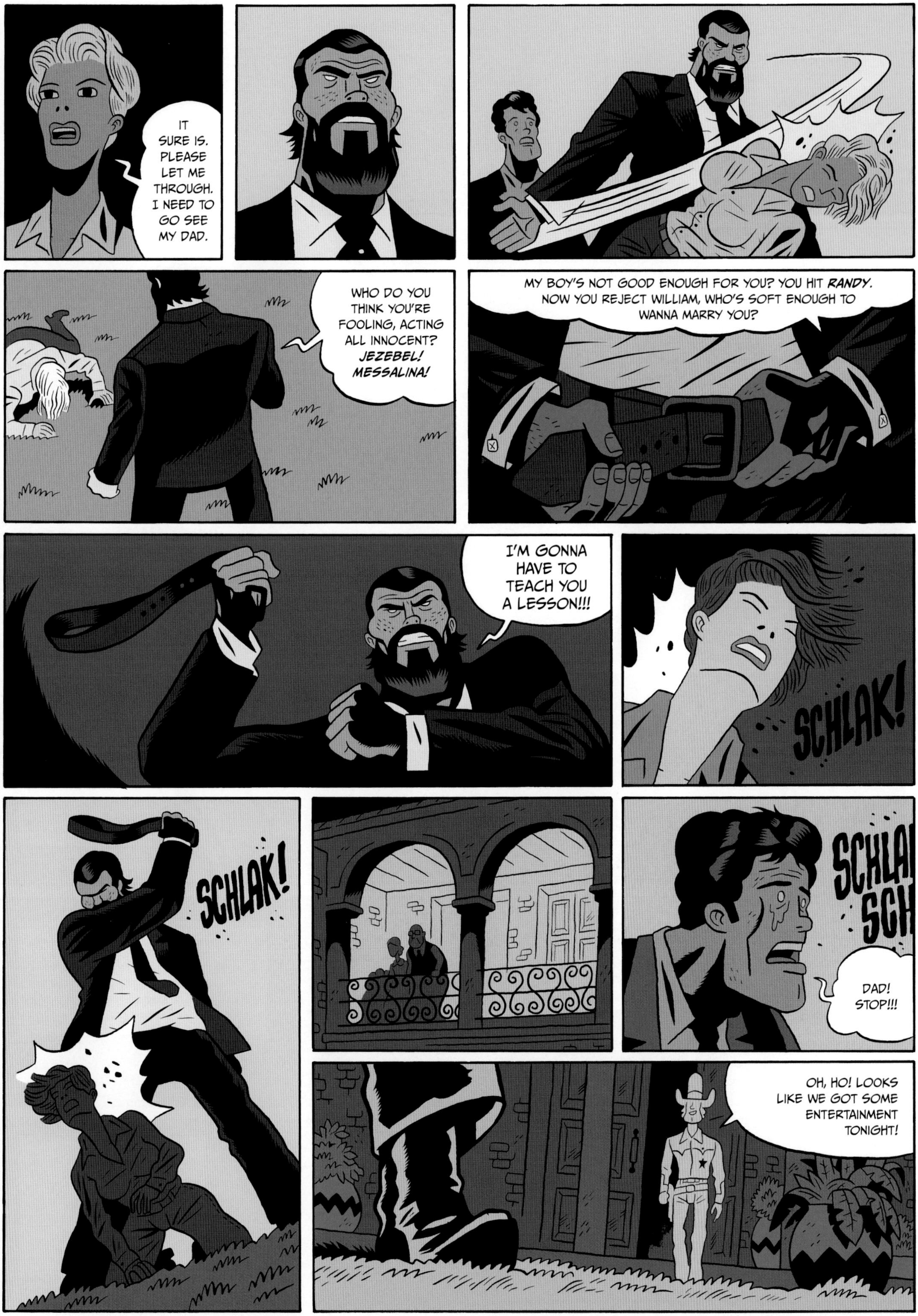
IT SURE IS. PLEASE LET ME THROUGH. I NEED TO GO SEE MY DAD.
WHO DO YOU THINK YOU'RE FOOLING, ACTING ALL INNOCENT? JEZEBEL! MESSALINA!
MY BOY'S NOT GOOD ENOUGH FOR YOU? YOU HIT RANDY. NOW YOU REJECT WILLIAM, WHO'S SOFT ENOUGH TO WANNA MARRY YOU?
I'M GONNA HAVE TO TEACH YOU A LESSON!!!
SCHLAK!
SCHLAK!
DAD! STOP!!!
OH, HO! LOOKS LIKE WE GOT SOME ENTERTAINMENT TONIGHT!

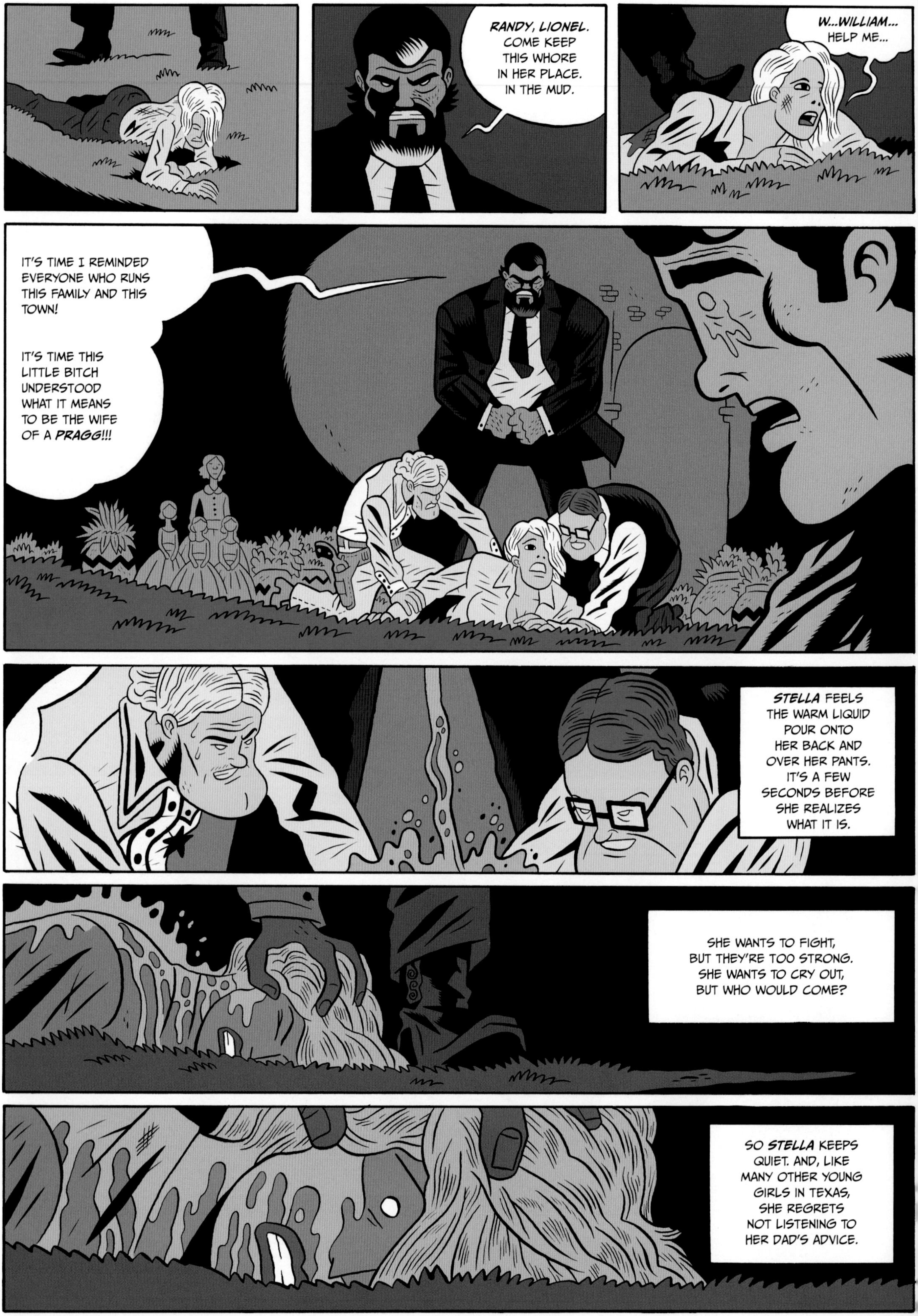
RANDY, LIONEL. COME KEEP THIS WHORE IN HER PLACE. IN THE MUD.
W...WILLIAM... HELP ME...
IT'S TIME I REMINDED EVERYONE WHO RUNS THIS FAMILY AND THIS TOWN!
IT'S TIME THIS LITTLE BITCH UNDERSTOOD WHAT IT MEANS TO BE THE WIFE OF A PRAGG!!!
STELLA FEELS THE WARM LIQUID POUR ONTO HER BACK AND OVER HER PANTS. IT'S A FEW SECONDS BEFORE SHE REALIZES WHAT IT IS.
SHE WANTS TO FIGHT, BUT THEY'RE TOO STRONG. SHE WANTS TO CRY OUT, BUT WHO WOULD COME?
SO STELLA KEEPS QUIET. AND, LIKE MANY OTHER YOUNG GIRLS IN TEXAS, SHE REGRETS NOT LISTENING TO HER DAD'S ADVICE.

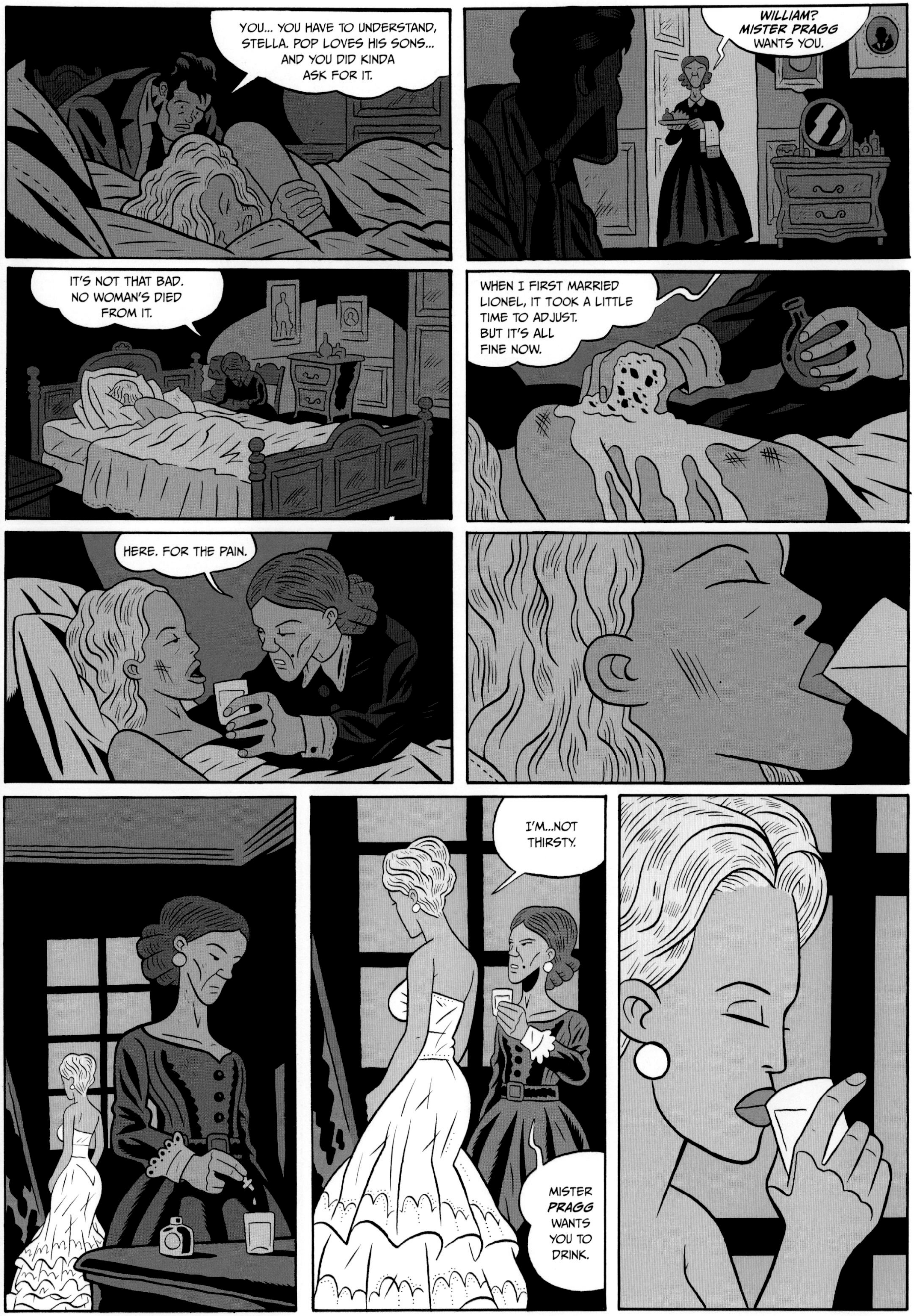
YOU... YOU HAVE TO UNDERSTAND, STELLA. POP LOVES HIS SONS... AND YOU DID KINDA ASK FOR IT.
WILLIAM? MISTER PRAGG WANTS YOU.
IT'S NOT THAT BAD. NO WOMAN'S DIED FROM IT.
WHEN I FIRST MARRIED LIONEL, IT TOOK A LITTLE TIME TO ADJUST. BUT IT'S ALL FINE NOW.
HERE. FOR THE PAIN.
I'M...NOT THIRSTY.
MISTER PRAGG WANTS YOU TO DRINK.

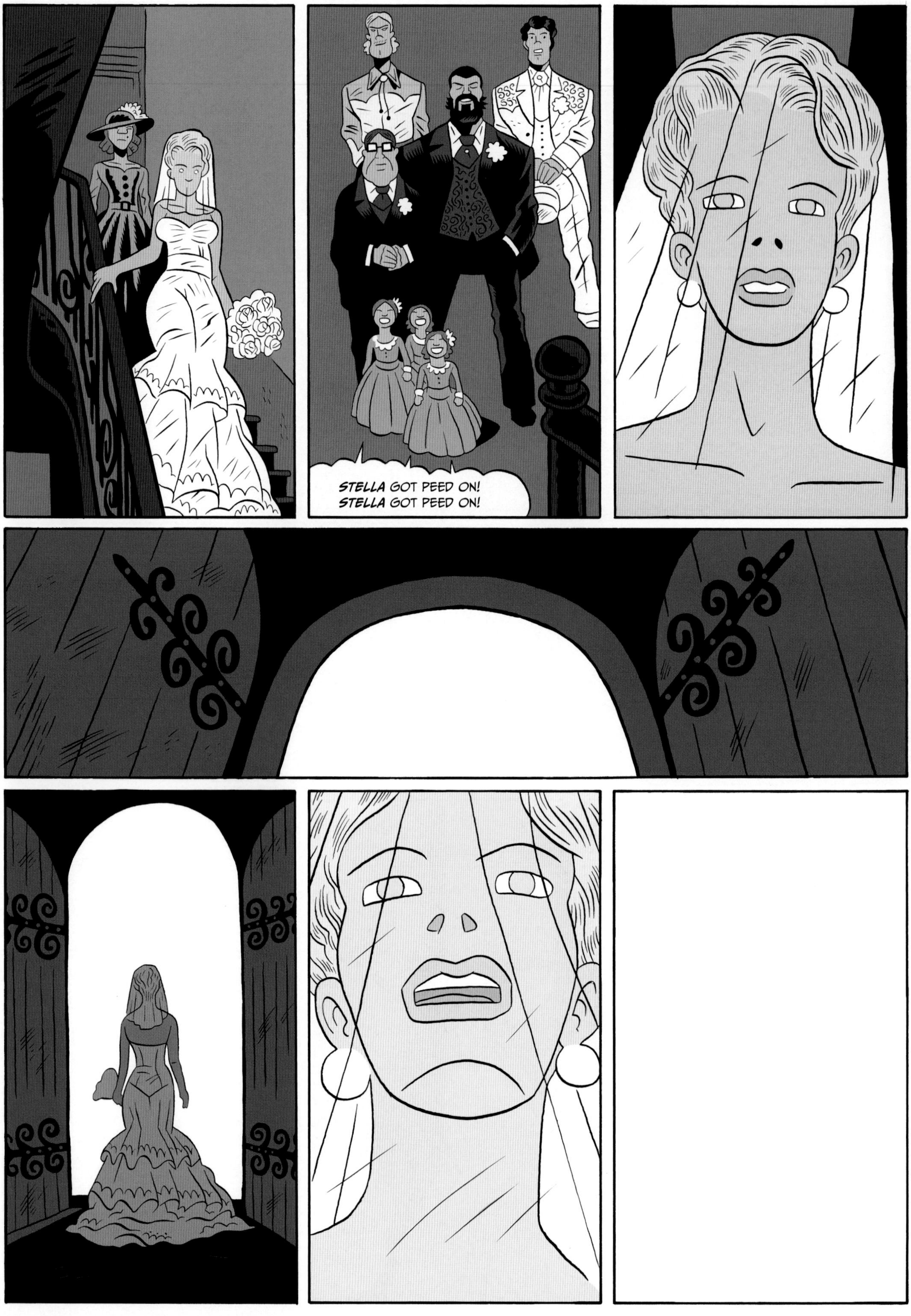
STELLA GOT PEED ON!
STELLA GOT PEED ON!

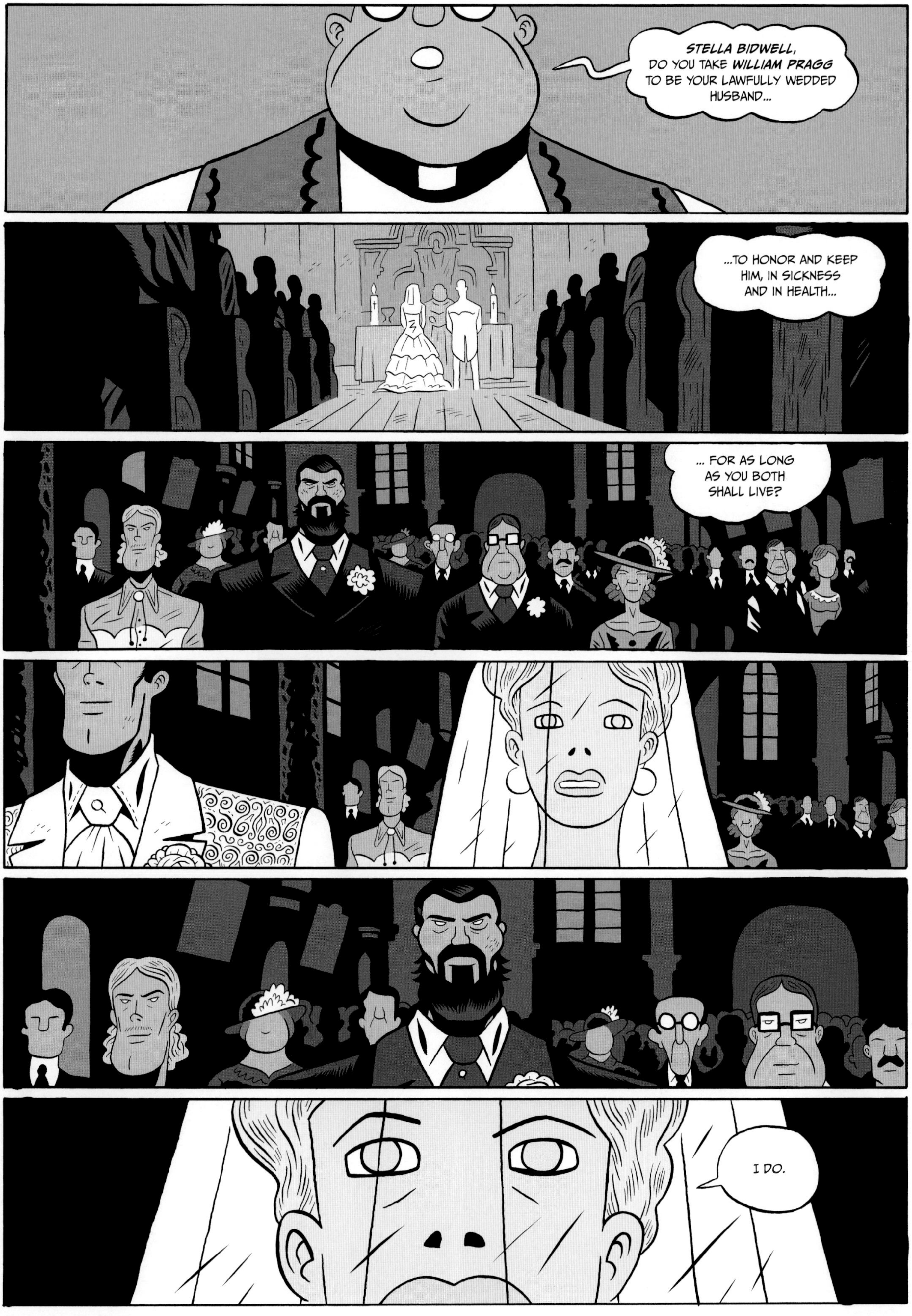
STELLA BIDWELL, DO YOU TAKE WILLIAM PRAGG TO BE YOUR LAWFULLY WEDDED HUSBAND...
...TO HONOR AND KEEP HIM, IN SICKNESS AND IN HEALTH...
... FOR AS LONG AS YOU BOTH SHALL LIVE?
I DO.

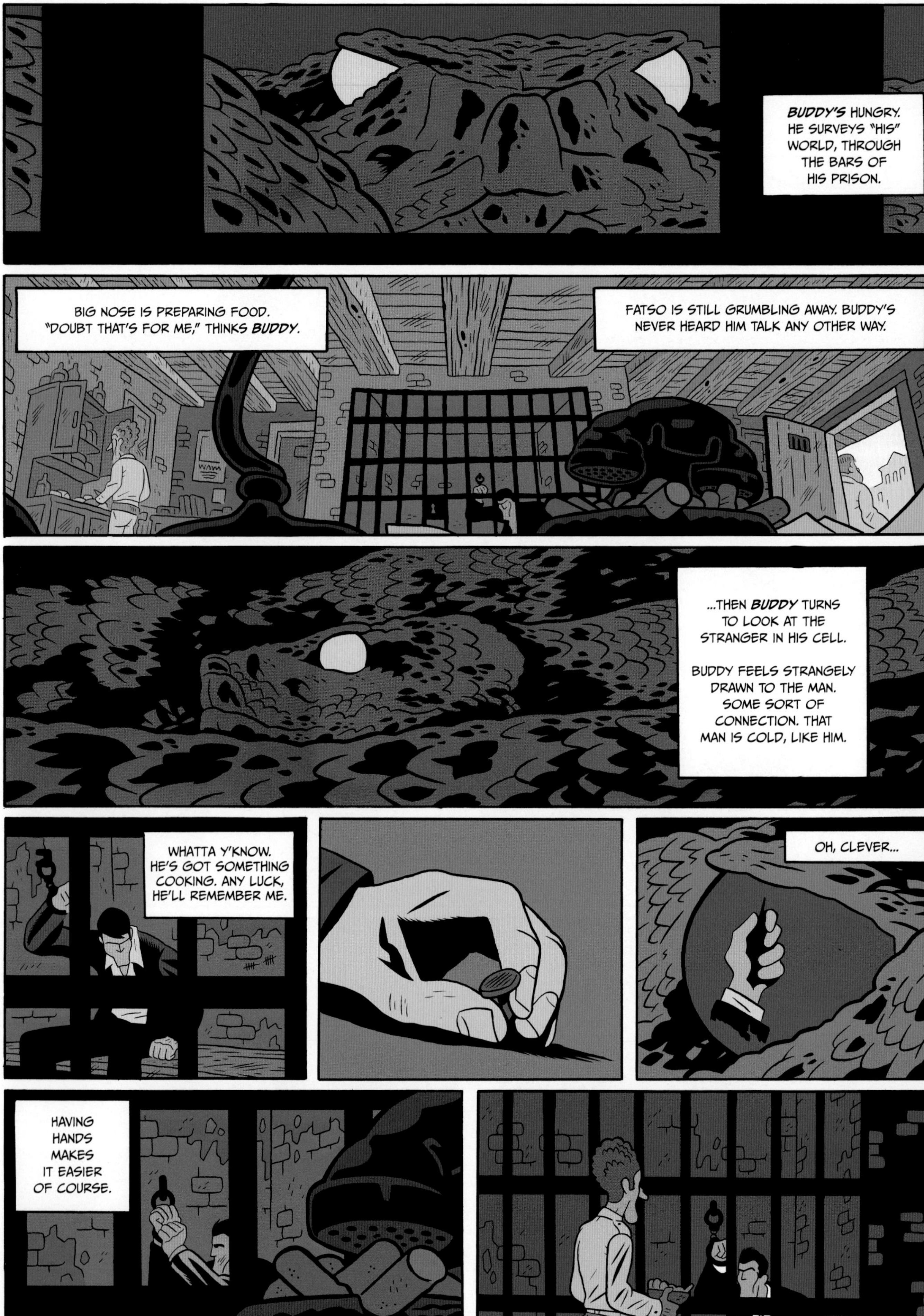
BUDDY'S HUNGRY. HE SURVEYS "HIS" WORLD, THROUGH THE BARS OF HIS PRISON.
BIG NOSE IS PREPARING FOOD. "DOUBT THAT'S FOR ME," THINKS BUDDY.
FATSO IS STILL GRUMBLING AWAY. BUDDY'S NEVER HEARD HIM TALK ANY OTHER WAY.
...THEN BUDDY TURNS TO LOOK AT THE STRANGER IN HIS CELL.
BUDDY FEELS STRANGELY DRAWN TO THE MAN. SOME SORT OF CONNECTION. THAT MAN IS COLD, LIKE HIM.
WHATTA Y'KNOW. HE'S GOT SOMETHING COOKING. ANY LUCK, HE'LL REMEMBER ME.
OH, CLEVER...
HAVING HANDS MAKES IT EASIER OF COURSE.

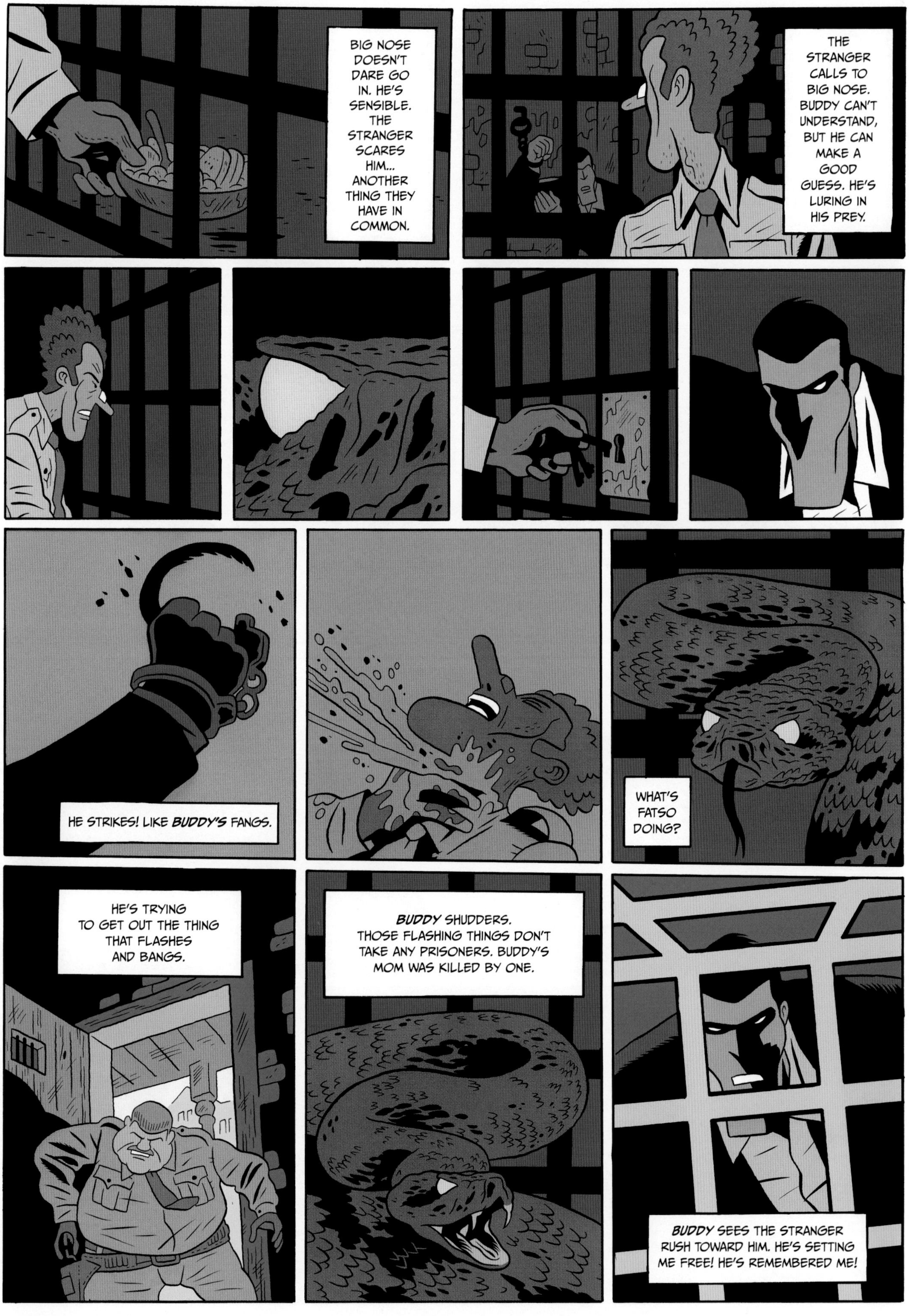
BIG NOSE DOESN'T DARE GO IN. HE'S SENSIBLE. THE STRANGER SCARES HIM... ANOTHER THING THEY HAVE IN COMMON.
THE STRANGER CALLS TO BIG NOSE. BUDDY CAN'T UNDERSTAND, BUT HE CAN MAKE A GOOD GUESS. HE'S LURING IN HIS PREY.
HE STRIKES! LIKE *BUDDY'S* FANGS.
WHAT'S FATSO DOING?
HE'S TRYING TO GET OUT THE THING THAT FLASHES AND BANGS.
BUDDY SHUDDERS. THOSE FLASHING THINGS DON'T TAKE ANY PRISONERS. BUDDY'S MOM WAS KILLED BY ONE.
BUDDY SEES THE STRANGER RUSH TOWARD HIM. HE'S SETTING ME FREE! HE'S REMEMBERED ME!

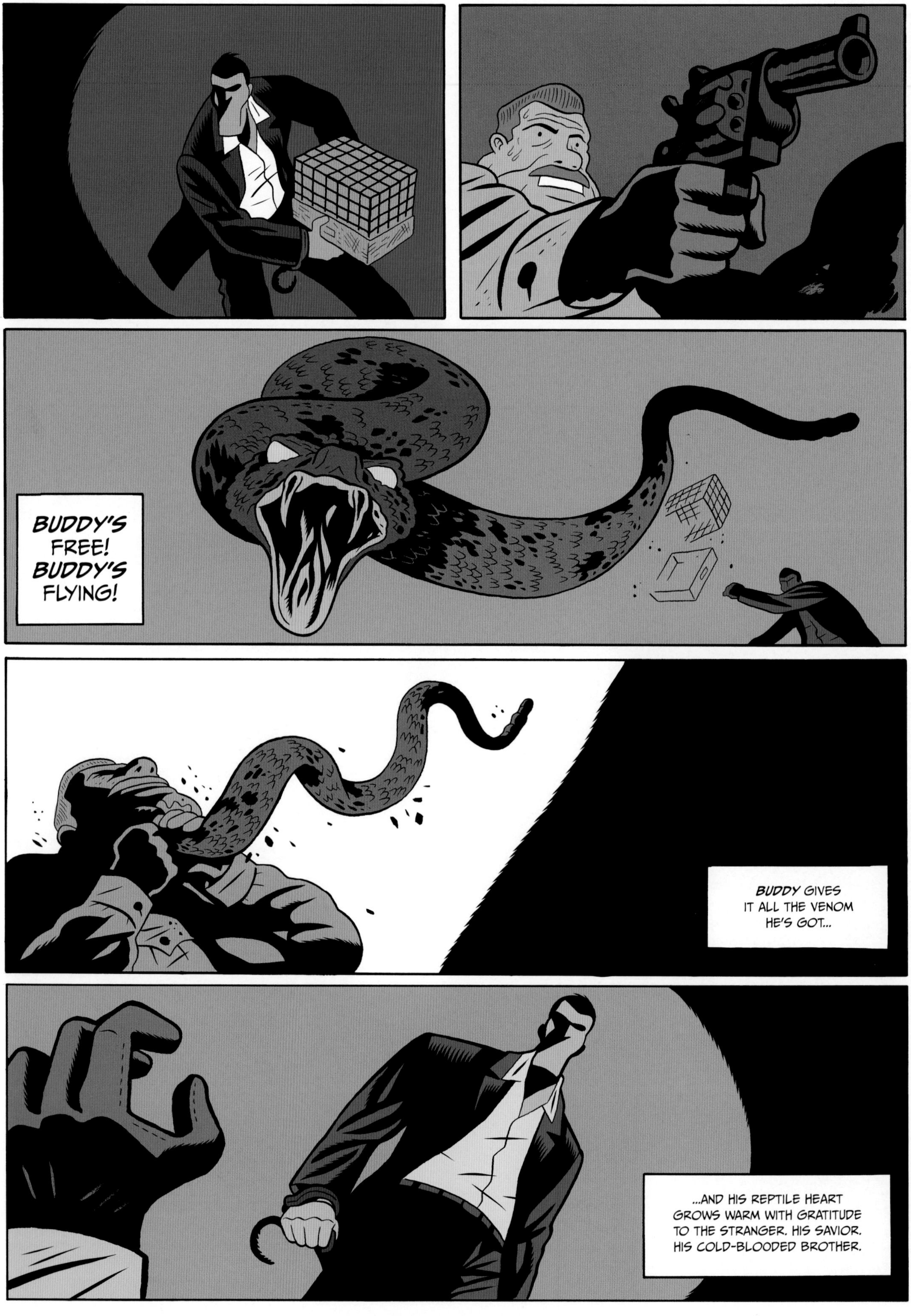

BUDDY'S FREE! BUDDY'S FLYING!
BUDDY GIVES IT ALL THE VENOM HE'S GOT...
...AND HIS REPTILE HEART GROWS WARM WITH GRATITUDE TO THE STRANGER. HIS SAVIOR. HIS COLD-BLOODED BROTHER.

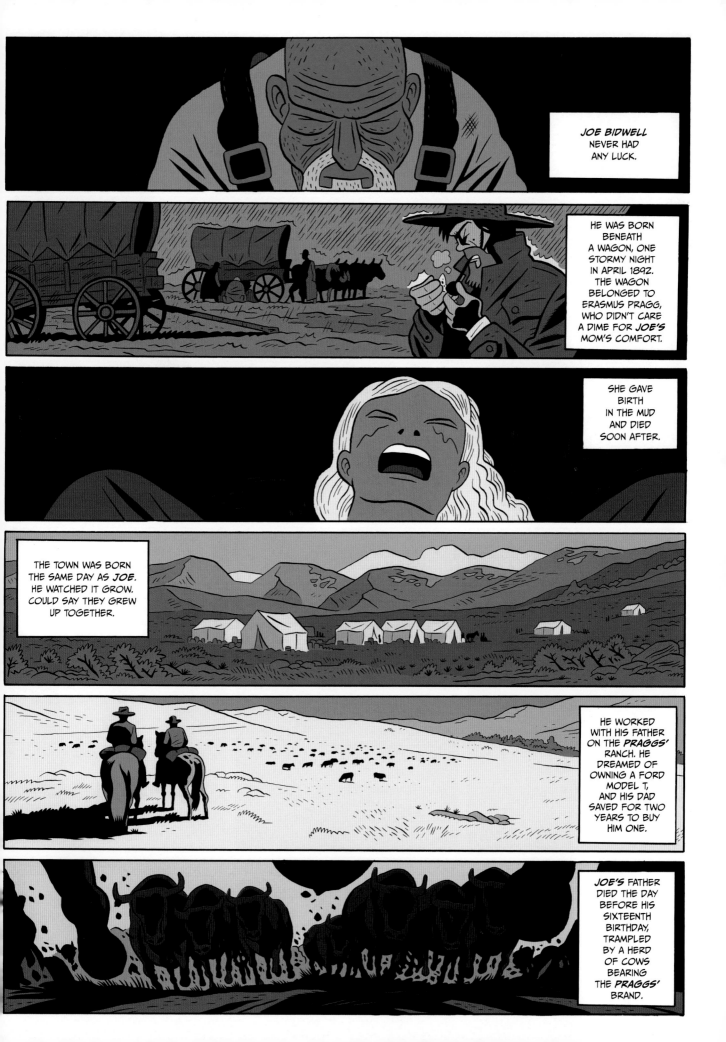

JOE BIDWELL NEVER HAD ANY LUCK.

HE WAS BORN BENEATH A WAGON, ONE STORMY NIGHT IN APRIL 1892. THE WAGON BELONGED TO ERASMUS PRAGG, WHO DIDN'T CARE A DIME FOR *JOE'S* MOM'S COMFORT.

SHE GAVE BIRTH IN THE MUD AND DIED SOON AFTER.

THE TOWN WAS BORN THE SAME DAY AS *JOE*. HE WATCHED IT GROW. COULD SAY THEY GREW UP TOGETHER.

HE WORKED WITH HIS FATHER ON THE *PRAGGS'* RANCH. HE DREAMED OF OWNING A FORD MODEL T, AND HIS DAD SAVED FOR TWO YEARS TO BUY HIM ONE.

JOE'S FATHER DIED THE DAY BEFORE HIS SIXTEENTH BIRTHDAY, TRAMPLED BY A HERD OF COWS BEARING THE *PRAGGS'* BRAND.

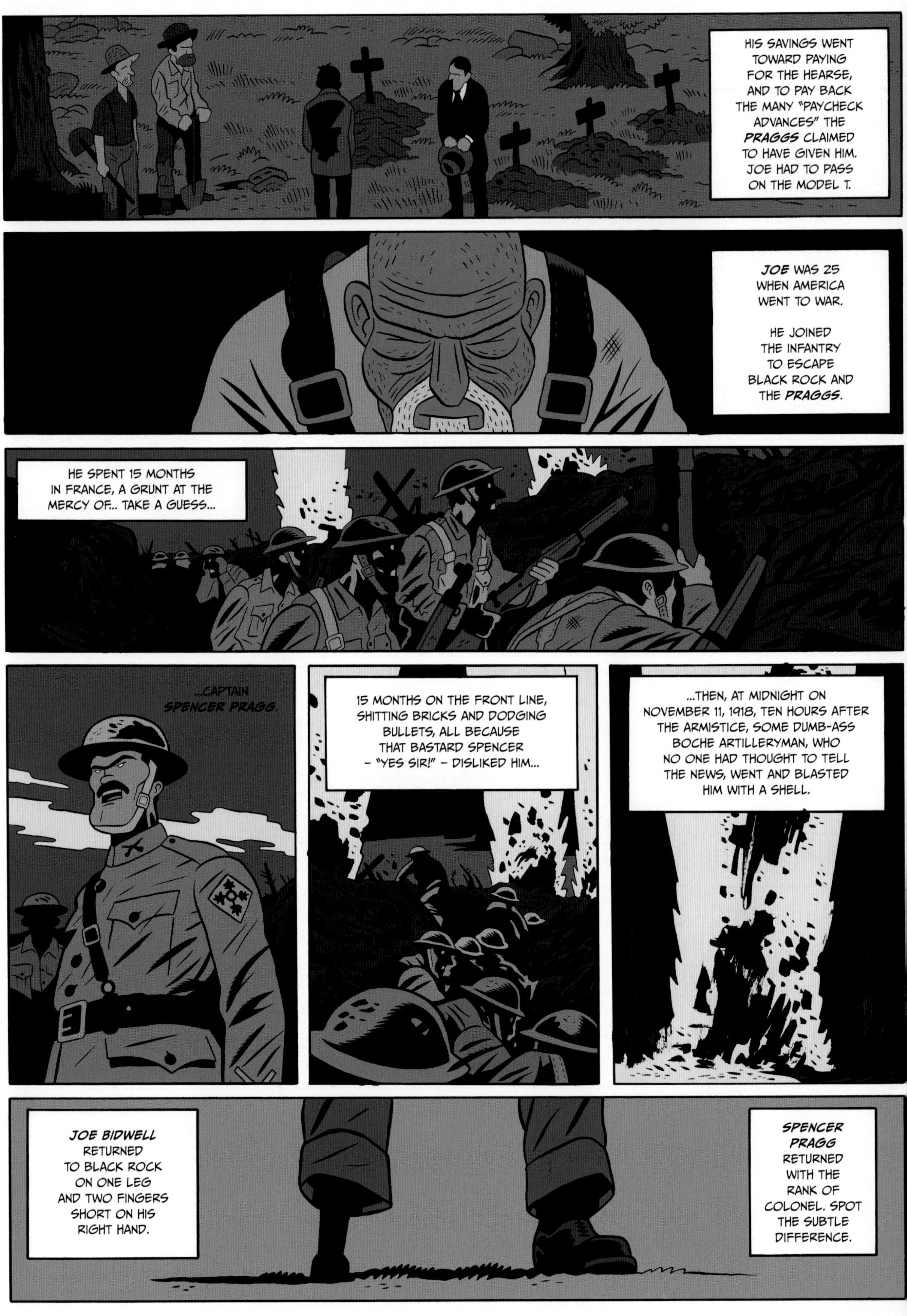
HIS SAVINGS WENT TOWARD PAYING FOR THE HEARSE, AND TO PAY BACK THE MANY "PAYCHECK ADVANCES" THE *PRAGGS* CLAIMED TO HAVE GIVEN HIM. JOE HAD TO PASS ON THE MODEL T.
JOE WAS 25 WHEN AMERICA WENT TO WAR.
HE JOINED THE INFANTRY TO ESCAPE BLACK ROCK AND THE *PRAGGS*.
HE SPENT 15 MONTHS IN FRANCE, A GRUNT AT THE MERCY OF... TAKE A GUESS...
...CAPTAIN *SPENCER PRAGG*.
15 MONTHS ON THE FRONT LINE, SHITTING BRICKS AND DODGING BULLETS, ALL BECAUSE THAT BASTARD SPENCER – "YES SIR!" – DISLIKED HIM...
...THEN, AT MIDNIGHT ON NOVEMBER 11, 1918, TEN HOURS AFTER THE ARMISTICE, SOME DUMB-ASS BOCHE ARTILLERYMAN, WHO NO ONE HAD THOUGHT TO TELL THE NEWS, WENT AND BLASTED HIM WITH A SHELL.
JOE BIDWELL RETURNED TO BLACK ROCK ON ONE LEG AND TWO FINGERS SHORT ON HIS RIGHT HAND.
SPENCER PRAGG RETURNED WITH THE RANK OF COLONEL. SPOT THE SUBTLE DIFFERENCE.

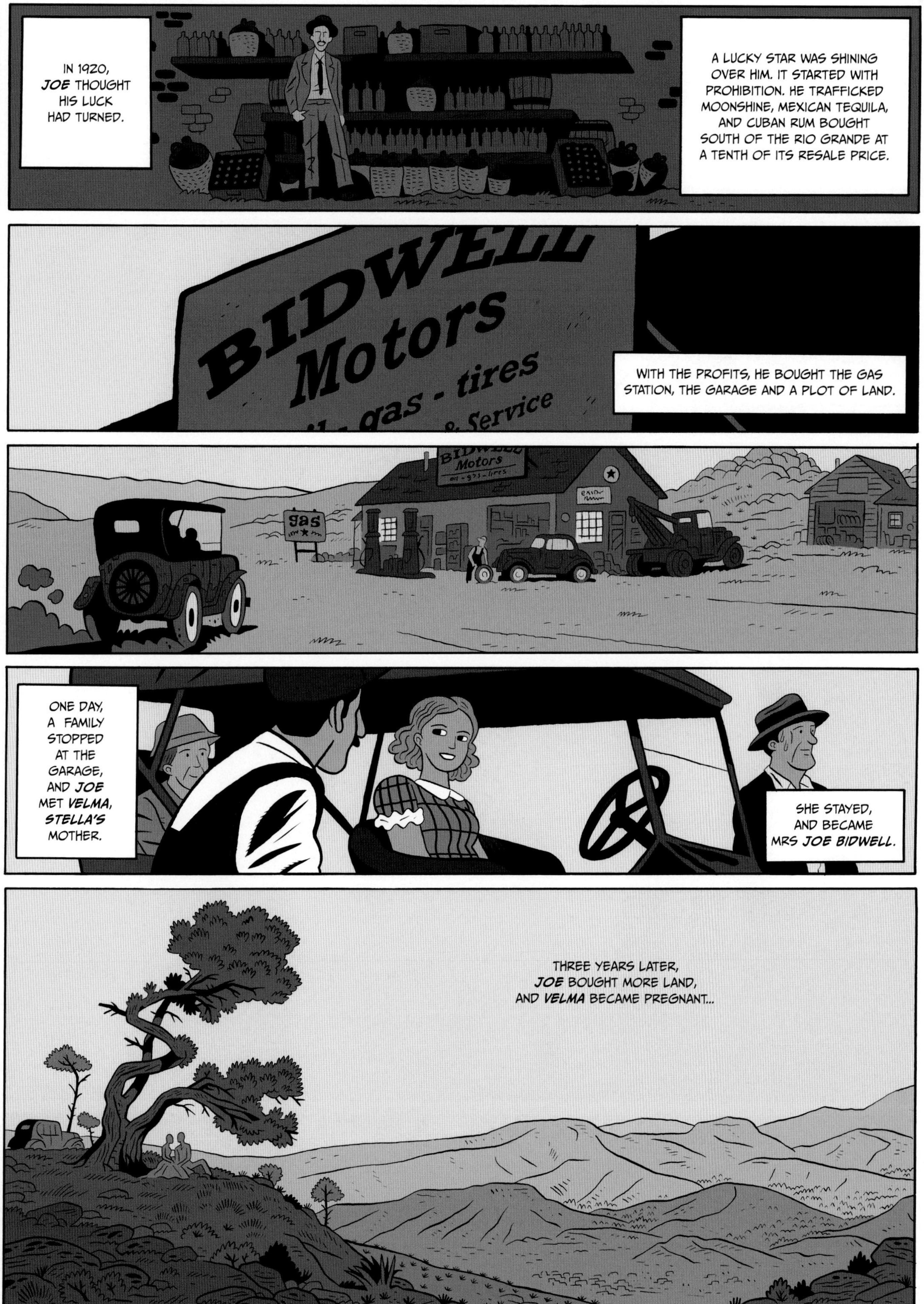
IN 1920, JOE THOUGHT HIS LUCK HAD TURNED.
A LUCKY STAR WAS SHINING OVER HIM. IT STARTED WITH PROHIBITION. HE TRAFFICKED MOONSHINE, MEXICAN TEQUILA, AND CUBAN RUM BOUGHT SOUTH OF THE RIO GRANDE AT A TENTH OF ITS RESALE PRICE.
BIDWELL
Motors
gas - tires
& Service
WITH THE PROFITS, HE BOUGHT THE GAS STATION, THE GARAGE AND A PLOT OF LAND.
Motors
gas
ONE DAY, A FAMILY STOPPED AT THE GARAGE, AND JOE MET VELMA, STELLA'S MOTHER.
SHE STAYED, AND BECAME MRS JOE BIDWELL.
THREE YEARS LATER, JOE BOUGHT MORE LAND, AND VELMA BECAME PREGNANT...

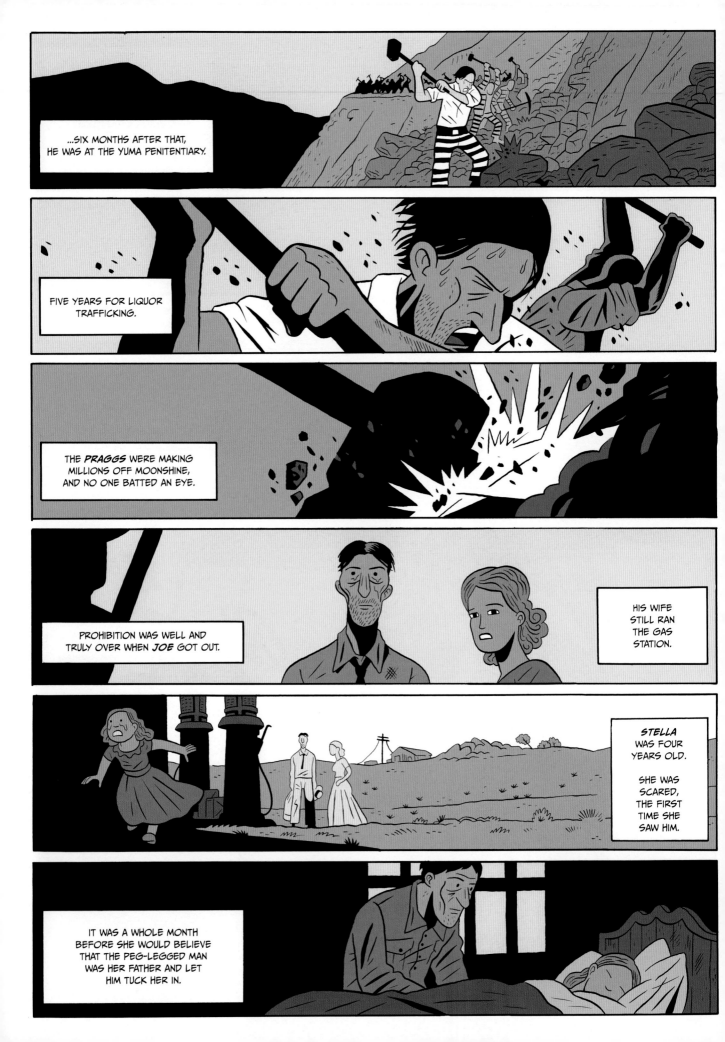

...SIX MONTHS AFTER THAT, HE WAS AT THE YUMA PENITENTIARY.

FIVE YEARS FOR LIQUOR TRAFFICKING.

THE *PRAGGS* WERE MAKING MILLIONS OFF MOONSHINE, AND NO ONE BATTED AN EYE.

PROHIBITION WAS WELL AND TRULY OVER WHEN *JOE* GOT OUT.

HIS WIFE STILL RAN THE GAS STATION.

STELLA WAS FOUR YEARS OLD.

SHE WAS SCARED, THE FIRST TIME SHE SAW HIM.

IT WAS A WHOLE MONTH BEFORE SHE WOULD BELIEVE THAT THE PEG-LEGGED MAN WAS HER FATHER AND LET HIM TUCK HER IN.

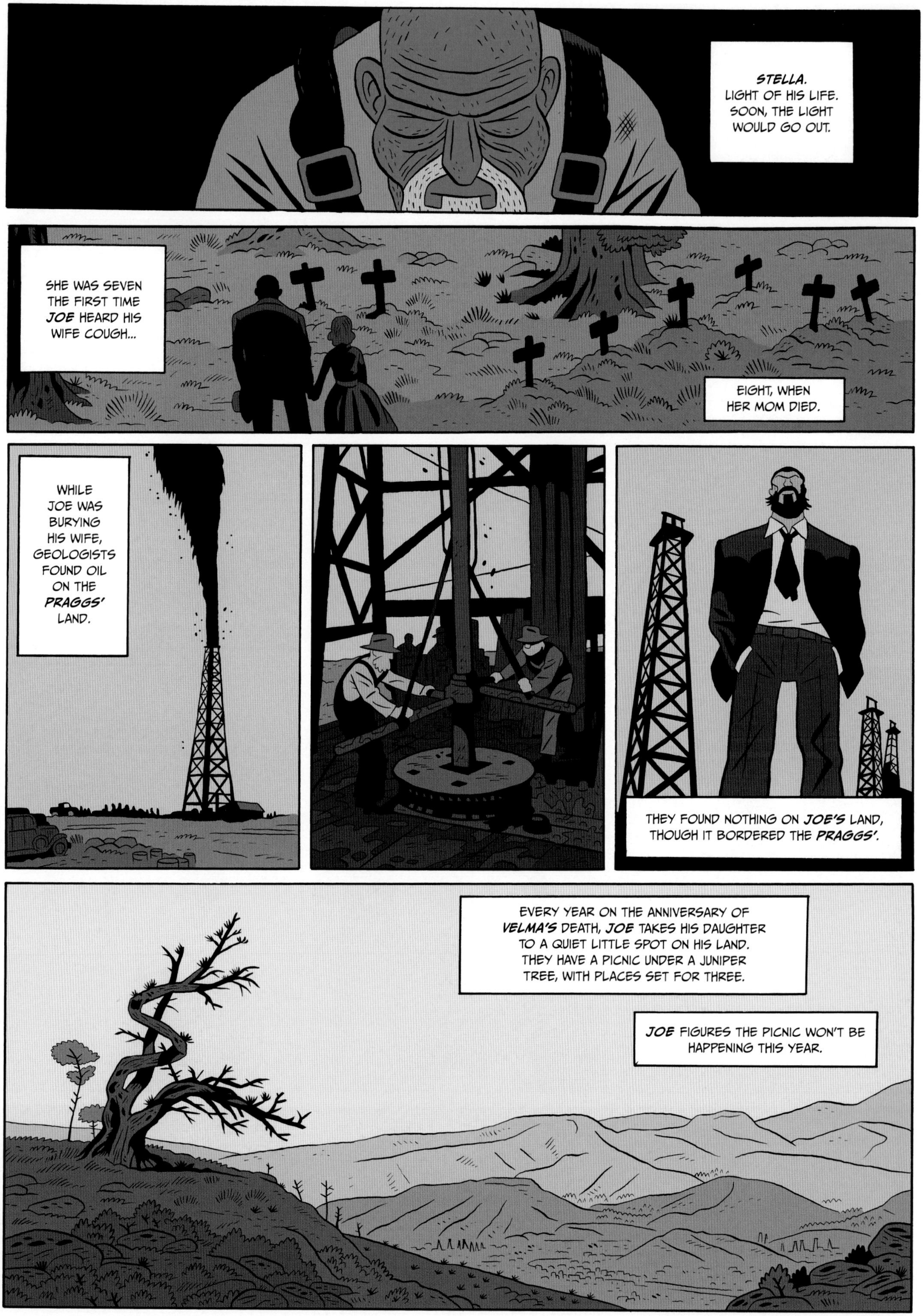
STELLA.
LIGHT OF HIS LIFE.
SOON, THE LIGHT
WOULD GO OUT.
SHE WAS SEVEN THE FIRST TIME JOE HEARD HIS WIFE COUGH...
EIGHT, WHEN HER MOM DIED.
WHILE JOE WAS BURYING HIS WIFE, GEOLOGISTS FOUND OIL ON THE PRAGGS' LAND.
THEY FOUND NOTHING ON JOE'S LAND, THOUGH IT BORDERED THE PRAGGS'.
EVERY YEAR ON THE ANNIVERSARY OF VELMA'S DEATH, JOE TAKES HIS DAUGHTER TO A QUIET LITTLE SPOT ON HIS LAND. THEY HAVE A PICNIC UNDER A JUNIPER TREE, WITH PLACES SET FOR THREE.
JOE FIGURES THE PICNIC WON'T BE HAPPENING THIS YEAR.

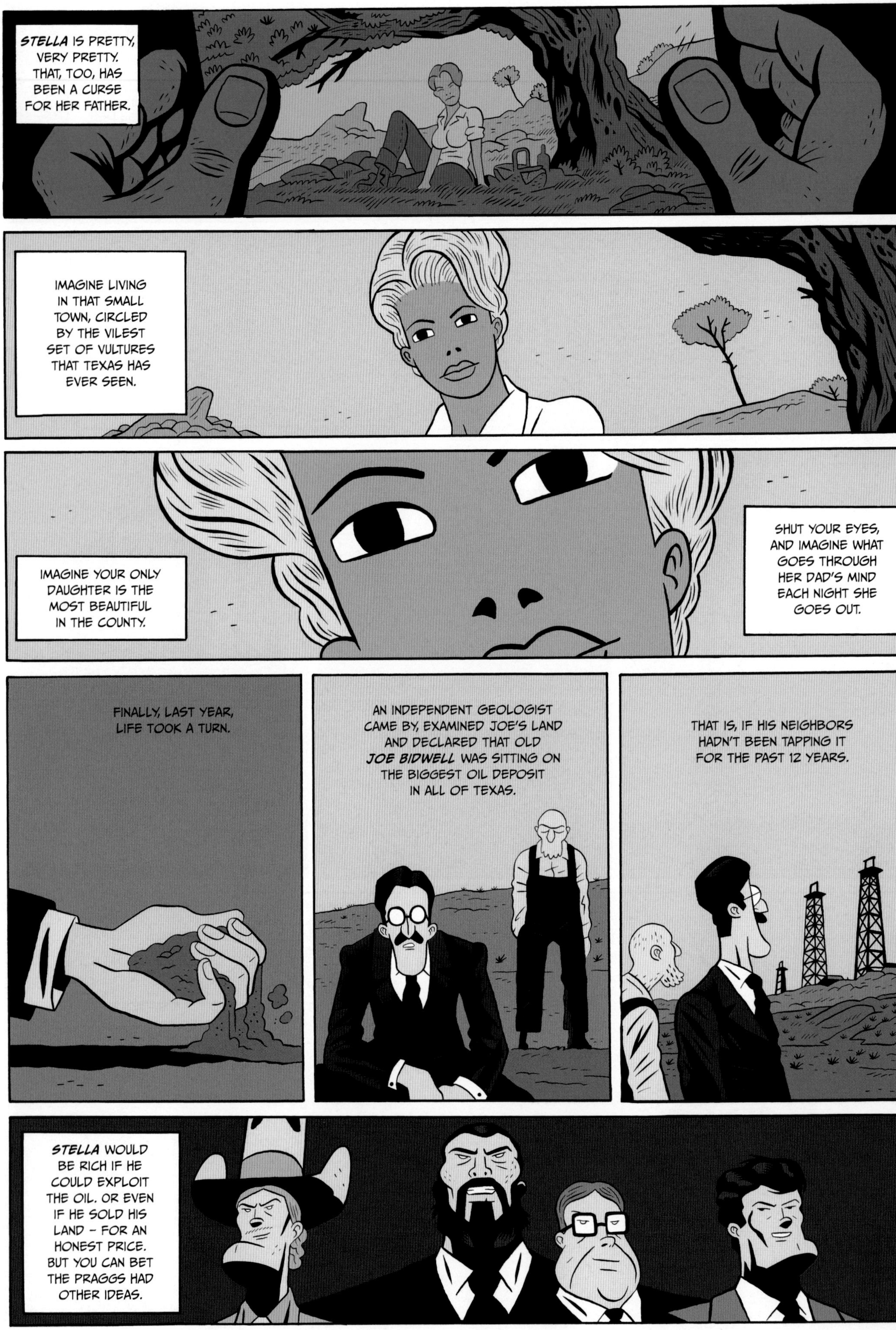
STELLA IS PRETTY, VERY PRETTY. THAT, TOO, HAS BEEN A CURSE FOR HER FATHER.
IMAGINE LIVING IN THAT SMALL TOWN, CIRCLED BY THE VILEST SET OF VULTURES THAT TEXAS HAS EVER SEEN.
IMAGINE YOUR ONLY DAUGHTER IS THE MOST BEAUTIFUL IN THE COUNTY.
SHUT YOUR EYES, AND IMAGINE WHAT GOES THROUGH HER DAD'S MIND EACH NIGHT SHE GOES OUT.
FINALLY, LAST YEAR, LIFE TOOK A TURN.
AN INDEPENDENT GEOLOGIST CAME BY, EXAMINED JOE'S LAND AND DECLARED THAT OLD JOE BIDWELL WAS SITTING ON THE BIGGEST OIL DEPOSIT IN ALL OF TEXAS.
THAT IS, IF HIS NEIGHBORS HADN'T BEEN TAPPING IT FOR THE PAST 12 YEARS.
STELLA WOULD BE RICH IF HE COULD EXPLOIT THE OIL. OR EVEN IF HE SOLD HIS LAND – FOR AN HONEST PRICE. BUT YOU CAN BET THE PRAGGS HAD OTHER IDEAS.

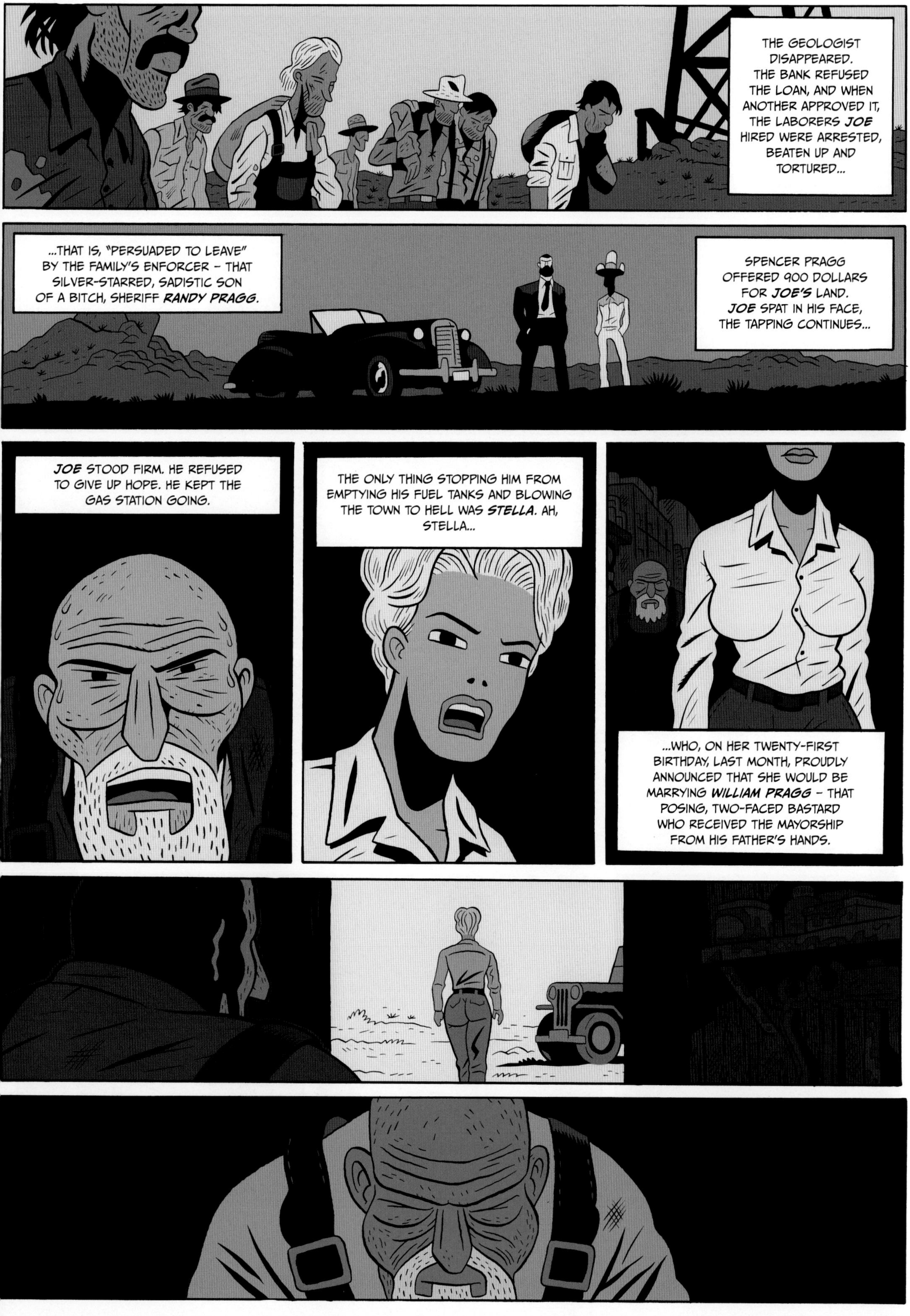
THE GEOLOGIST DISAPPEARED. THE BANK REFUSED THE LOAN, AND WHEN ANOTHER APPROVED IT, THE LABORERS JOE HIRED WERE ARRESTED, BEATEN UP AND TORTURED...
...THAT IS, "PERSUADED TO LEAVE" BY THE FAMILY'S ENFORCER – THAT SILVER-STARRED, SADISTIC SON OF A BITCH, SHERIFF RANDY PRAGG.
SPENCER PRAGG OFFERED 900 DOLLARS FOR JOE'S LAND. JOE SPAT IN HIS FACE, THE TAPPING CONTINUES...
JOE STOOD FIRM. HE REFUSED TO GIVE UP HOPE. HE KEPT THE GAS STATION GOING.
THE ONLY THING STOPPING HIM FROM EMPTYING HIS FUEL TANKS AND BLOWING THE TOWN TO HELL WAS STELLA. AH, STELLA...
...WHO, ON HER TWENTY-FIRST BIRTHDAY, LAST MONTH, PROUDLY ANNOUNCED THAT SHE WOULD BE MARRYING WILLIAM PRAGG – THAT POSING, TWO-FACED BASTARD WHO RECEIVED THE MAYORSHIP FROM HIS FATHER'S HANDS.

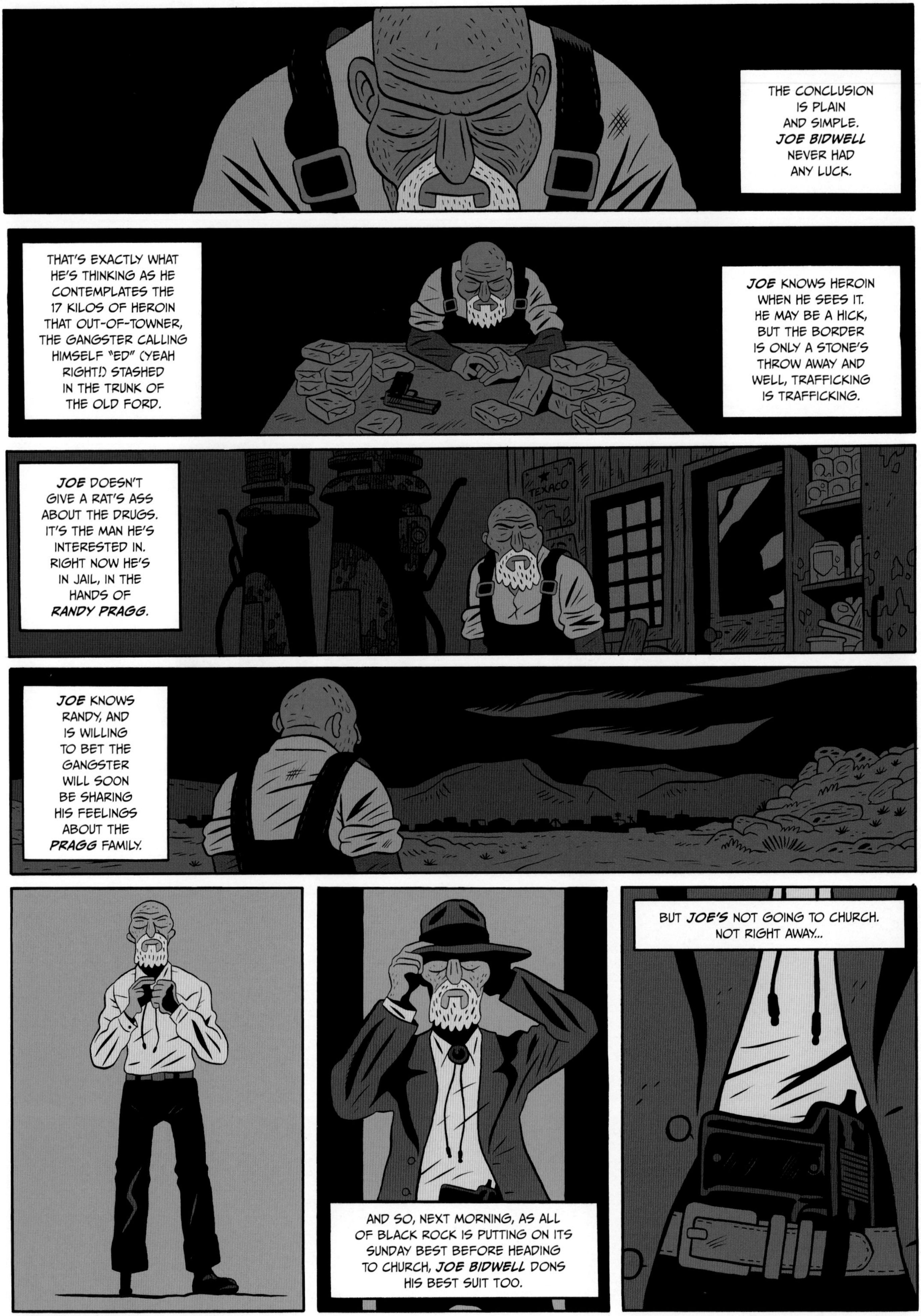

THE CONCLUSION IS PLAIN AND SIMPLE. JOE BIDWELL NEVER HAD ANY LUCK.
THAT'S EXACTLY WHAT HE'S THINKING AS HE CONTEMPLATES THE 17 KILOS OF HEROIN THAT OUT-OF-TOWNER, THE GANGSTER CALLING HIMSELF "ED" (YEAH RIGHT!) STASHED IN THE TRUNK OF THE OLD FORD.
JOE KNOWS HEROIN WHEN HE SEES IT. HE MAY BE A HICK, BUT THE BORDER IS ONLY A STONE'S THROW AWAY AND WELL, TRAFFICKING IS TRAFFICKING.
JOE DOESN'T GIVE A RAT'S ASS ABOUT THE DRUGS. IT'S THE MAN HE'S INTERESTED IN. RIGHT NOW HE'S IN JAIL, IN THE HANDS OF RANDY PRAGG.
TEXACO
JOE KNOWS RANDY, AND IS WILLING TO BET THE GANGSTER WILL SOON BE SHARING HIS FEELINGS ABOUT THE PRAGG FAMILY.
AND SO, NEXT MORNING, AS ALL OF BLACK ROCK IS PUTTING ON ITS SUNDAY BEST BEFORE HEADING TO CHURCH, JOE BIDWELL DONS HIS BEST SUIT TOO.
BUT JOE'S NOT GOING TO CHURCH. NOT RIGHT AWAY...

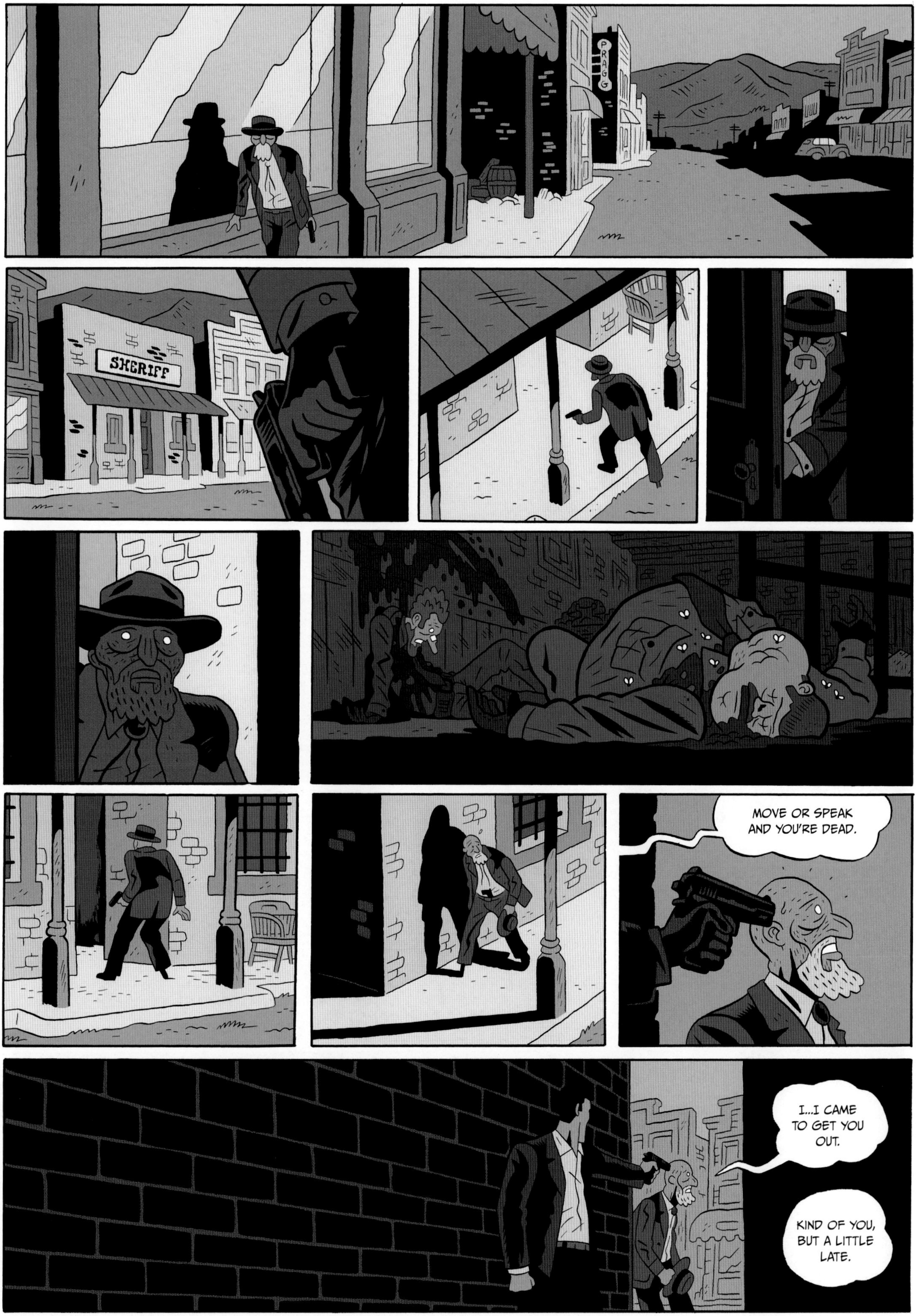
PRAGG
SHERIFF
MOVE OR SPEAK AND YOU'RE DEAD.
I...I CAME TO GET YOU OUT.
KIND OF YOU, BUT A LITTLE LATE.

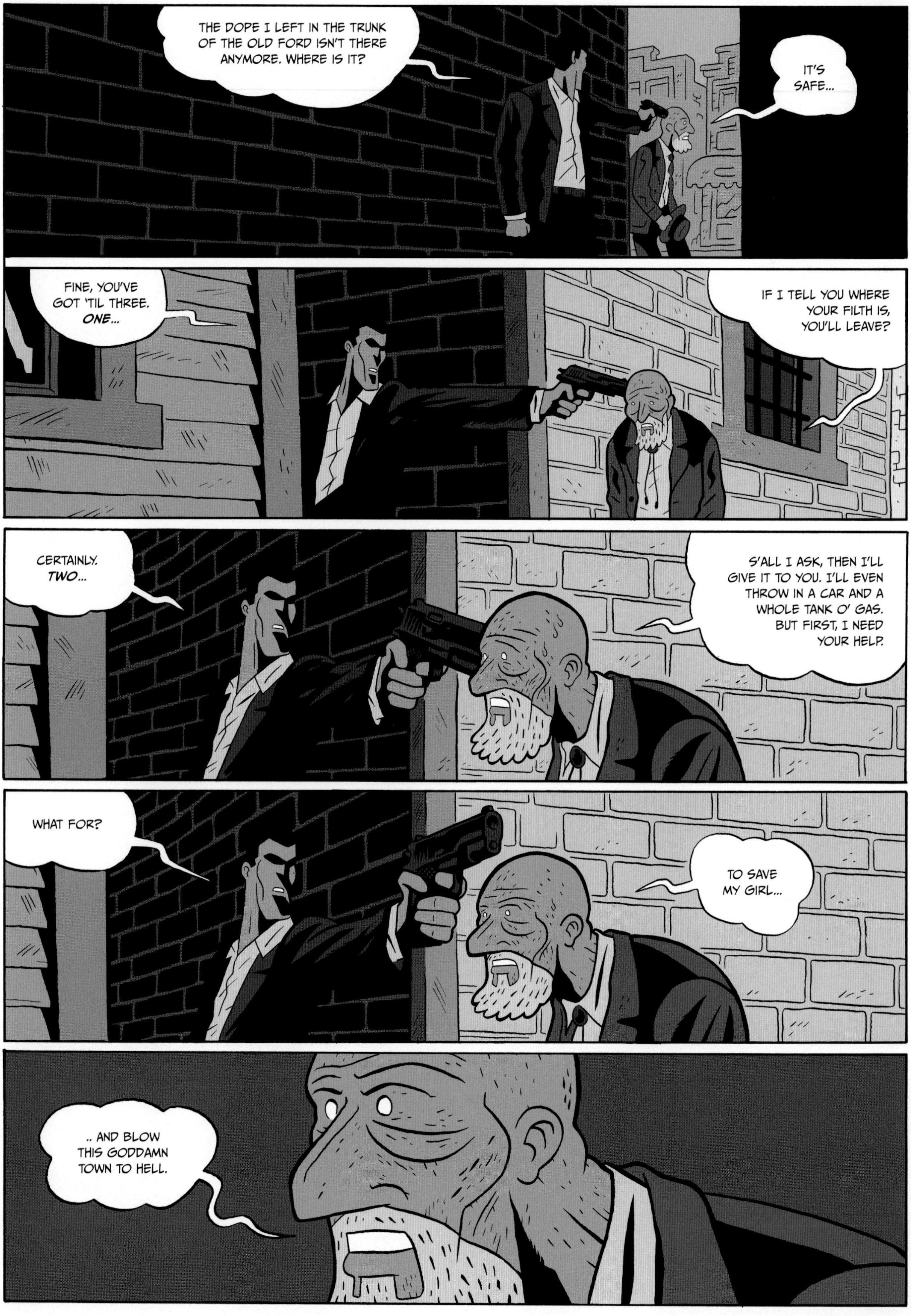
THE DOPE I LEFT IN THE TRUNK OF THE OLD FORD ISN'T THERE ANYMORE. WHERE IS IT?
IT'S SAFE...
FINE, YOU'VE GOT 'TIL THREE. ONE...
IF I TELL YOU WHERE YOUR FILTH IS, YOU'LL LEAVE?
CERTAINLY. TWO...
S'ALL I ASK, THEN I'LL GIVE IT TO YOU. I'LL EVEN THROW IN A CAR AND A WHOLE TANK O' GAS. BUT FIRST, I NEED YOUR HELP.
WHAT FOR?
TO SAVE MY GIRL...
.. AND BLOW THIS GODDAMN TOWN TO HELL.

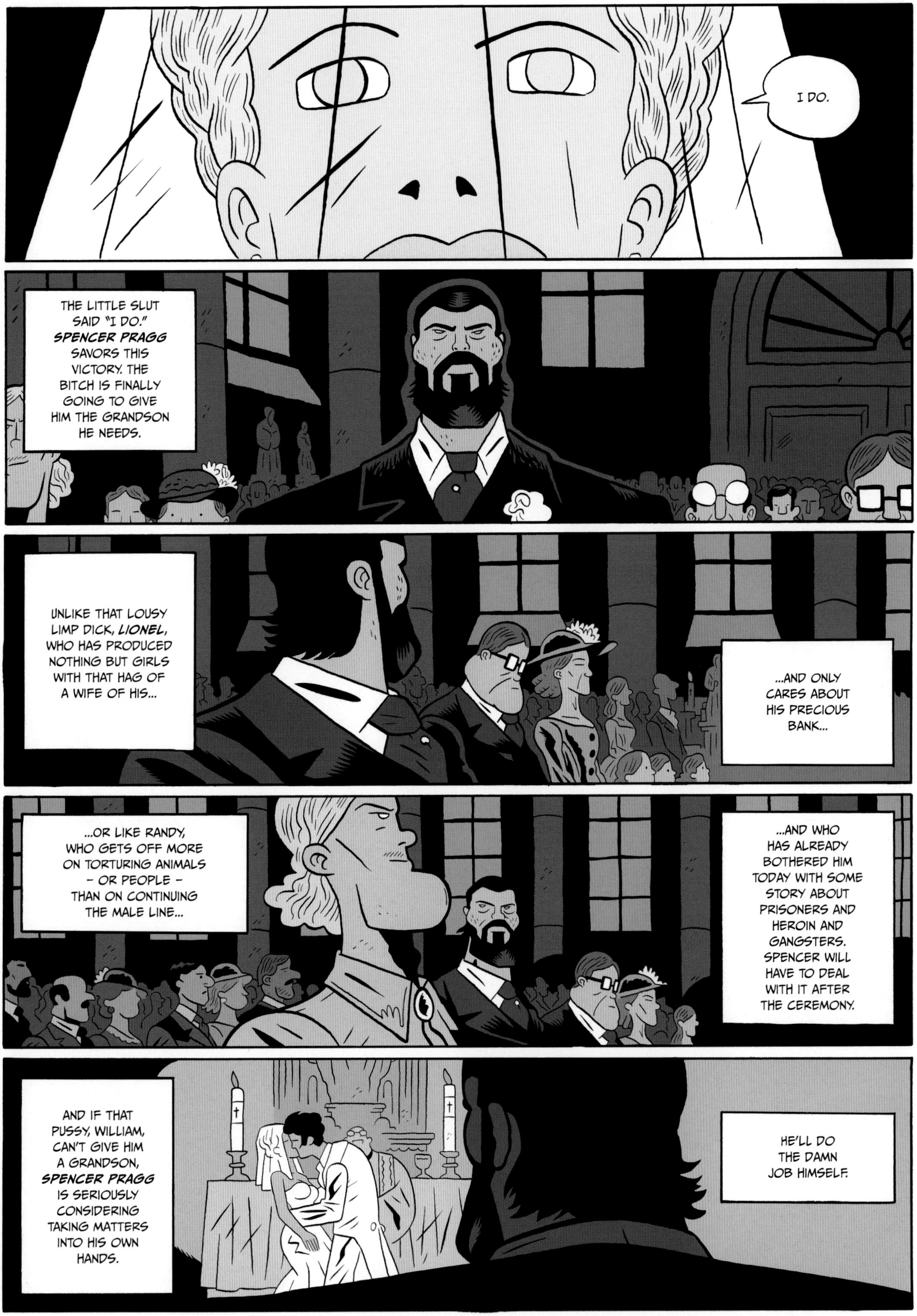
I DO.
THE LITTLE SLUT SAID "I DO." **SPENCER PRAGG** SAVORS THIS VICTORY. THE BITCH IS FINALLY GOING TO GIVE HIM THE GRANDSON HE NEEDS.
UNLIKE THAT LOUSY LIMP DICK, **LIONEL**, WHO HAS PRODUCED NOTHING BUT GIRLS WITH THAT HAG OF A WIFE OF HIS...
...AND ONLY CARES ABOUT HIS PRECIOUS BANK...
...OR LIKE RANDY, WHO GETS OFF MORE ON TORTURING ANIMALS – OR PEOPLE – THAN ON CONTINUING THE MALE LINE...
...AND WHO HAS ALREADY BOTHERED HIM TODAY WITH SOME STORY ABOUT PRISONERS AND HEROIN AND GANGSTERS. SPENCER WILL HAVE TO DEAL WITH IT AFTER THE CEREMONY.
AND IF THAT PUSSY, WILLIAM, CAN'T GIVE HIM A GRANDSON, **SPENCER PRAGG** IS SERIOUSLY CONSIDERING TAKING MATTERS INTO HIS OWN HANDS.
HE'LL DO THE DAMN JOB HIMSELF.

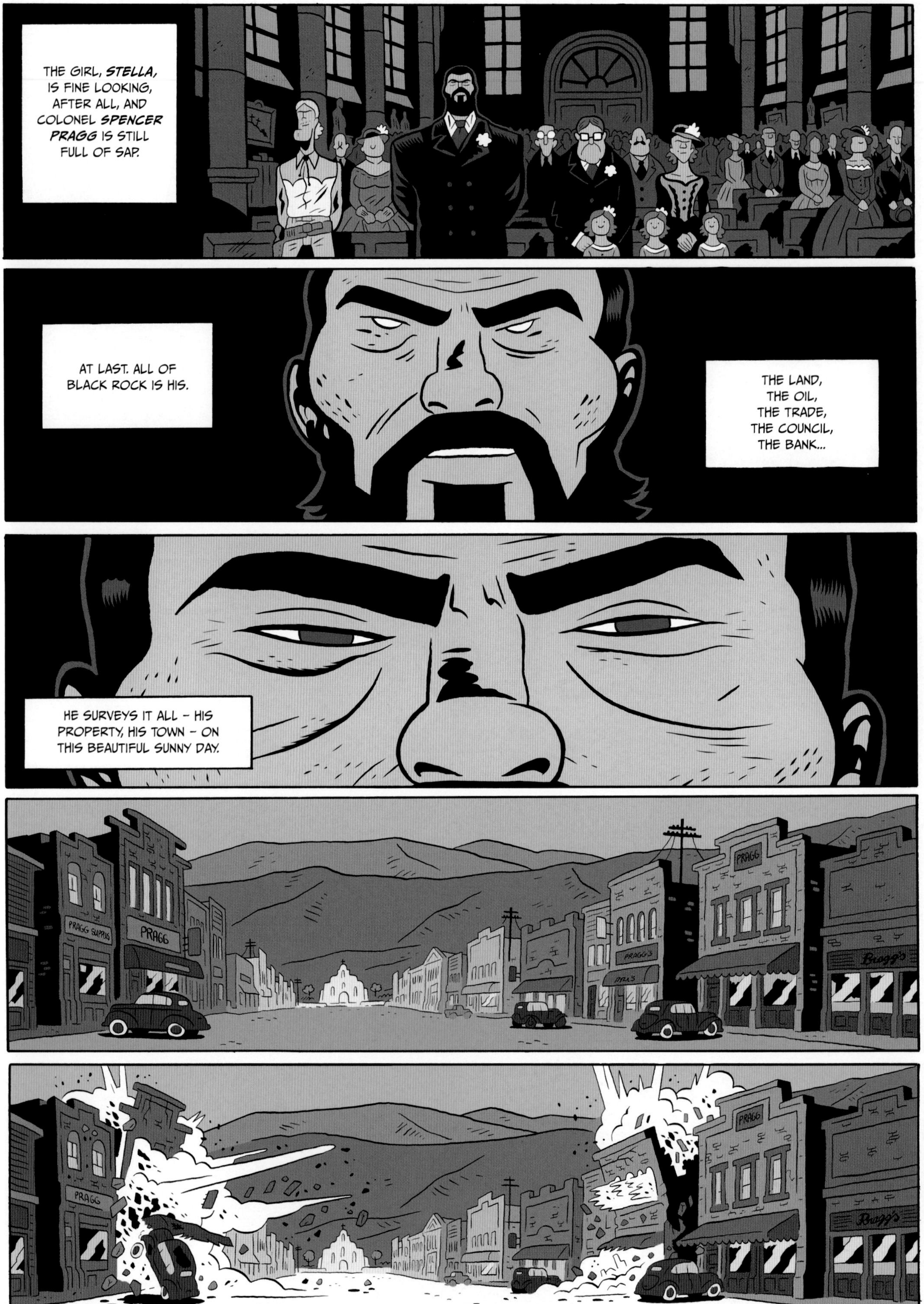

THE GIRL, STELLA, IS FINE LOOKING, AFTER ALL, AND COLONEL SPENCER PRAGG IS STILL FULL OF SAP.
AT LAST. ALL OF BLACK ROCK IS HIS.
THE LAND, THE OIL, THE TRADE, THE COUNCIL, THE BANK...
HE SURVEYS IT ALL – HIS PROPERTY, HIS TOWN – ON THIS BEAUTIFUL SUNNY DAY.
PRAGG
PRAGG
Bragg's
PRAGG
PRAGG
Bragg's

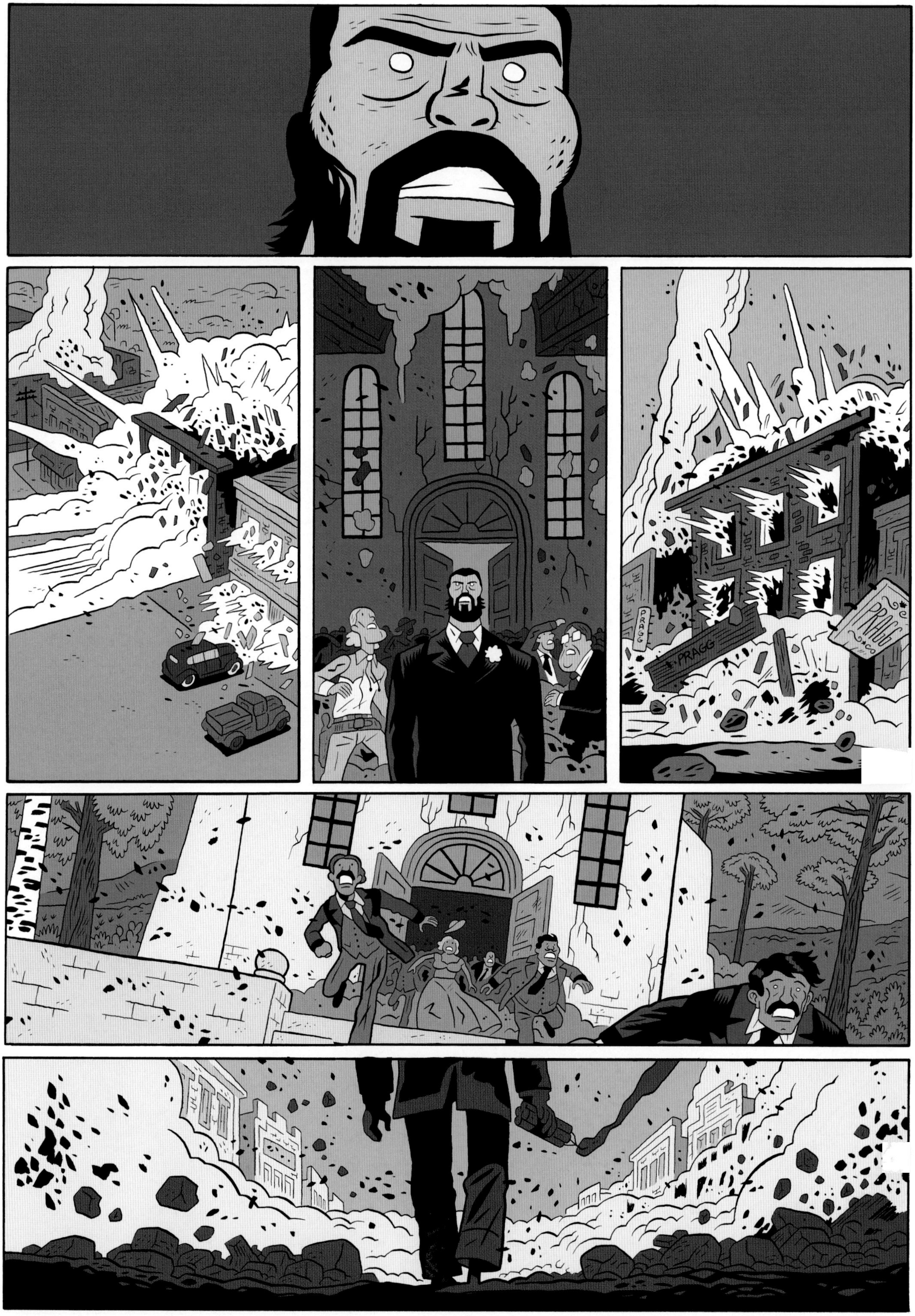
PRAGG
PRAGG
PRAGG

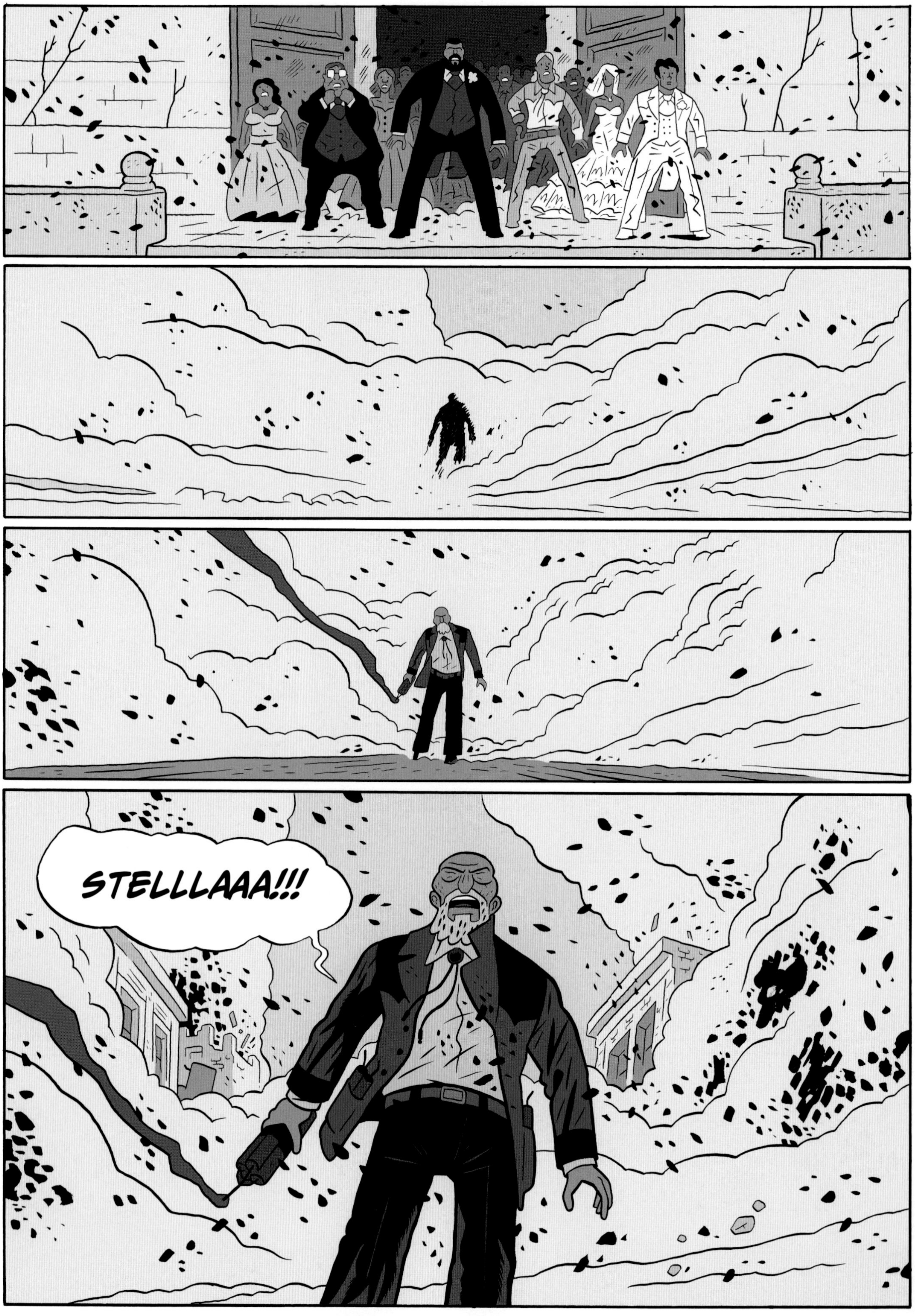
STELLLAAA!!!

3. HONEYMOON

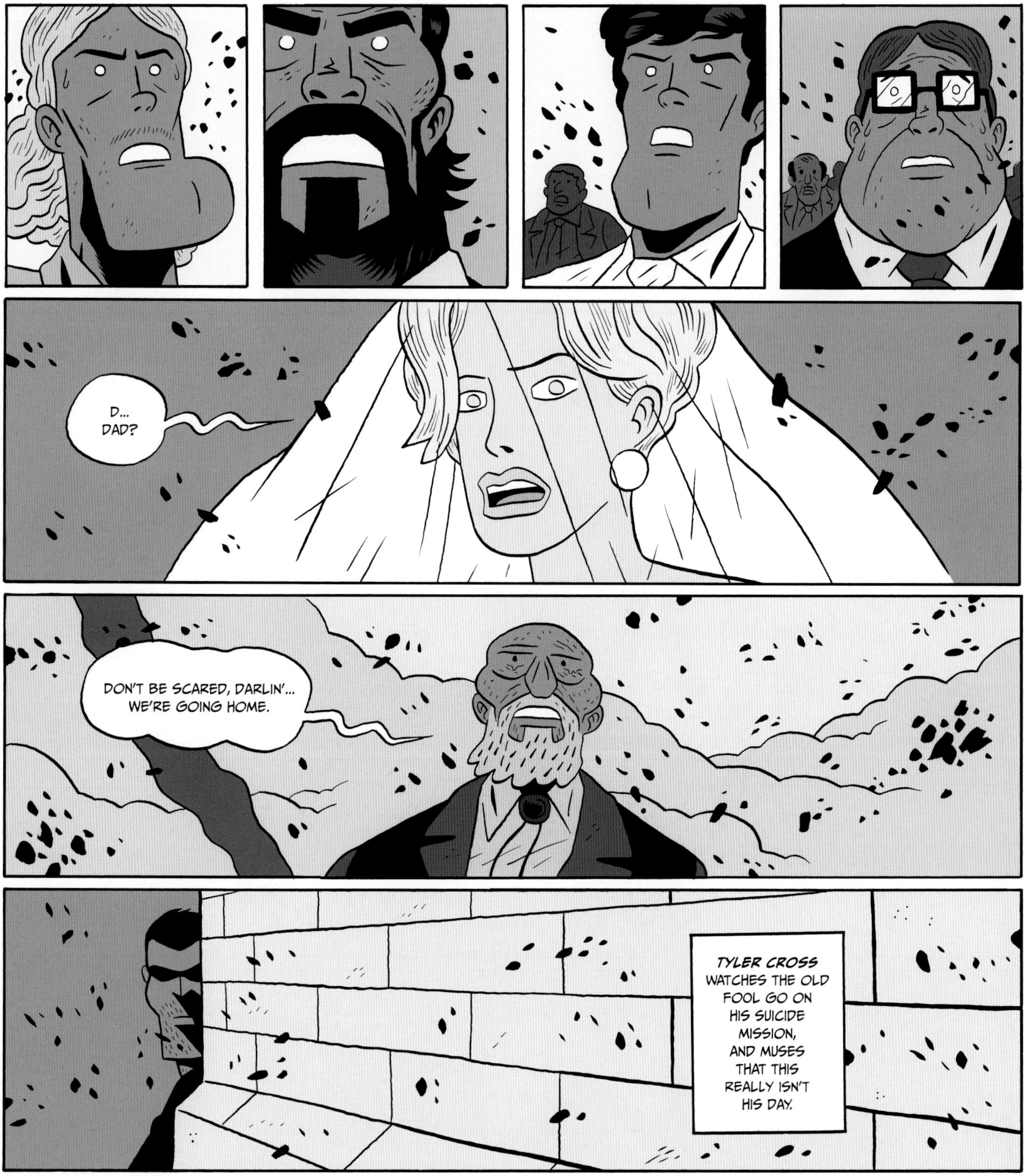

D... DAD?
DON'T BE SCARED, DARLIN'... WE'RE GOING HOME.
TYLER CROSS WATCHES THE OLD FOOL GO ON HIS SUICIDE MISSION, AND MUSES THAT THIS REALLY ISN'T HIS DAY.

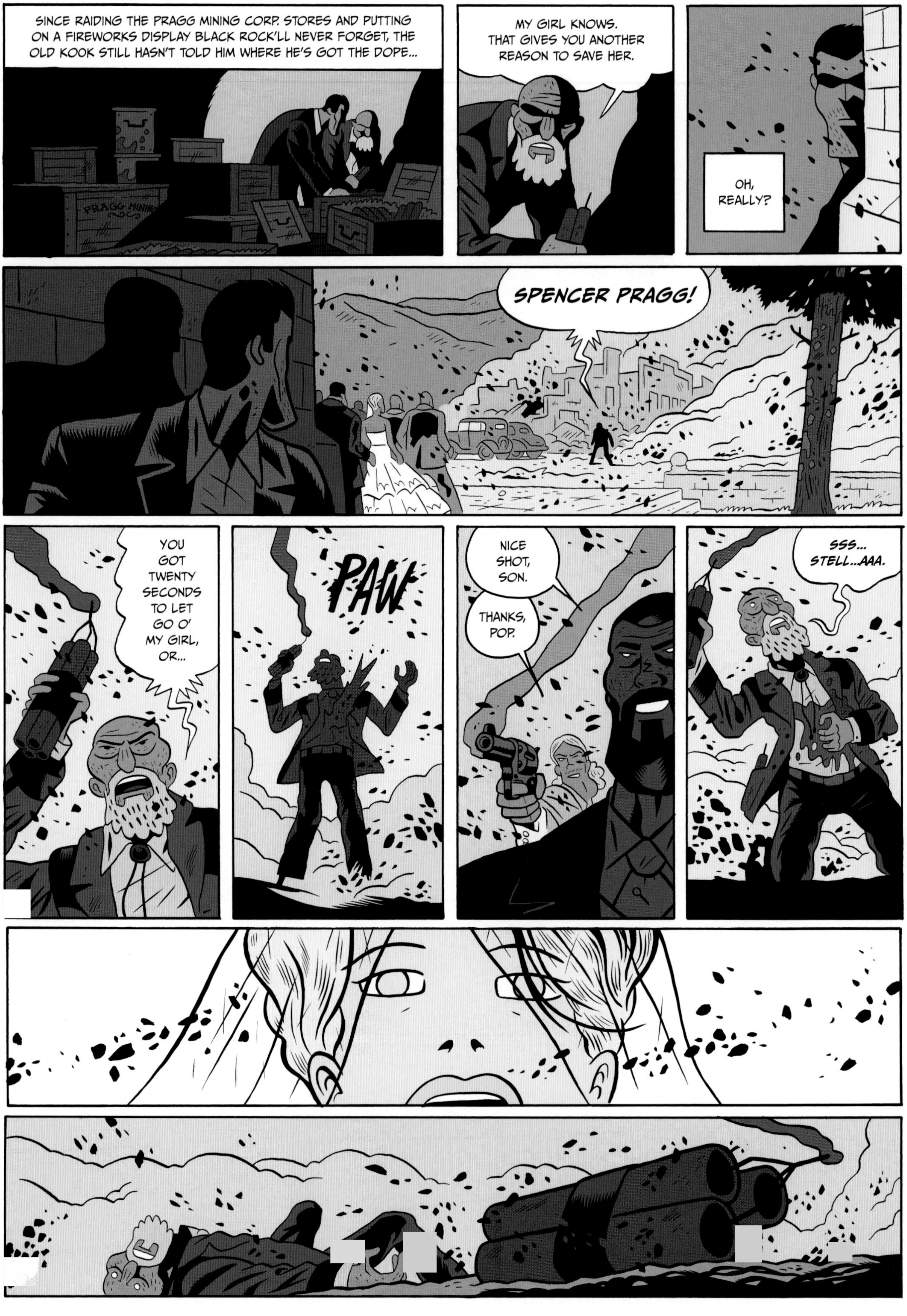

SINCE RAIDING THE PRAGG MINING CORP. STORES AND PUTTING ON A FIREWORKS DISPLAY BLACK ROCK'LL NEVER FORGET, THE OLD KOOK STILL HASN'T TOLD HIM WHERE HE'S GOT THE DOPE...
PRAGG MINING
MY GIRL KNOWS. THAT GIVES YOU ANOTHER REASON TO SAVE HER.
OH, REALLY?
SPENCER PRAGG!
YOU GOT TWENTY SECONDS TO LET GO O' MY GIRL, OR...
PAW
NICE SHOT, SON.
THANKS, POP.
SSS... STELL...AAA.

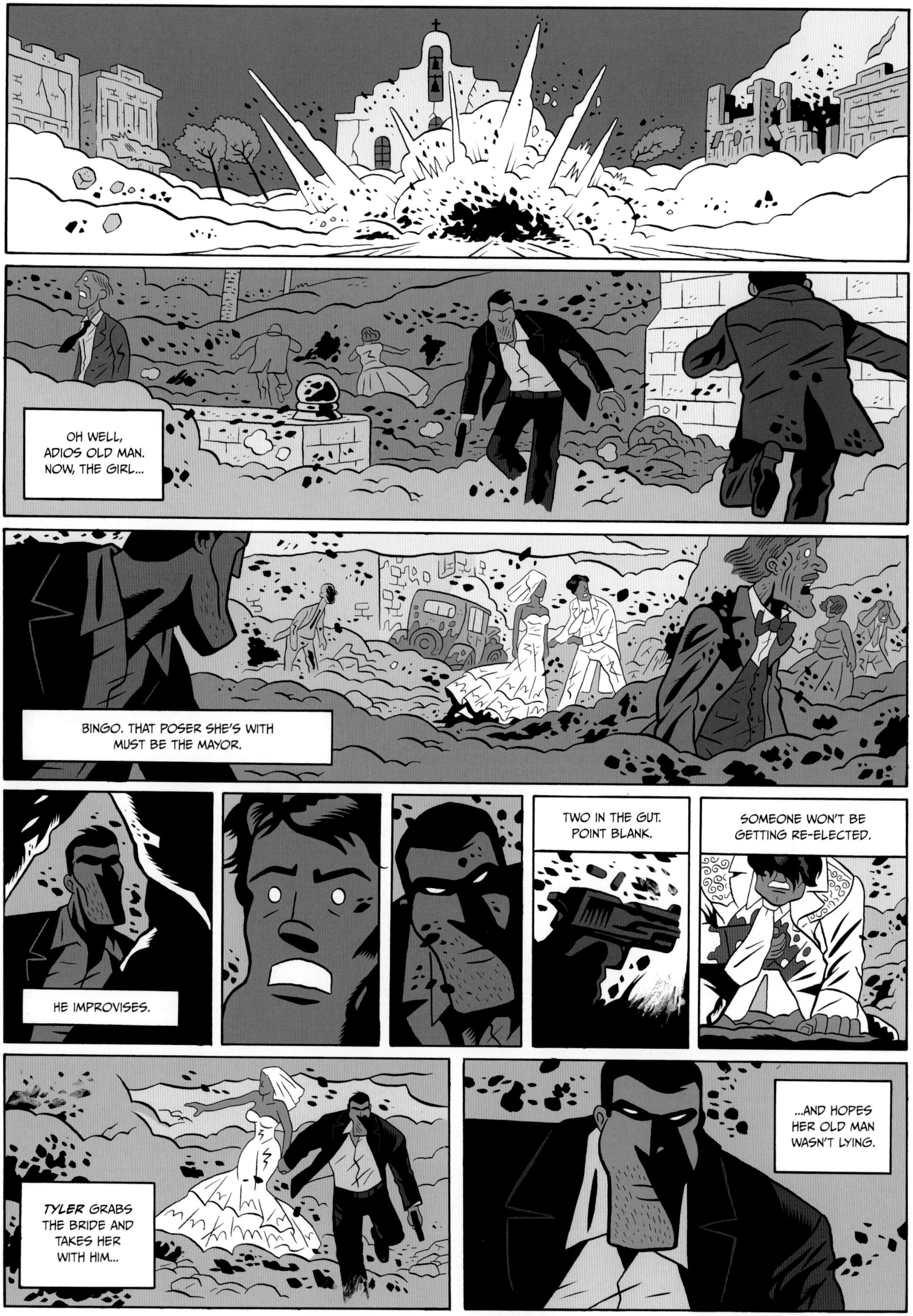
OH WELL, ADIOS OLD MAN. NOW, THE GIRL...
BINGO. THAT POSER SHE'S WITH MUST BE THE MAYOR.
HE IMPROVISES.
TWO IN THE GUT. POINT BLANK.
SOMEONE WON'T BE GETTING RE-ELECTED.
TYLER GRABS THE BRIDE AND TAKES HER WITH HIM...
...AND HOPES HER OLD MAN WASN'T LYING.

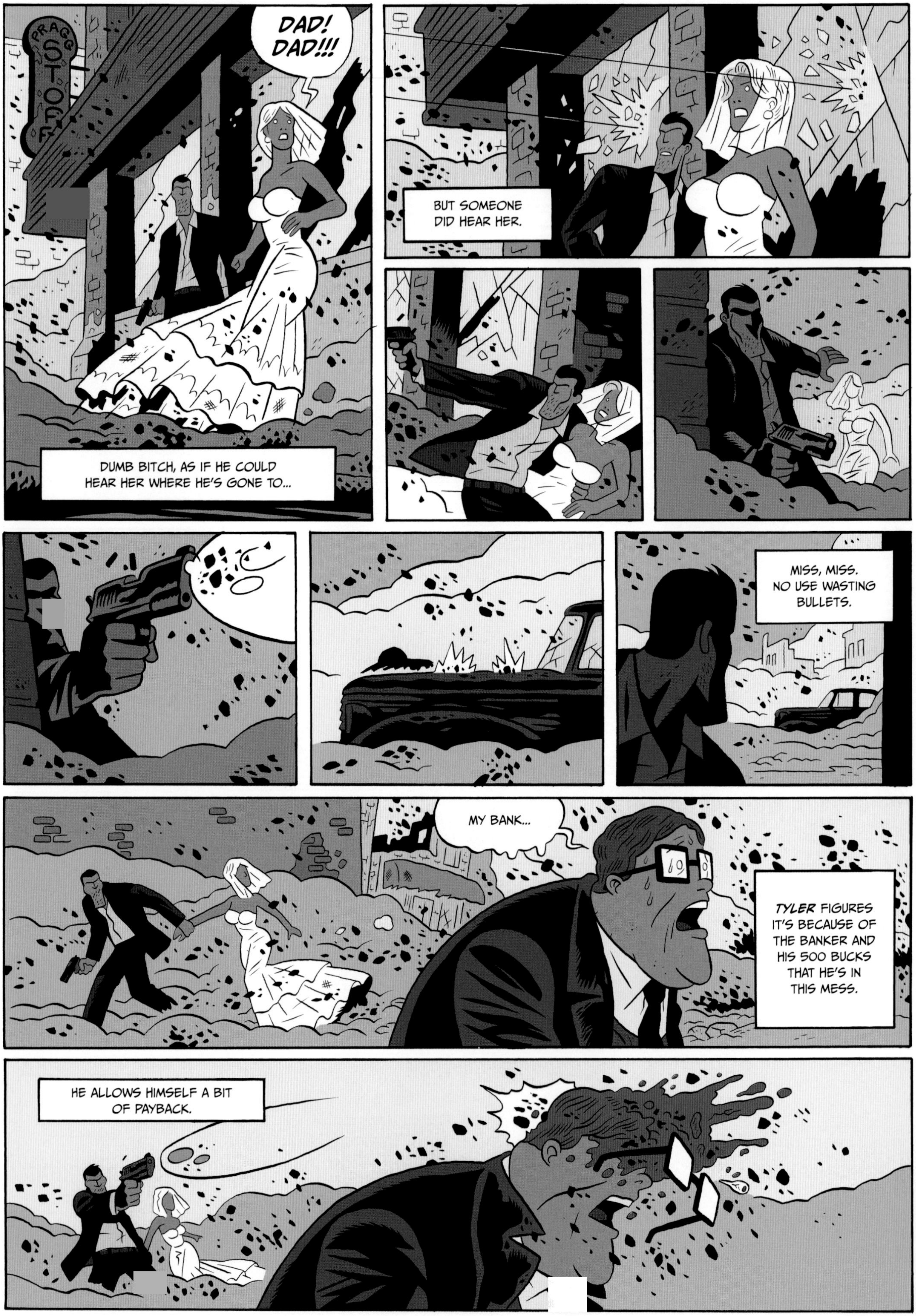
DAD!
DAD!!!
PRAGG
STOFF
DUMB BITCH, AS IF HE COULD HEAR HER WHERE HE'S GONE TO...
BUT SOMEONE DID HEAR HER.
MISS, MISS. NO USE WASTING BULLETS.
MY BANK...
TYLER FIGURES IT'S BECAUSE OF THE BANKER AND HIS 500 BUCKS THAT HE'S IN THIS MESS.
HE ALLOWS HIMSELF A BIT OF PAYBACK.

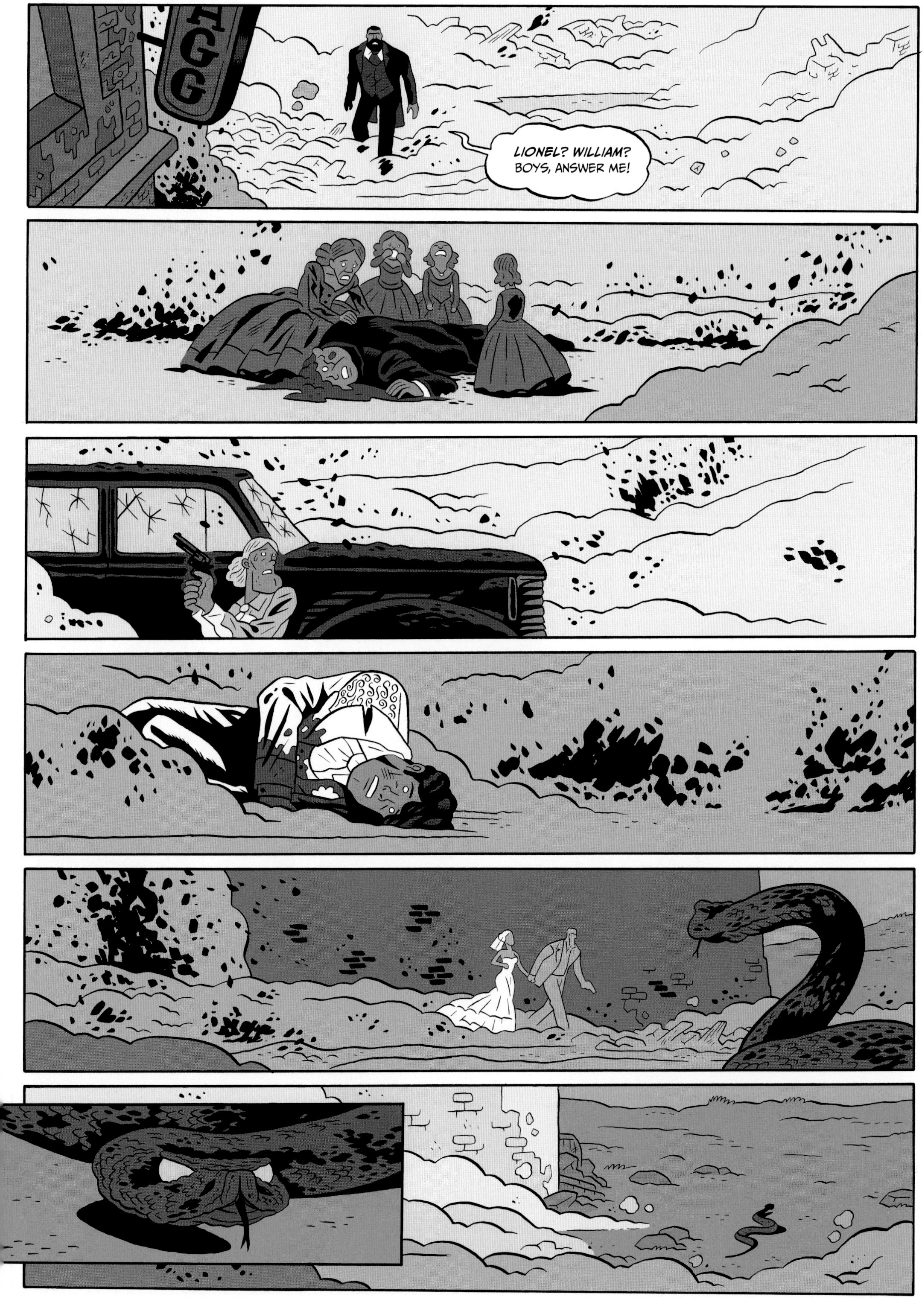
AGG
LIONEL? WILLIAM?
BOYS, ANSWER ME!

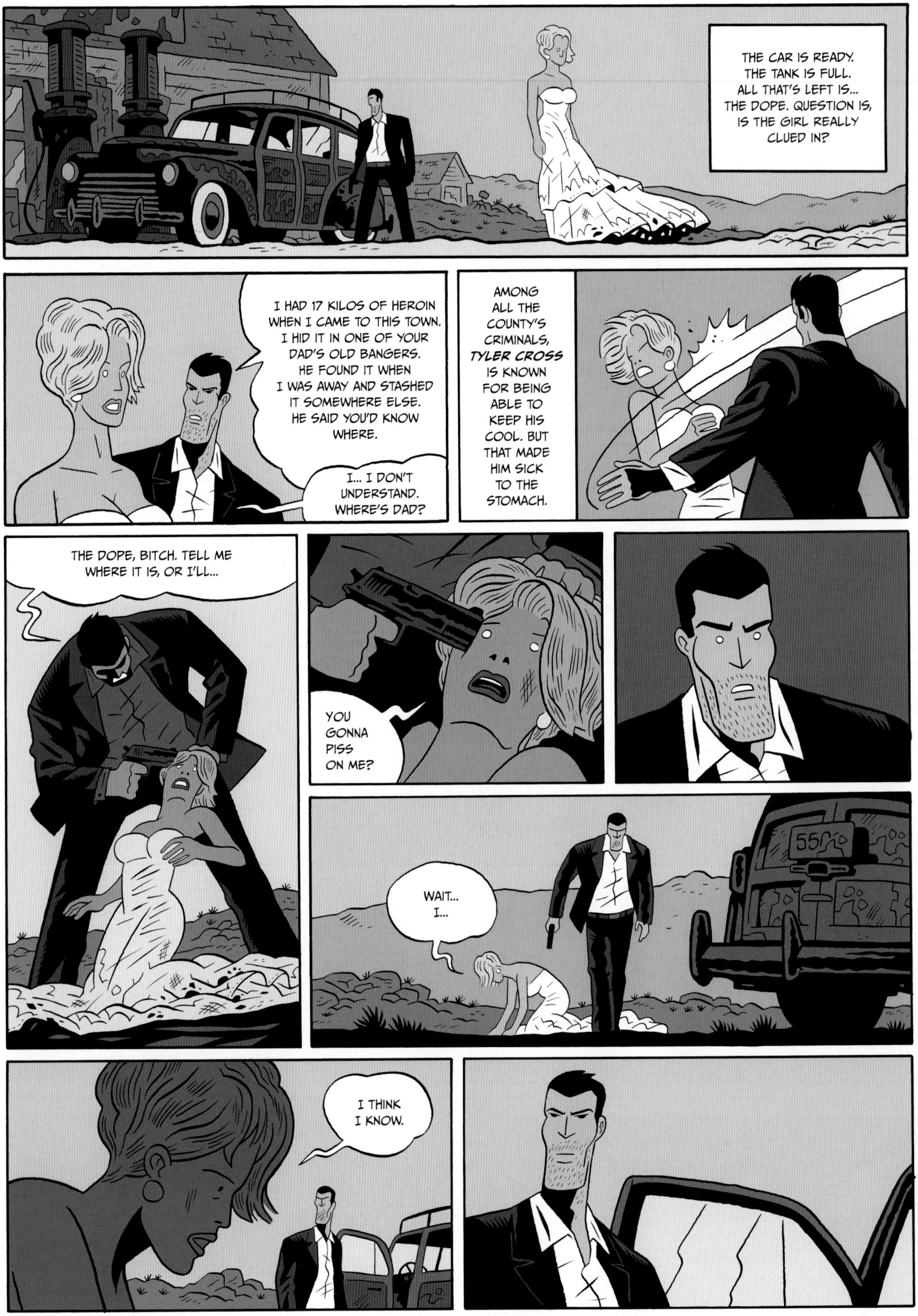
THE CAR IS READY. THE TANK IS FULL. ALL THAT'S LEFT IS... THE DOPE. QUESTION IS, IS THE GIRL REALLY CLUED IN?
I HAD 17 KILOS OF HEROIN WHEN I CAME TO THIS TOWN. I HID IT IN ONE OF YOUR DAD'S OLD BANGERS. HE FOUND IT WHEN I WAS AWAY AND STASHED IT SOMEWHERE ELSE. HE SAID YOU'D KNOW WHERE.
I... I DON'T UNDERSTAND. WHERE'S DAD?
AMONG ALL THE COUNTY'S CRIMINALS, TYLER CROSS IS KNOWN FOR BEING ABLE TO KEEP HIS COOL. BUT THAT MADE HIM SICK TO THE STOMACH.
THE DOPE, BITCH. TELL ME WHERE IT IS, OR I'LL...
YOU GONNA PISS ON ME?
55
WAIT... I...
I THINK I KNOW.

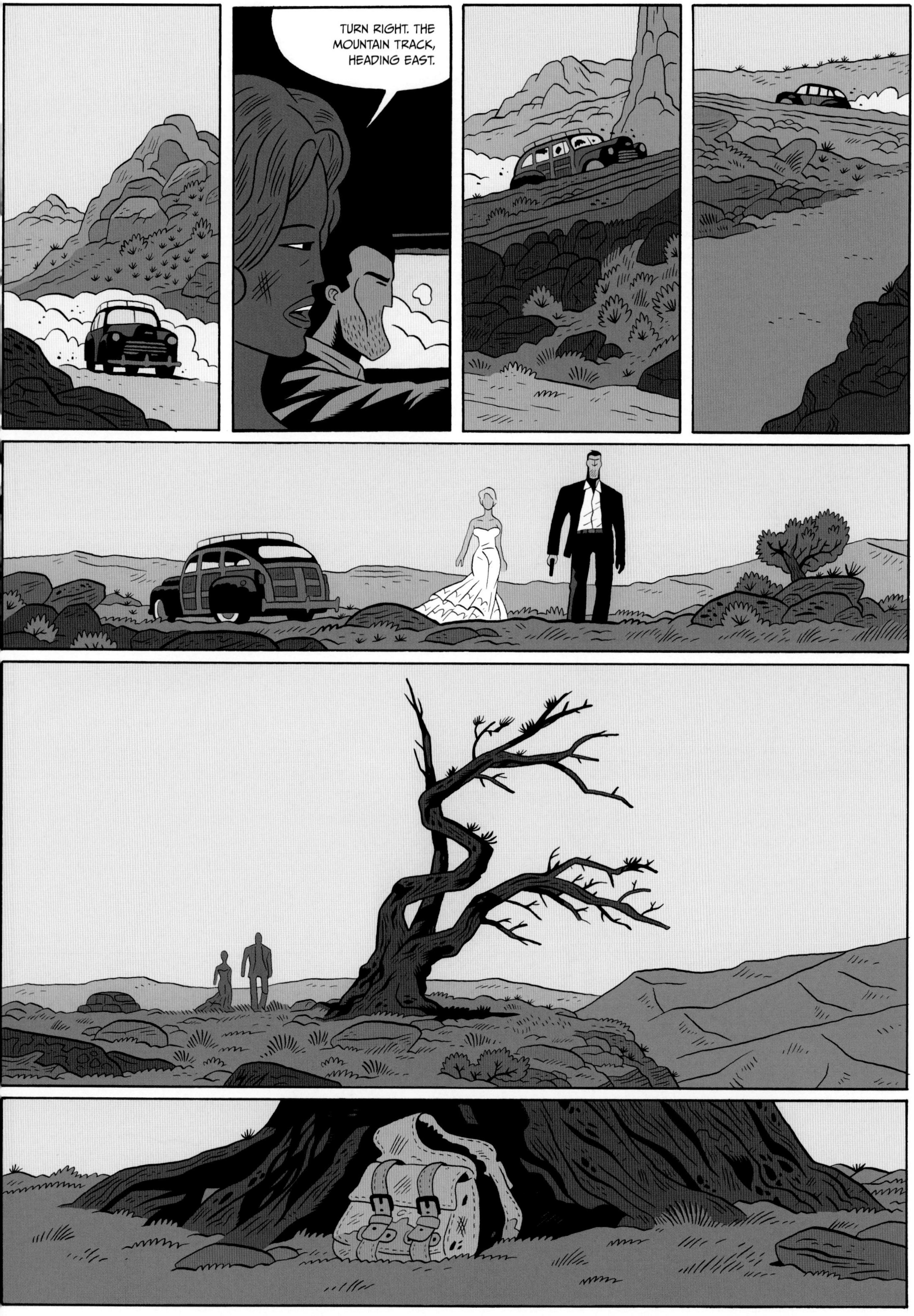
TURN RIGHT. THE MOUNTAIN TRACK, HEADING EAST.

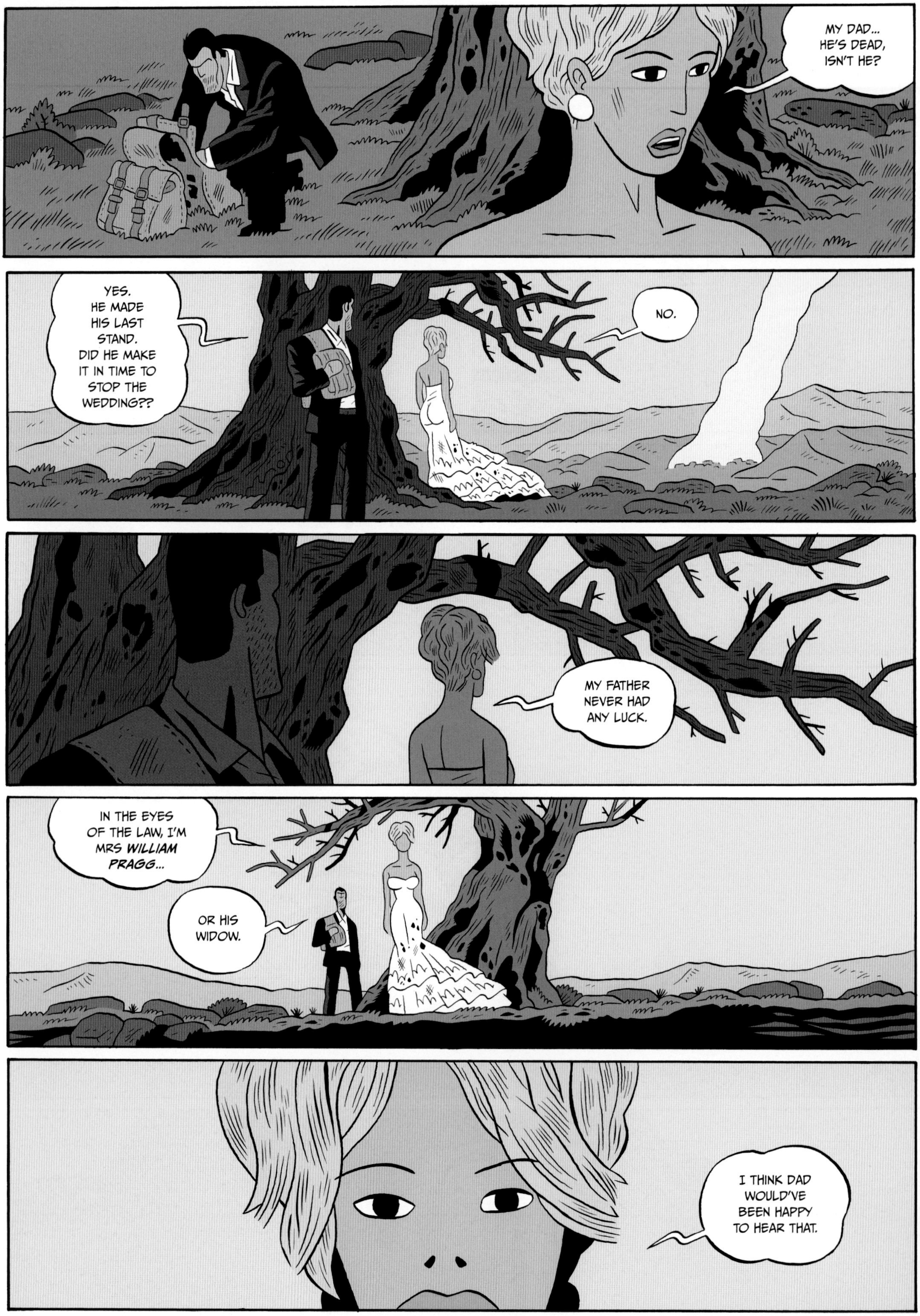
MY DAD... HE'S DEAD, ISN'T HE?
YES. HE MADE HIS LAST STAND. DID HE MAKE IT IN TIME TO STOP THE WEDDING??
NO.
MY FATHER NEVER HAD ANY LUCK.
IN THE EYES OF THE LAW, I'M MRS *WILLIAM PRAGG*...
OR HIS WIDOW.
I THINK DAD WOULD'VE BEEN HAPPY TO HEAR THAT.

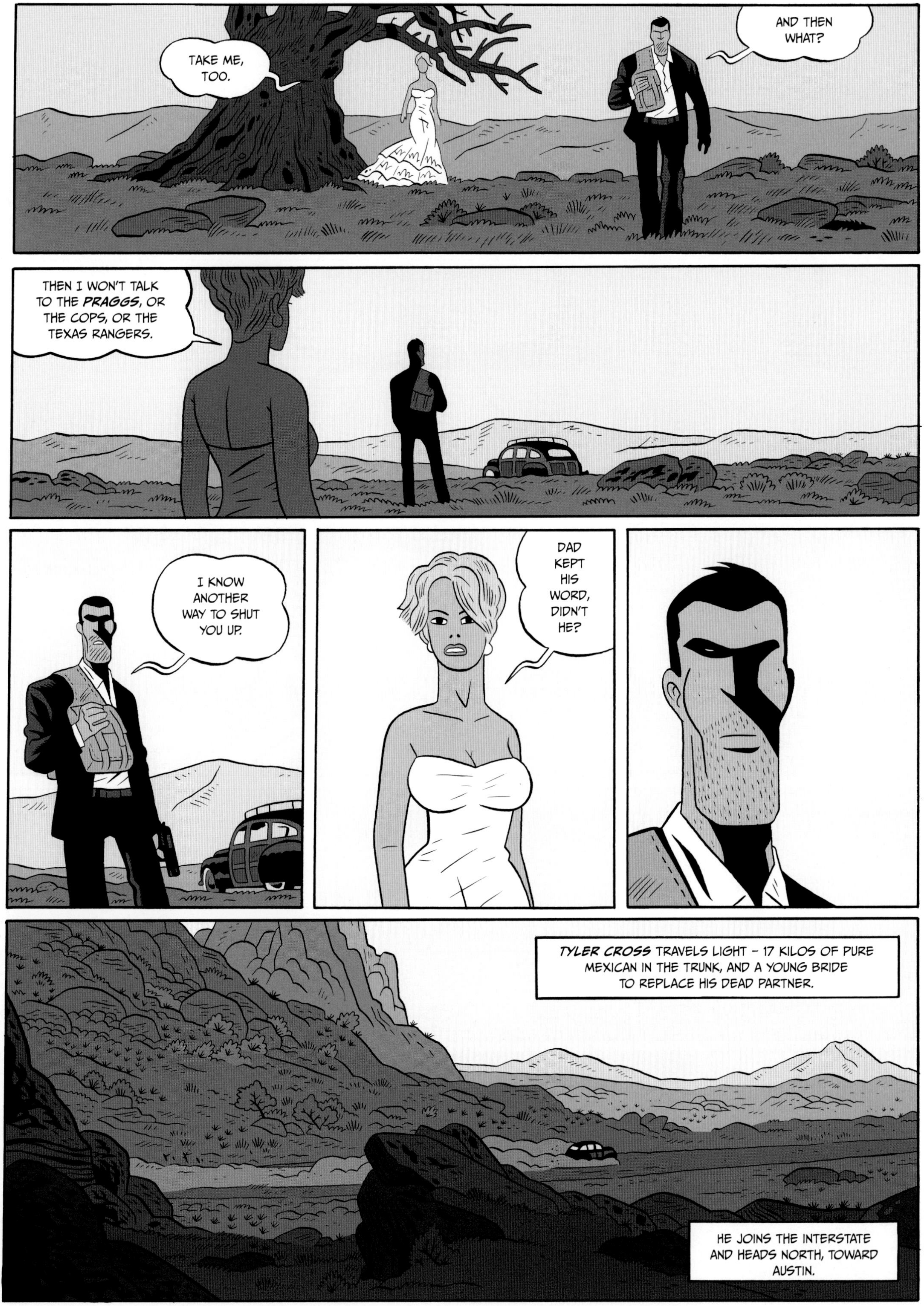
TAKE ME, TOO.
AND THEN WHAT?
THEN I WON'T TALK TO THE *PRAGGS*, OR THE COPS, OR THE TEXAS RANGERS.
I KNOW ANOTHER WAY TO SHUT YOU UP.
DAD KEPT HIS WORD, DIDN'T HE?
TYLER CROSS TRAVELS LIGHT – 17 KILOS OF PURE MEXICAN IN THE TRUNK, AND A YOUNG BRIDE TO REPLACE HIS DEAD PARTNER.
HE JOINS THE INTERSTATE AND HEADS NORTH, TOWARD AUSTIN.

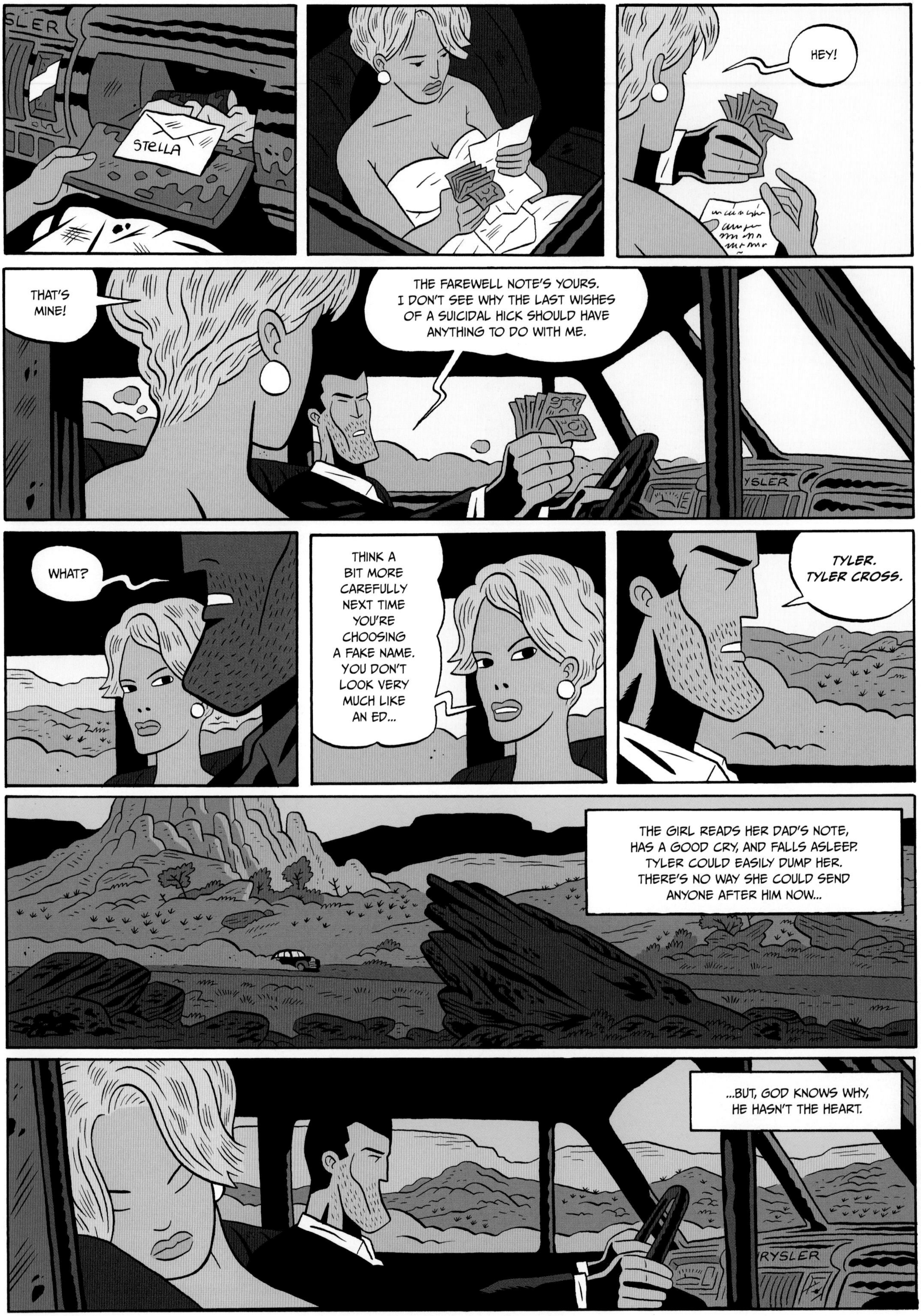
STELLA
HEY!
THAT'S MINE!
THE FAREWELL NOTE'S YOURS. I DON'T SEE WHY THE LAST WISHES OF A SUICIDAL HICK SHOULD HAVE ANYTHING TO DO WITH ME.
WHAT?
THINK A BIT MORE CAREFULLY NEXT TIME YOU'RE CHOOSING A FAKE NAME. YOU DON'T LOOK VERY MUCH LIKE AN ED...
TYLER. TYLER CROSS.
THE GIRL READS HER DAD'S NOTE, HAS A GOOD CRY, AND FALLS ASLEEP. TYLER COULD EASILY DUMP HER. THERE'S NO WAY SHE COULD SEND ANYONE AFTER HIM NOW...
...BUT, GOD KNOWS WHY, HE HASN'T THE HEART.

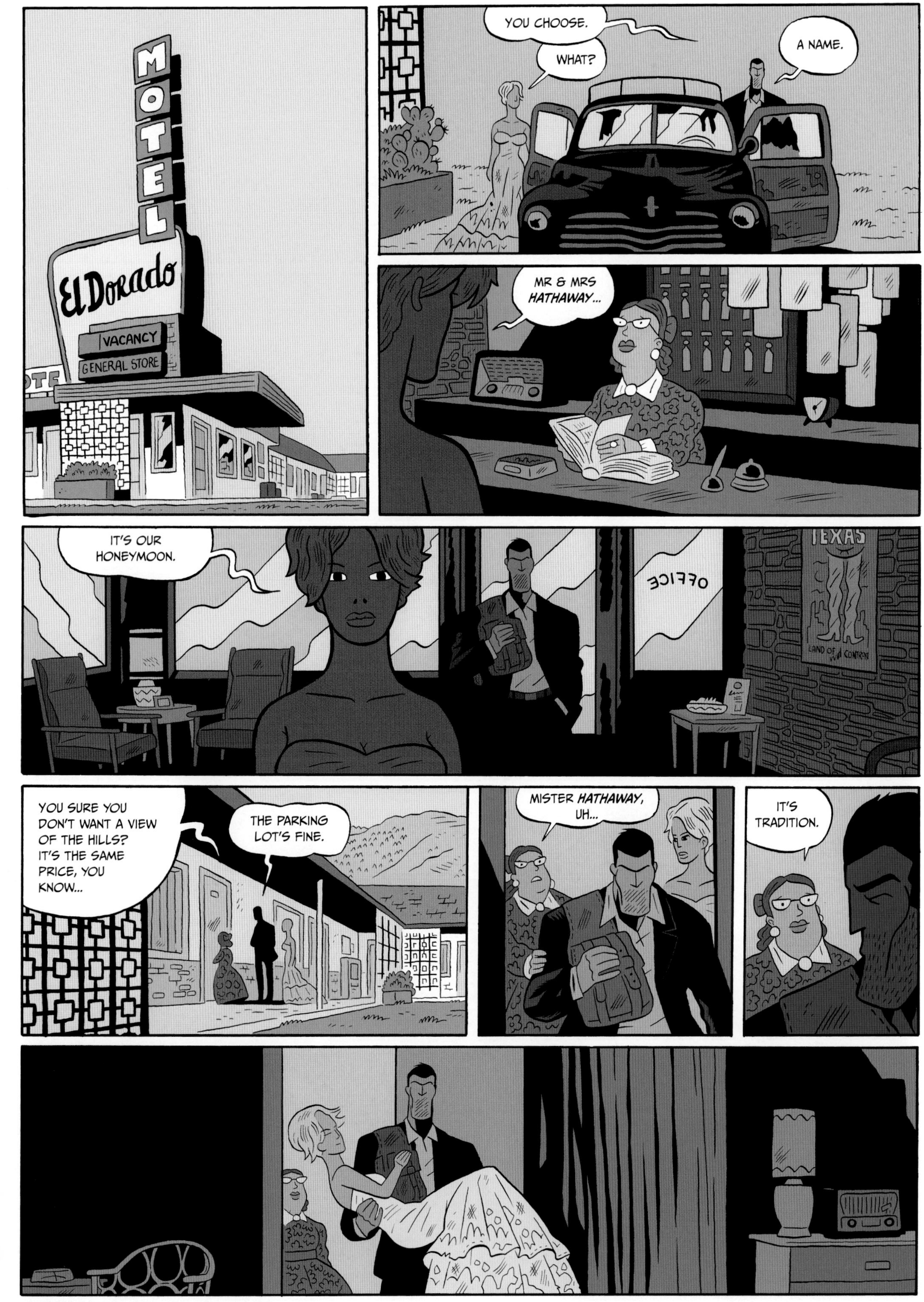
MOTEL
El Dorado
VACANCY
GENERAL STORE
YOU CHOOSE.
WHAT?
A NAME.
MR & MRS *HATHAWAY*...
IT'S OUR HONEYMOON.
OFFICE
TEXAS
YOU SURE YOU DON'T WANT A VIEW OF THE HILLS? IT'S THE SAME PRICE, YOU KNOW...
THE PARKING LOT'S FINE.
MISTER *HATHAWAY*, UH...
IT'S TRADITION.

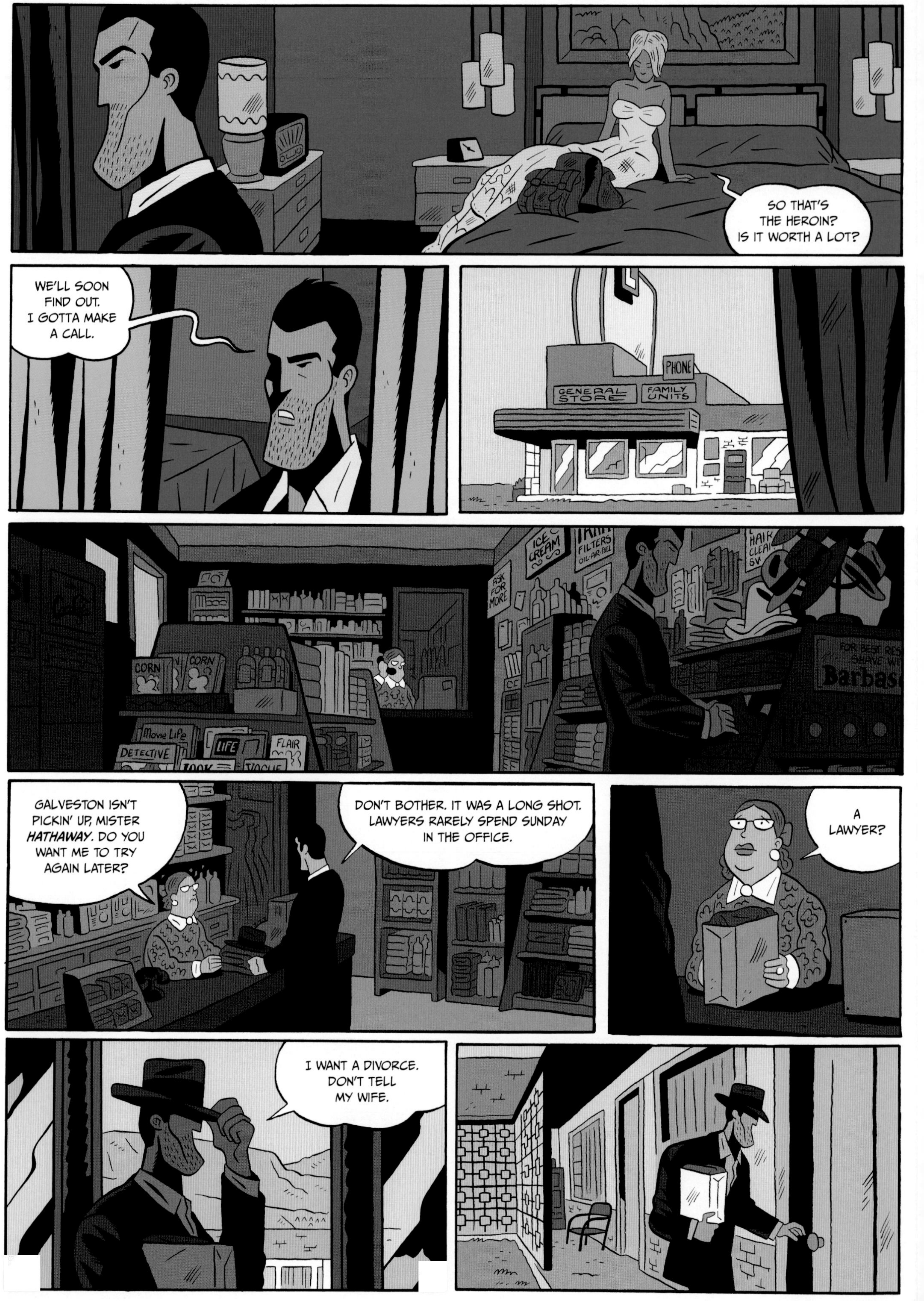
SO THAT'S THE HEROIN? IS IT WORTH A LOT?
WE'LL SOON FIND OUT. I GOTTA MAKE A CALL.
PHONE
GENERAL STORE
FAMILY UNITS
ICE CREAM
FILTERS
ASK FOR MORE
CORN
CORN
Movie Life
DETECTIVE
LIFE
FLAIR
GALVESTON ISN'T PICKIN' UP, MISTER *HATHAWAY*. DO YOU WANT ME TO TRY AGAIN LATER?
DON'T BOTHER. IT WAS A LONG SHOT. LAWYERS RARELY SPEND SUNDAY IN THE OFFICE.
A LAWYER?
I WANT A DIVORCE. DON'T TELL MY WIFE.

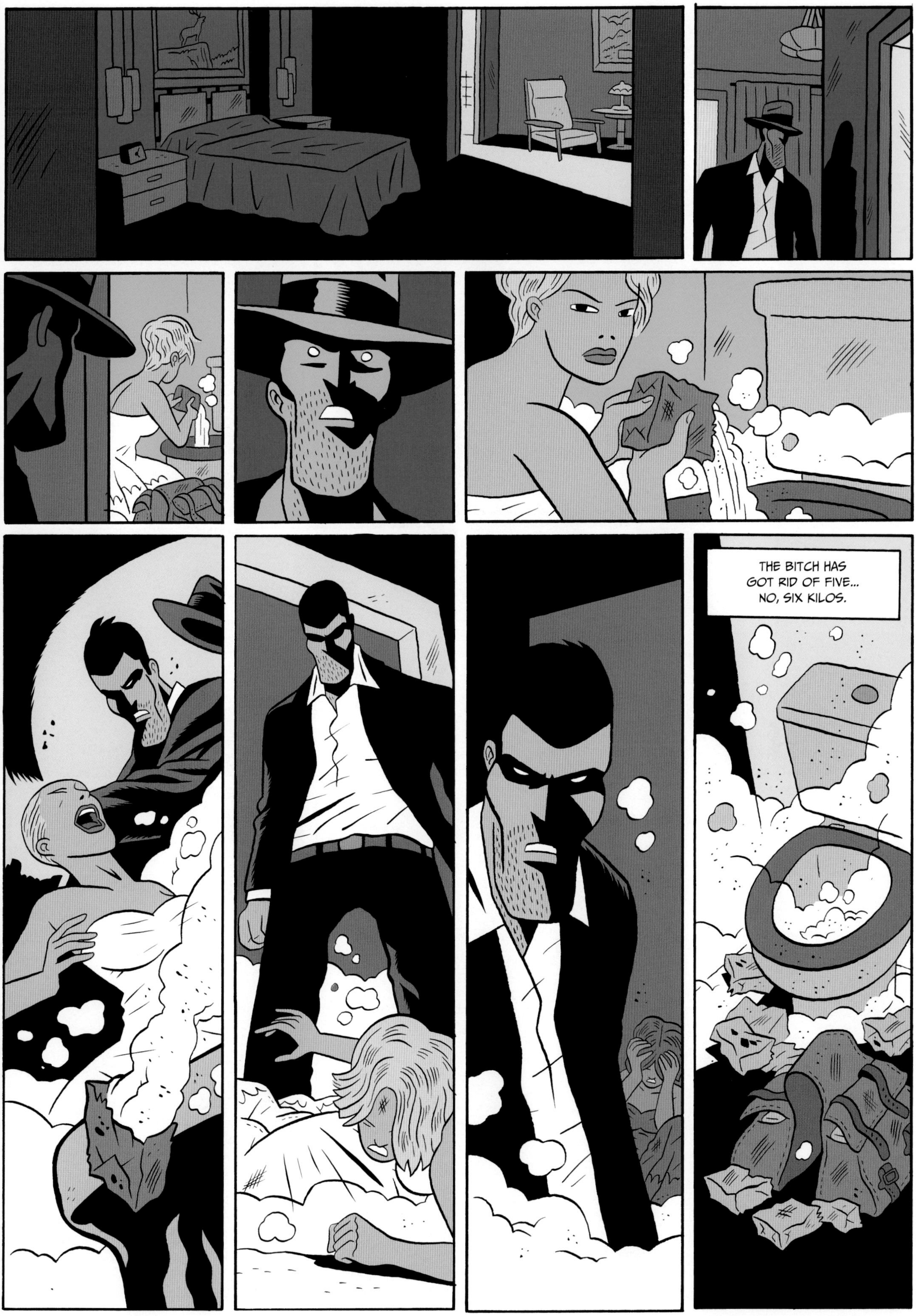
THE BITCH HAS
GOT RID OF FIVE...
NO, SIX KILOS.

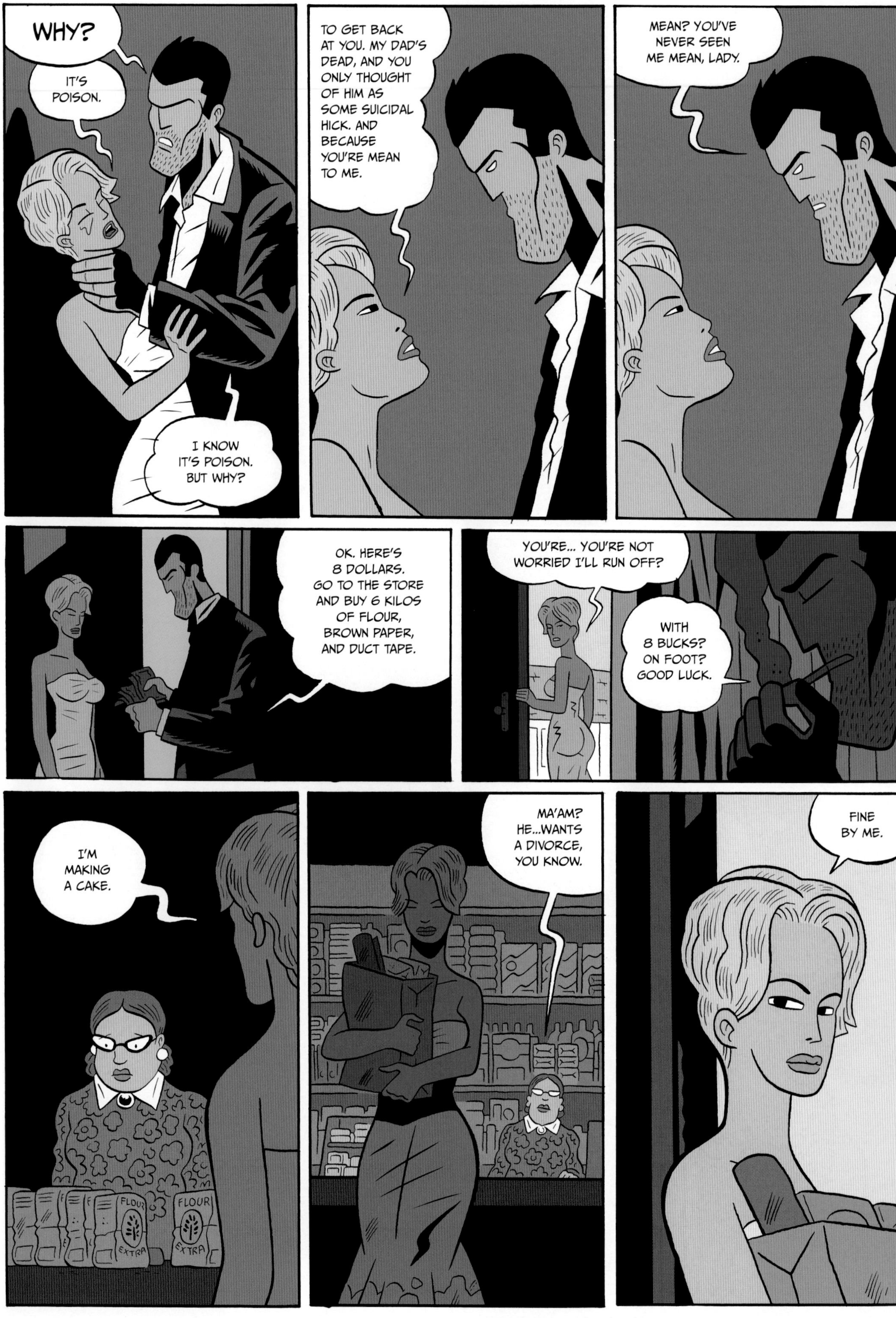
WHY?
IT'S POISON.
I KNOW IT'S POISON. BUT WHY?
TO GET BACK AT YOU. MY DAD'S DEAD, AND YOU ONLY THOUGHT OF HIM AS SOME SUICIDAL HICK. AND BECAUSE YOU'RE MEAN TO ME.
MEAN? YOU'VE NEVER SEEN ME MEAN, LADY.
OK. HERE'S 8 DOLLARS. GO TO THE STORE AND BUY 6 KILOS OF FLOUR, BROWN PAPER, AND DUCT TAPE.
YOU'RE... YOU'RE NOT WORRIED I'LL RUN OFF?
WITH 8 BUCKS? ON FOOT? GOOD LUCK.
I'M MAKING A CAKE.
FLOUR
EXTRA
FLOUR
EXTRA
MA'AM? HE...WANTS A DIVORCE, YOU KNOW.
FINE BY ME.

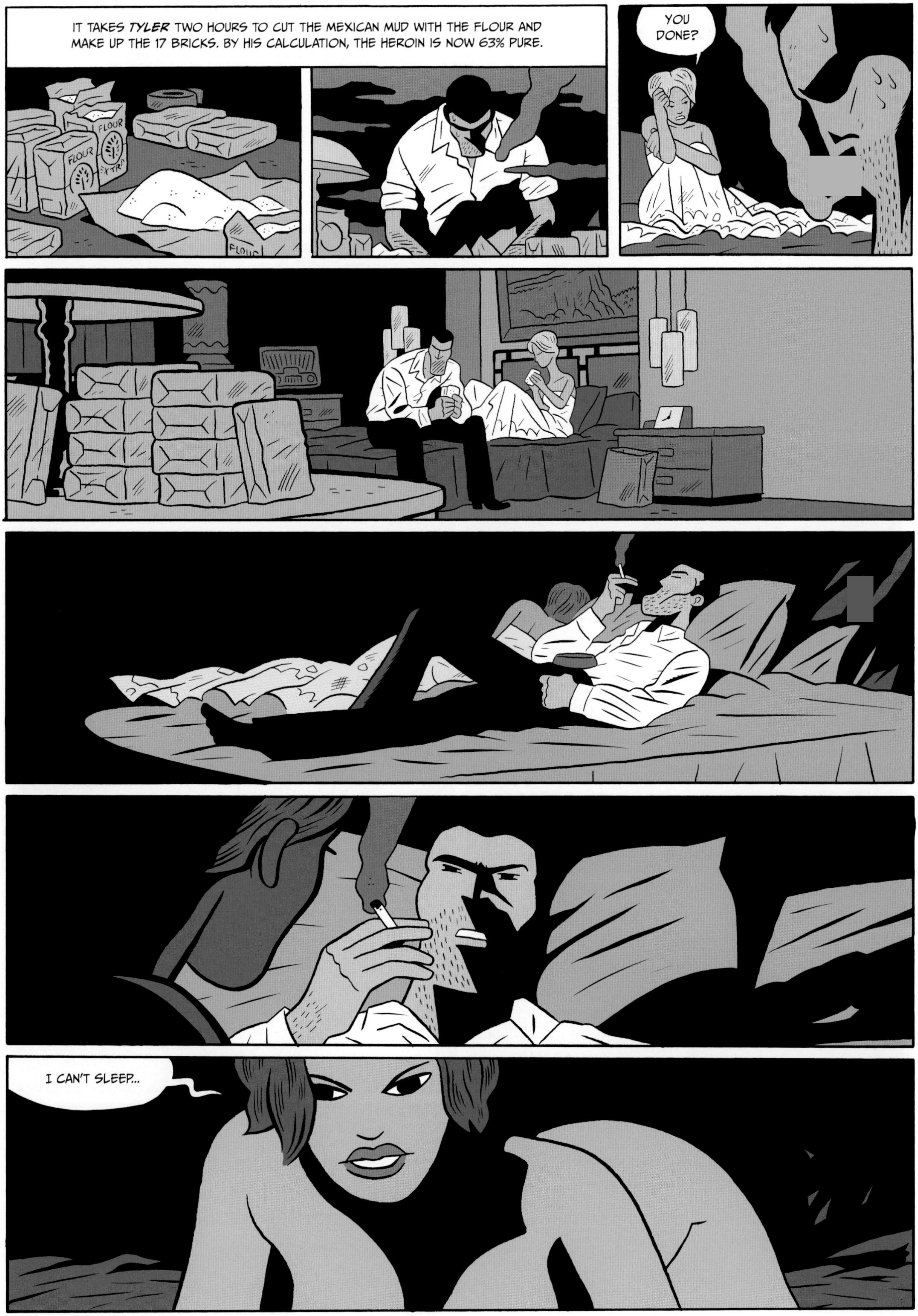
IT TAKES TYLER TWO HOURS TO CUT THE MEXICAN MUD WITH THE FLOUR AND MAKE UP THE 17 BRICKS. BY HIS CALCULATION, THE HEROIN IS NOW 63% PURE.
FLOUR
FLOUR
FLOUR
YOU DONE?
I CAN'T SLEEP...

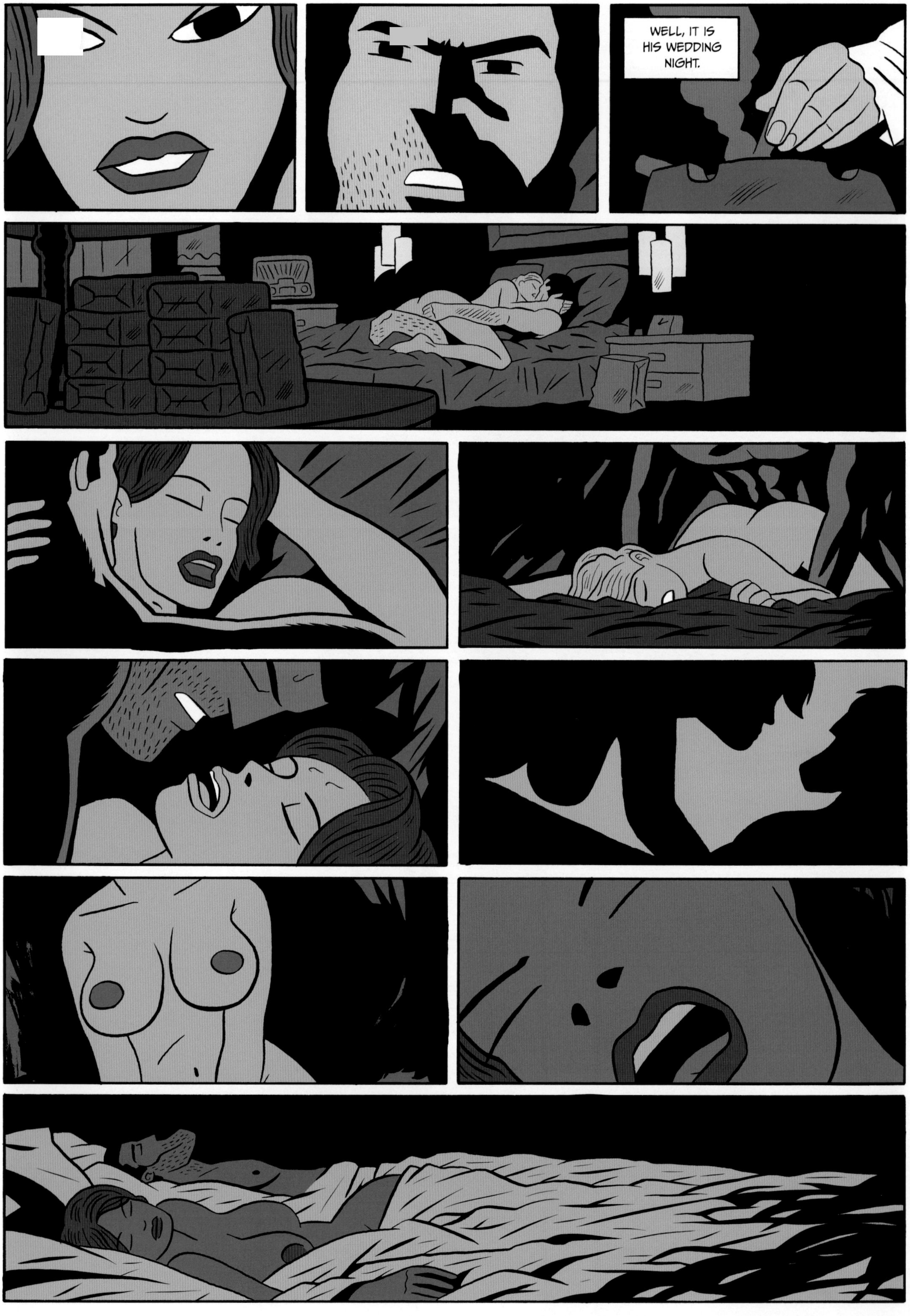
WELL, IT IS HIS WEDDING NIGHT.

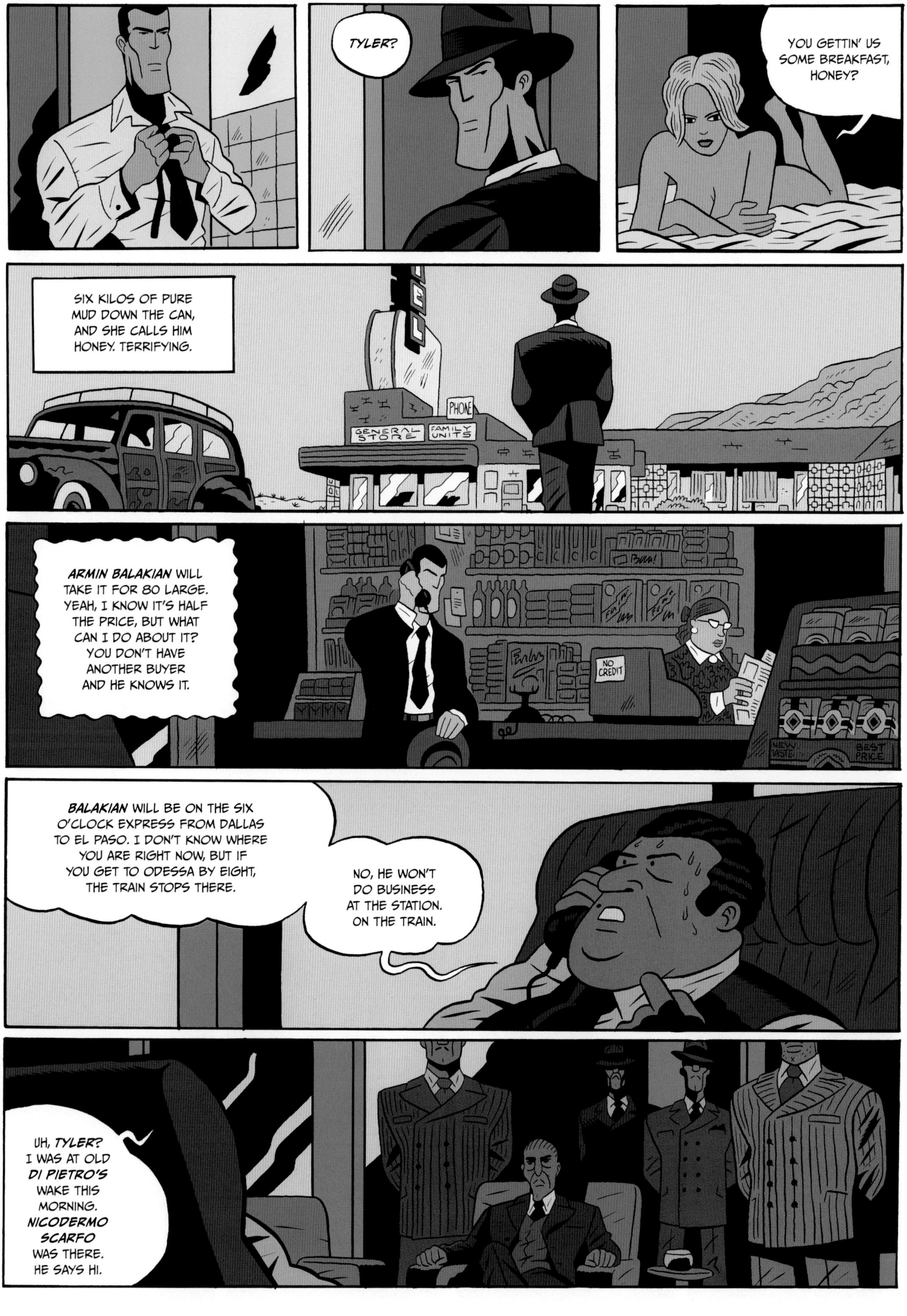
TYLER?
YOU GETTIN' US SOME BREAKFAST, HONEY?
SIX KILOS OF PURE MUD DOWN THE CAN, AND SHE CALLS HIM HONEY. TERRIFYING.
PHONE
GENERAL STORE
FAMILY UNITS
ARMIN BALAKIAN WILL TAKE IT FOR 80 LARGE. YEAH, I KNOW IT'S HALF THE PRICE, BUT WHAT CAN I DO ABOUT IT? YOU DON'T HAVE ANOTHER BUYER AND HE KNOWS IT.
NO CREDIT
NEW TASTE
BEST PRICE
BALAKIAN WILL BE ON THE SIX O'CLOCK EXPRESS FROM DALLAS TO EL PASO. I DON'T KNOW WHERE YOU ARE RIGHT NOW, BUT IF YOU GET TO ODESSA BY EIGHT, THE TRAIN STOPS THERE.
NO, HE WON'T DO BUSINESS AT THE STATION. ON THE TRAIN.
UH, TYLER? I WAS AT OLD DI PIETRO'S WAKE THIS MORNING. NICODERMO SCARFO WAS THERE. HE SAYS HI.

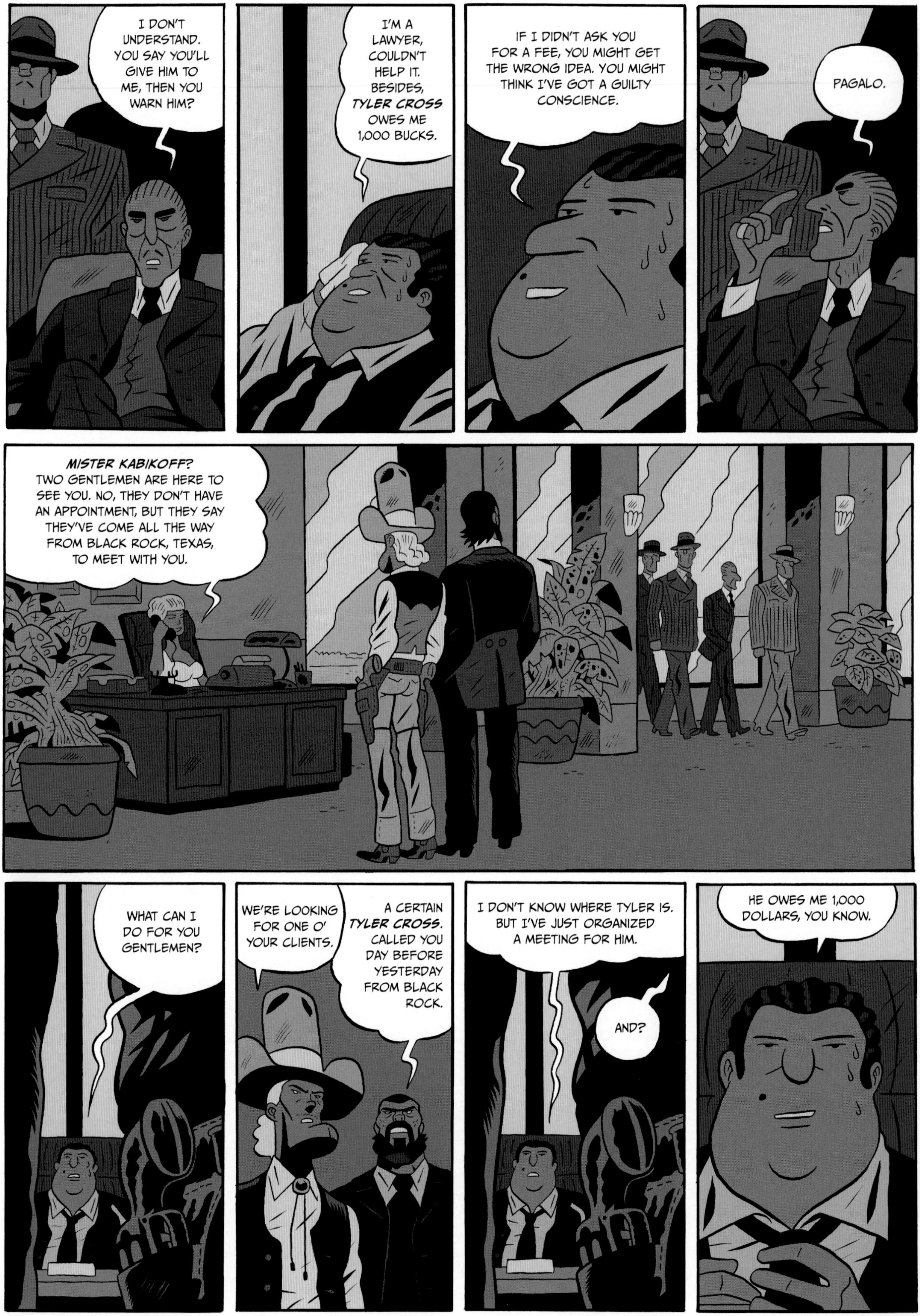

I DON'T UNDERSTAND. YOU SAY YOU'LL GIVE HIM TO ME, THEN YOU WARN HIM?
I'M A LAWYER, COULDN'T HELP IT. BESIDES, *TYLER CROSS* OWES ME 1,000 BUCKS.
IF I DIDN'T ASK YOU FOR A FEE, YOU MIGHT GET THE WRONG IDEA. YOU MIGHT THINK I'VE GOT A GUILTY CONSCIENCE.
PAGALO.
MISTER KABIKOFF? TWO GENTLEMEN ARE HERE TO SEE YOU. NO, THEY DON'T HAVE AN APPOINTMENT, BUT THEY SAY THEY'VE COME ALL THE WAY FROM BLACK ROCK, TEXAS, TO MEET WITH YOU.
WHAT CAN I DO FOR YOU GENTLEMEN?
WE'RE LOOKING FOR ONE O' YOUR CLIENTS.
A CERTAIN *TYLER CROSS*. CALLED YOU DAY BEFORE YESTERDAY FROM BLACK ROCK.
I DON'T KNOW WHERE TYLER IS. BUT I'VE JUST ORGANIZED A MEETING FOR HIM.
AND?
HE OWES ME 1,000 DOLLARS, YOU KNOW.

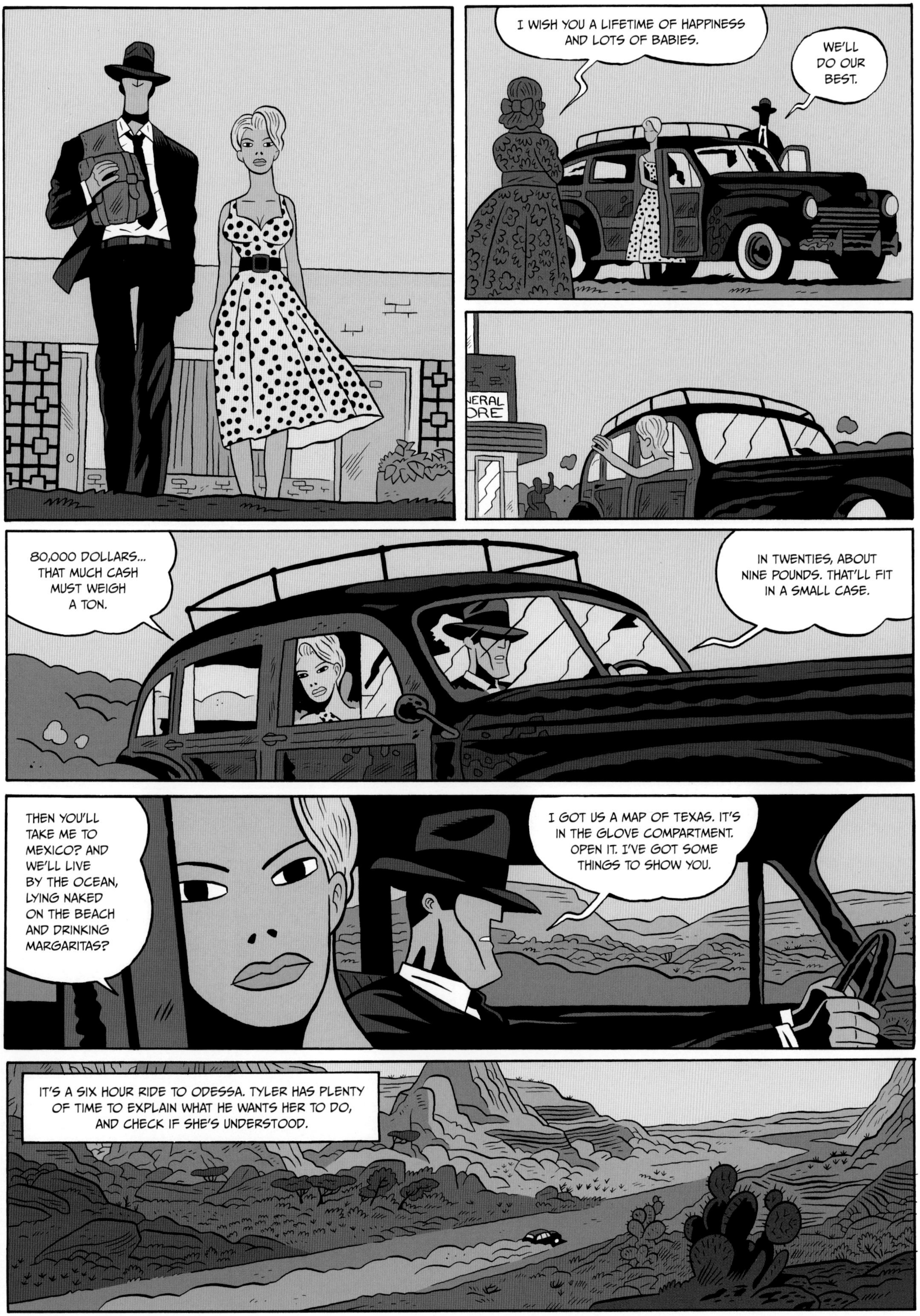
I WISH YOU A LIFETIME OF HAPPINESS AND LOTS OF BABIES.
WE'LL DO OUR BEST.
80,000 DOLLARS... THAT MUCH CASH MUST WEIGH A TON.
IN TWENTIES, ABOUT NINE POUNDS. THAT'LL FIT IN A SMALL CASE.
THEN YOU'LL TAKE ME TO MEXICO? AND WE'LL LIVE BY THE OCEAN, LYING NAKED ON THE BEACH AND DRINKING MARGARITAS?
I GOT US A MAP OF TEXAS. IT'S IN THE GLOVE COMPARTMENT. OPEN IT. I'VE GOT SOME THINGS TO SHOW YOU.
IT'S A SIX HOUR RIDE TO ODESSA. TYLER HAS PLENTY OF TIME TO EXPLAIN WHAT HE WANTS HER TO DO, AND CHECK IF SHE'S UNDERSTOOD.

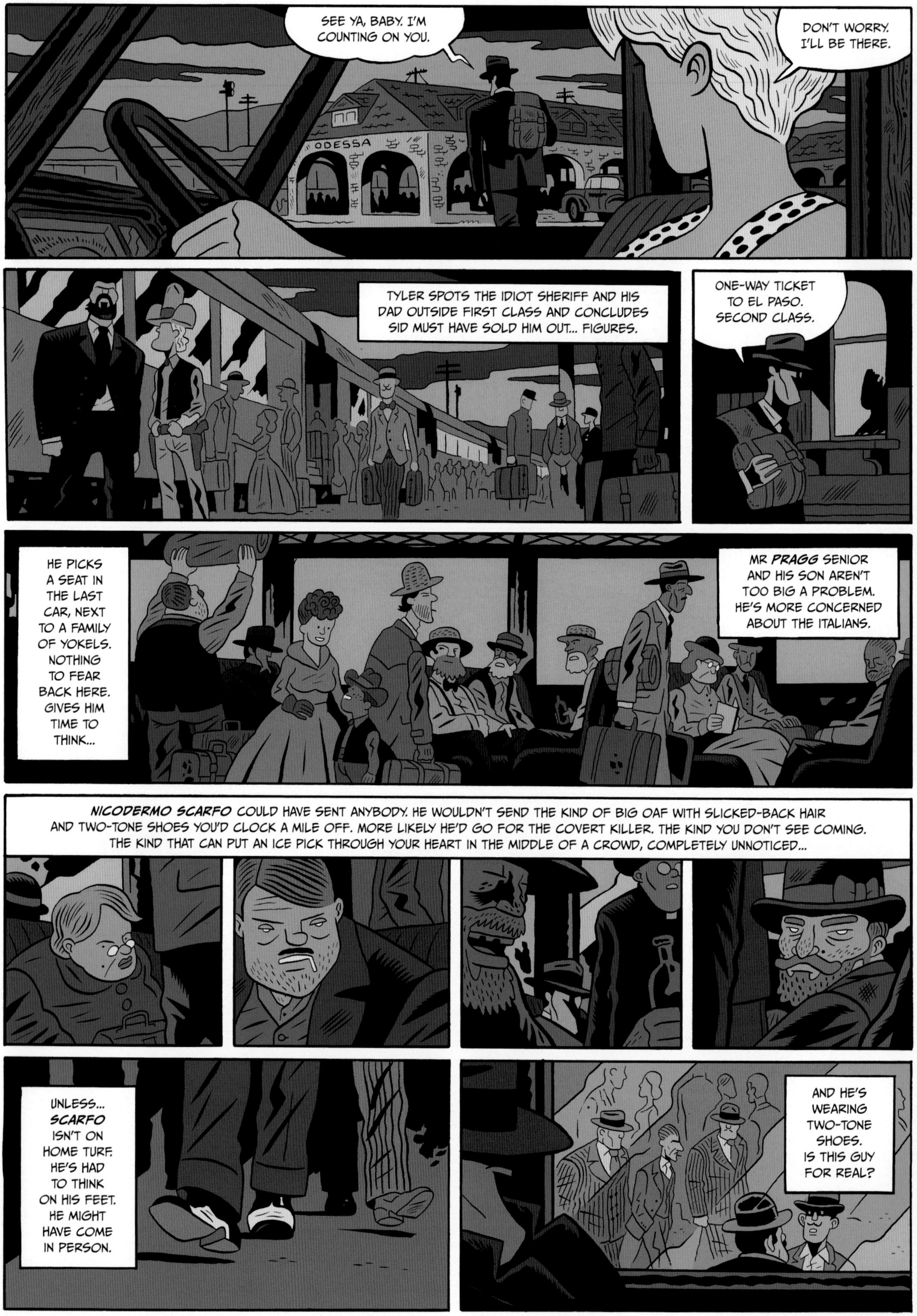
SEE YA, BABY. I'M COUNTING ON YOU.
DON'T WORRY. I'LL BE THERE.
ODESSA
TYLER SPOTS THE IDIOT SHERIFF AND HIS DAD OUTSIDE FIRST CLASS AND CONCLUDES SID MUST HAVE SOLD HIM OUT... FIGURES.
ONE-WAY TICKET TO EL PASO. SECOND CLASS.
HE PICKS A SEAT IN THE LAST CAR, NEXT TO A FAMILY OF YOKELS. NOTHING TO FEAR BACK HERE. GIVES HIM TIME TO THINK...
MR PRAGG SENIOR AND HIS SON AREN'T TOO BIG A PROBLEM. HE'S MORE CONCERNED ABOUT THE ITALIANS.
NICODERMO SCARFO COULD HAVE SENT ANYBODY. HE WOULDN'T SEND THE KIND OF BIG OAF WITH SLICKED-BACK HAIR AND TWO-TONE SHOES YOU'D CLOCK A MILE OFF. MORE LIKELY HE'D GO FOR THE COVERT KILLER. THE KIND YOU DON'T SEE COMING. THE KIND THAT CAN PUT AN ICE PICK THROUGH YOUR HEART IN THE MIDDLE OF A CROWD, COMPLETELY UNNOTICED...
UNLESS... SCARFO ISN'T ON HOME TURF. HE'S HAD TO THINK ON HIS FEET. HE MIGHT HAVE COME IN PERSON.
AND HE'S WEARING TWO-TONE SHOES. IS THIS GUY FOR REAL?

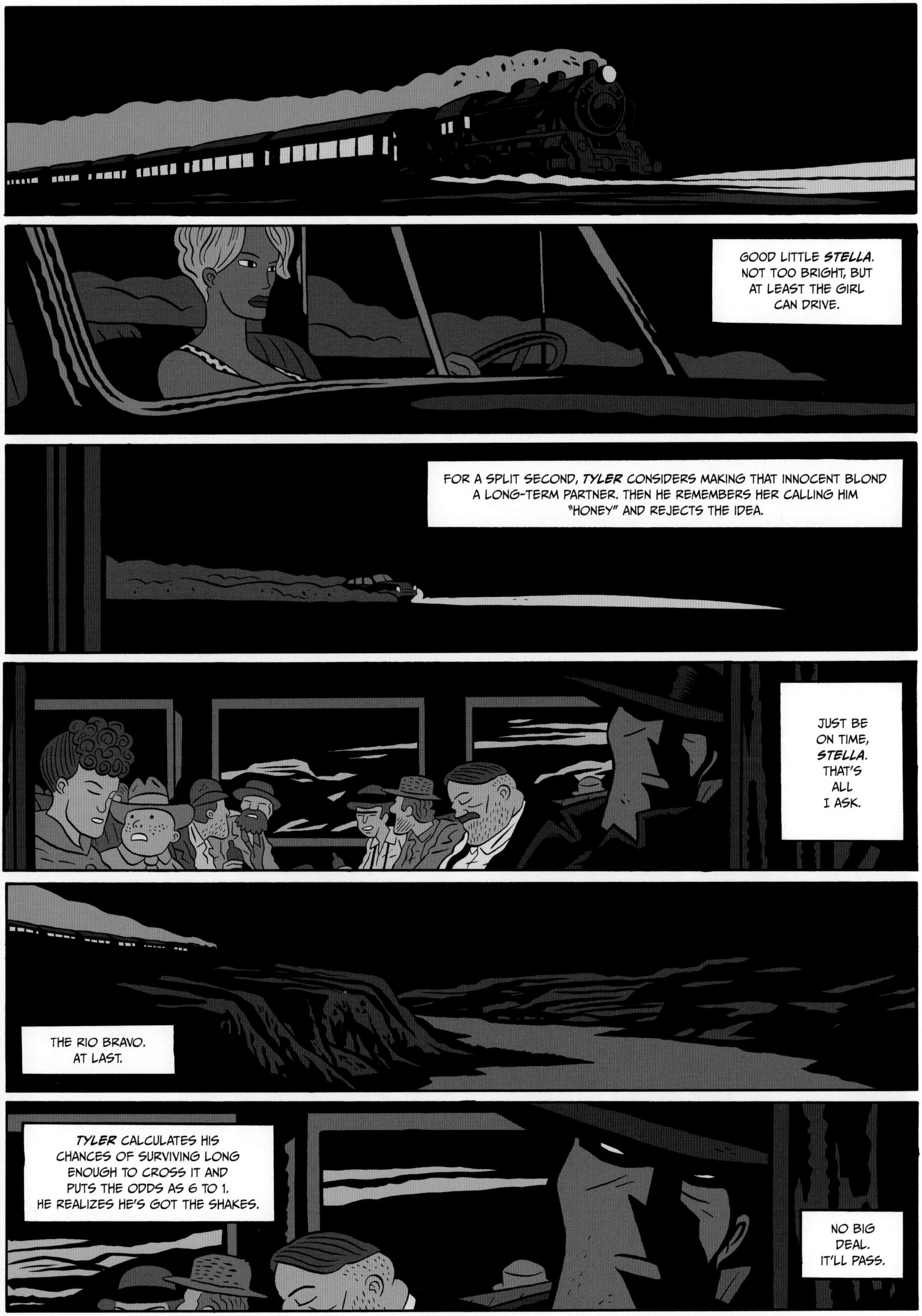
GOOD LITTLE STELLA. NOT TOO BRIGHT, BUT AT LEAST THE GIRL CAN DRIVE.
FOR A SPLIT SECOND, TYLER CONSIDERS MAKING THAT INNOCENT BLOND A LONG-TERM PARTNER. THEN HE REMEMBERS HER CALLING HIM "HONEY" AND REJECTS THE IDEA.
JUST BE ON TIME, STELLA. THAT'S ALL I ASK.
THE RIO BRAVO. AT LAST.
TYLER CALCULATES HIS CHANCES OF SURVIVING LONG ENOUGH TO CROSS IT AND PUTS THE ODDS AS 6 TO 1. HE REALIZES HE'S GOT THE SHAKES.
NO BIG DEAL. IT'LL PASS.

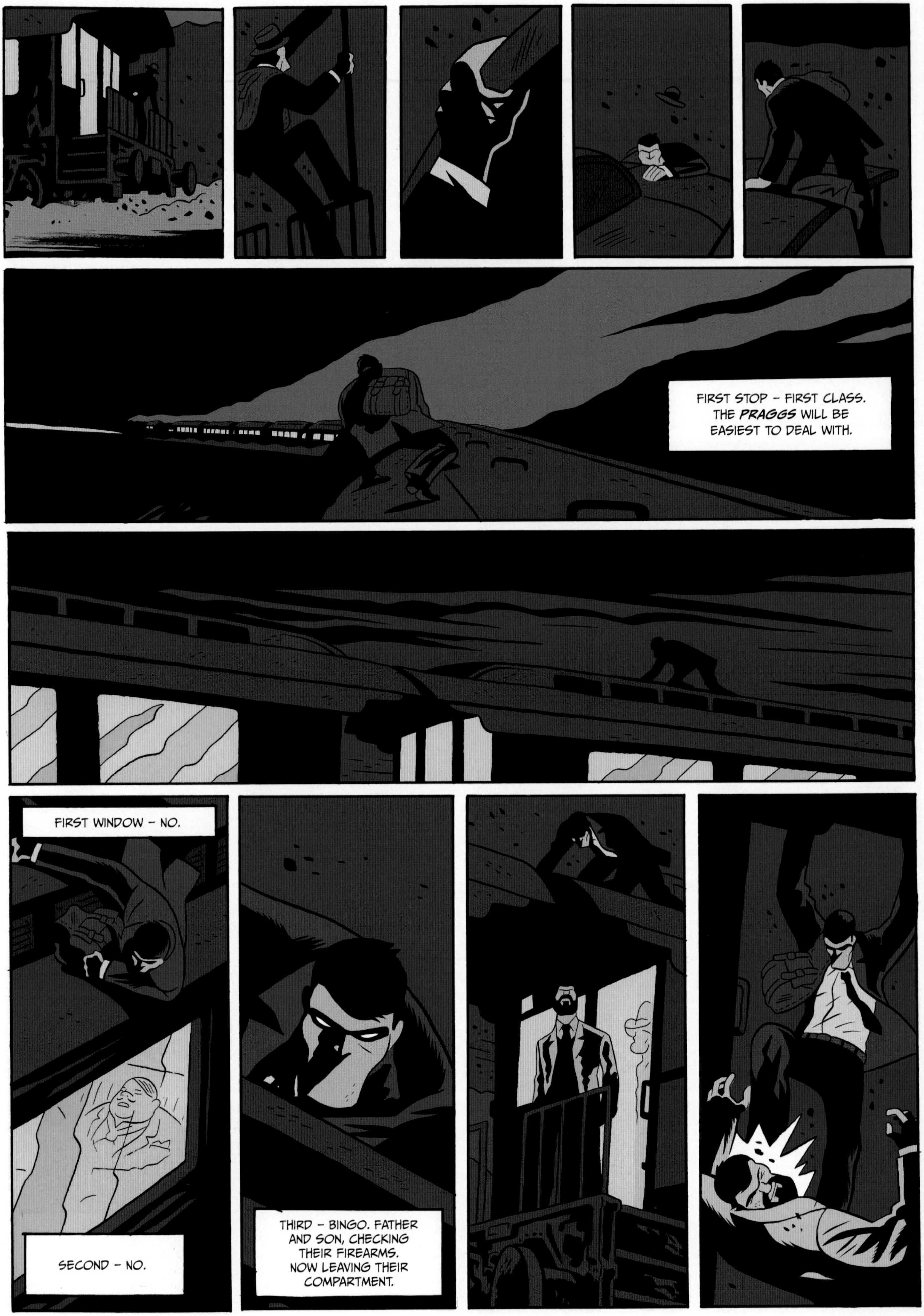
FIRST STOP – FIRST CLASS. THE PRAGGS WILL BE EASIEST TO DEAL WITH.
FIRST WINDOW – NO.
SECOND – NO.
THIRD – BINGO. FATHER AND SON, CHECKING THEIR FIREARMS. NOW LEAVING THEIR COMPARTMENT.

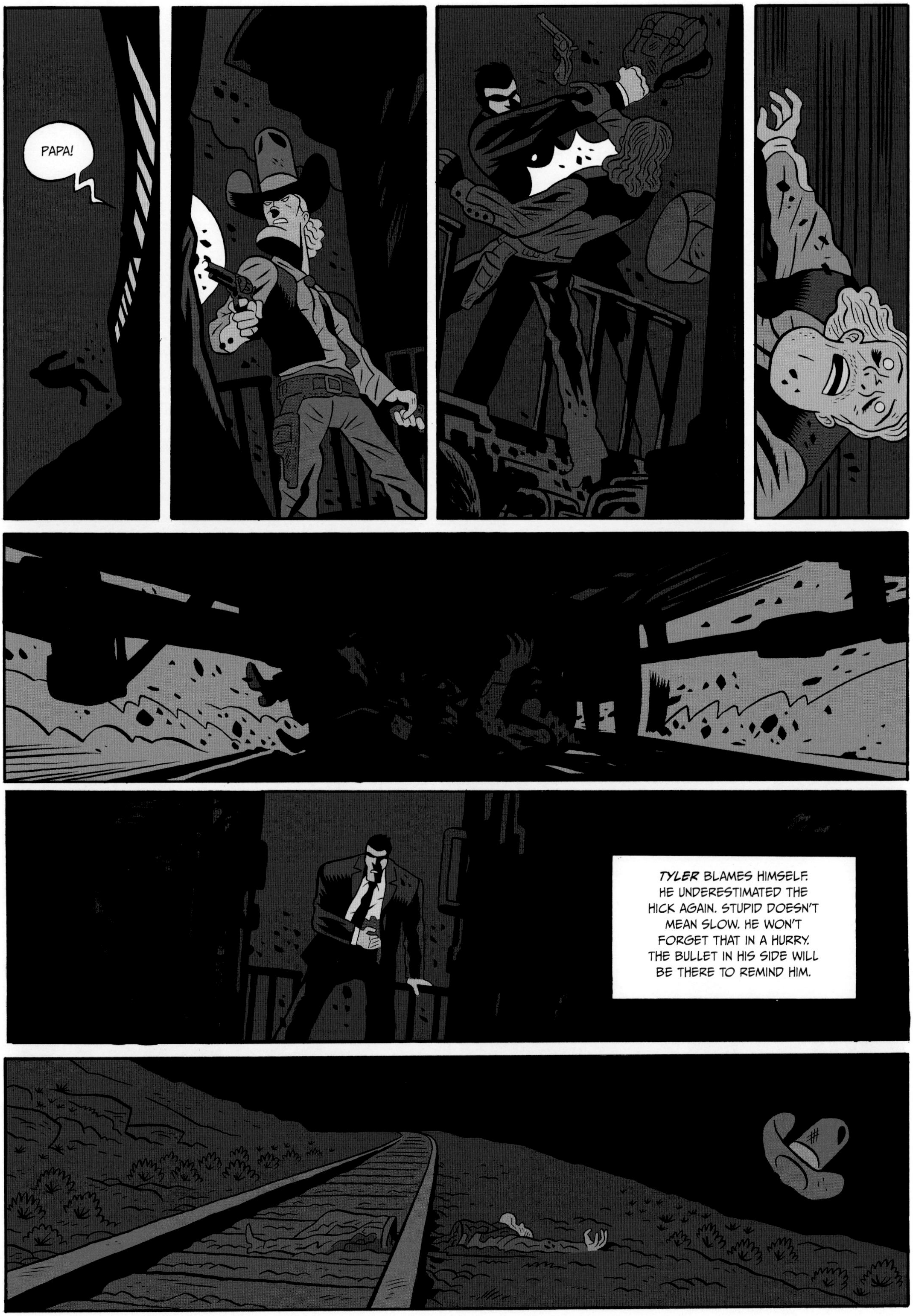
PAPA!
TYLER BLAMES HIMSELF. HE UNDERESTIMATED THE HICK AGAIN. STUPID DOESN'T MEAN SLOW. HE WON'T FORGET THAT IN A HURRY. THE BULLET IN HIS SIDE WILL BE THERE TO REMIND HIM.

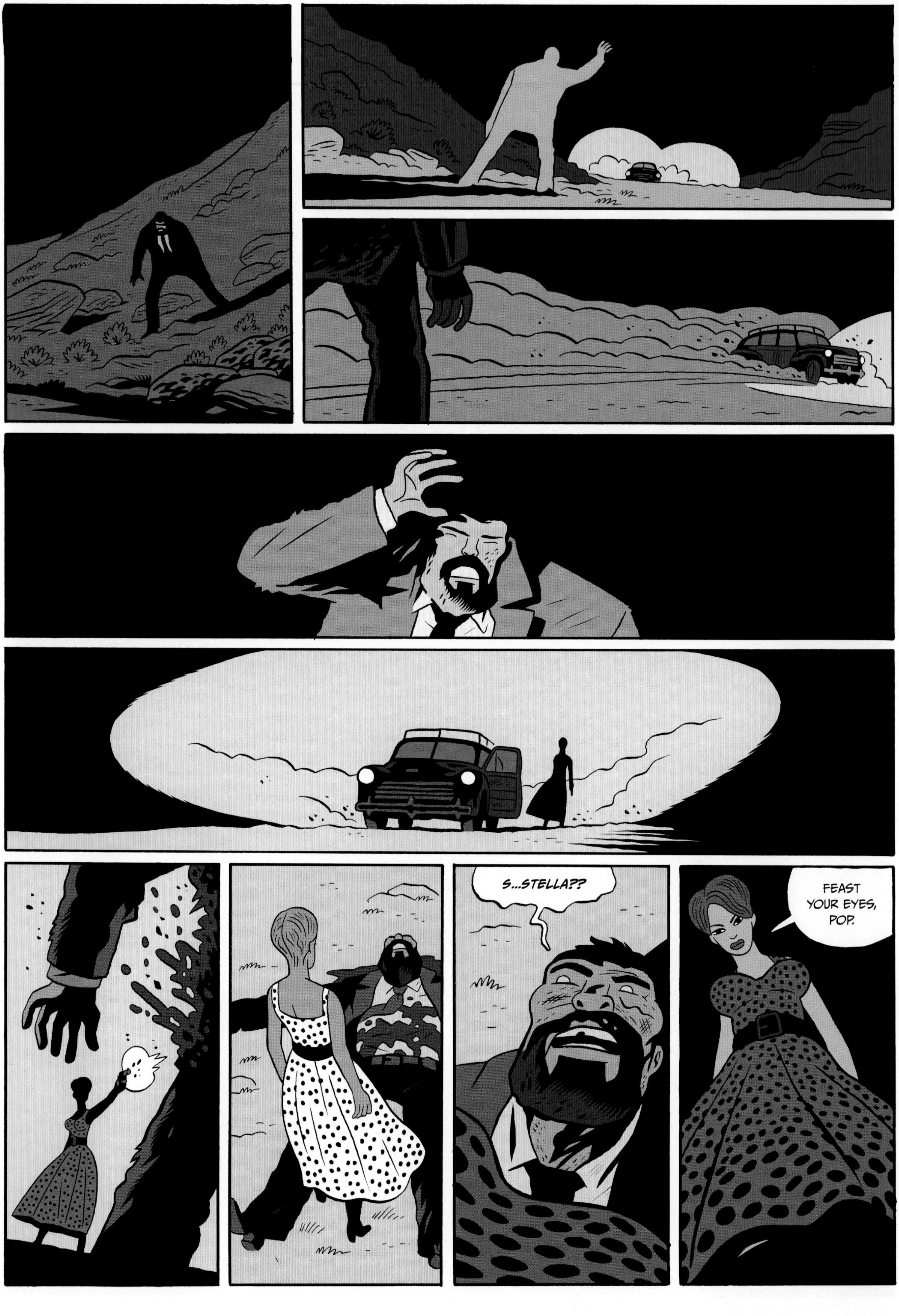
S...STELLA??
FEAST YOUR EYES, POP.

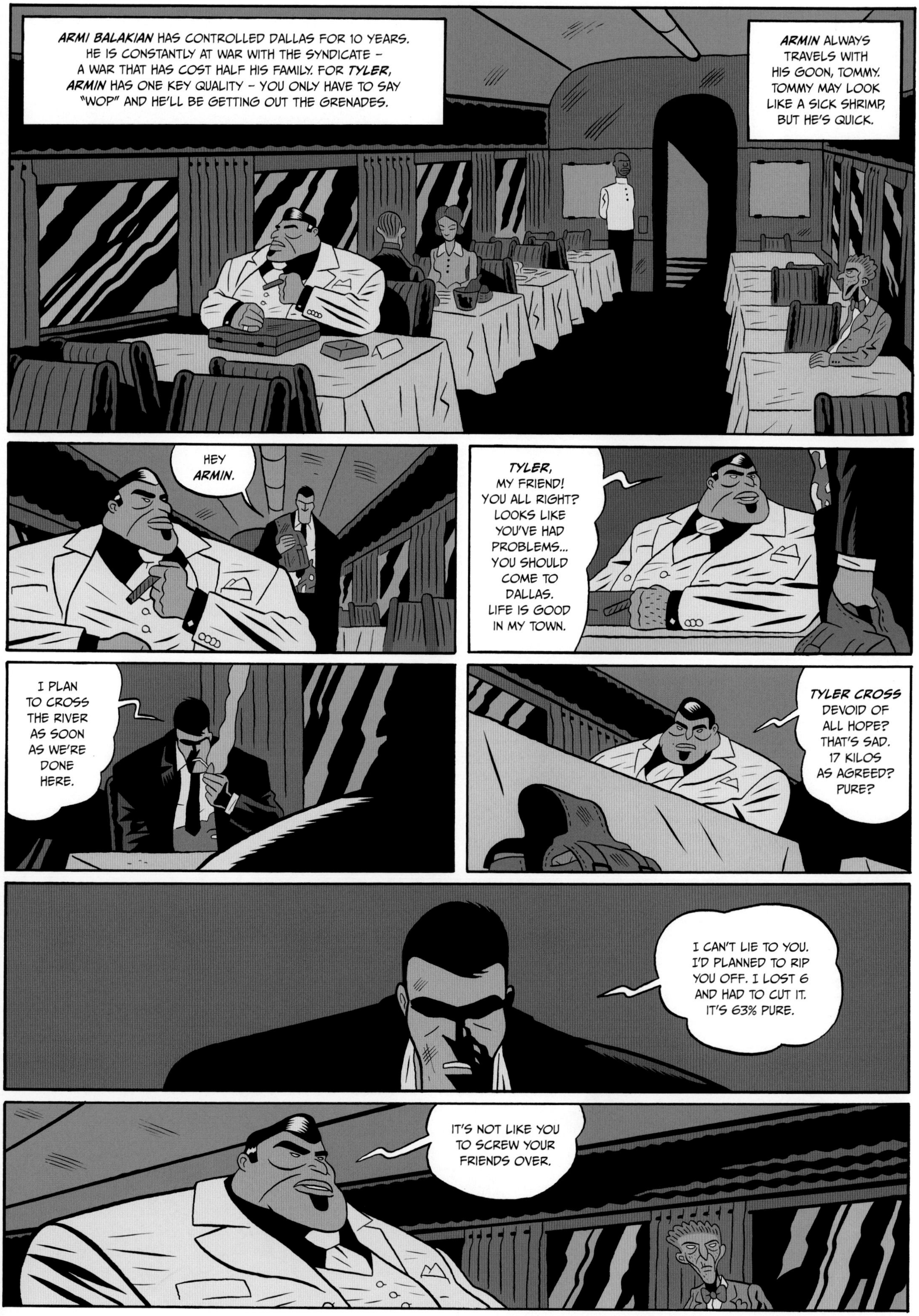
ARMI BALAKIAN HAS CONTROLLED DALLAS FOR 10 YEARS. HE IS CONSTANTLY AT WAR WITH THE SYNDICATE – A WAR THAT HAS COST HALF HIS FAMILY. FOR TYLER, ARMIN HAS ONE KEY QUALITY – YOU ONLY HAVE TO SAY "WOP" AND HE'LL BE GETTING OUT THE GRENADES.
ARMIN ALWAYS TRAVELS WITH HIS GOON, TOMMY. TOMMY MAY LOOK LIKE A SICK SHRIMP, BUT HE'S QUICK.
HEY ARMIN.
TYLER, MY FRIEND! YOU ALL RIGHT? LOOKS LIKE YOU'VE HAD PROBLEMS... YOU SHOULD COME TO DALLAS. LIFE IS GOOD IN MY TOWN.
I PLAN TO CROSS THE RIVER AS SOON AS WE'RE DONE HERE.
TYLER CROSS DEVOID OF ALL HOPE? THAT'S SAD. 17 KILOS AS AGREED? PURE?
I CAN'T LIE TO YOU. I'D PLANNED TO RIP YOU OFF. I LOST 6 AND HAD TO CUT IT. IT'S 63% PURE.
IT'S NOT LIKE YOU TO SCREW YOUR FRIENDS OVER.

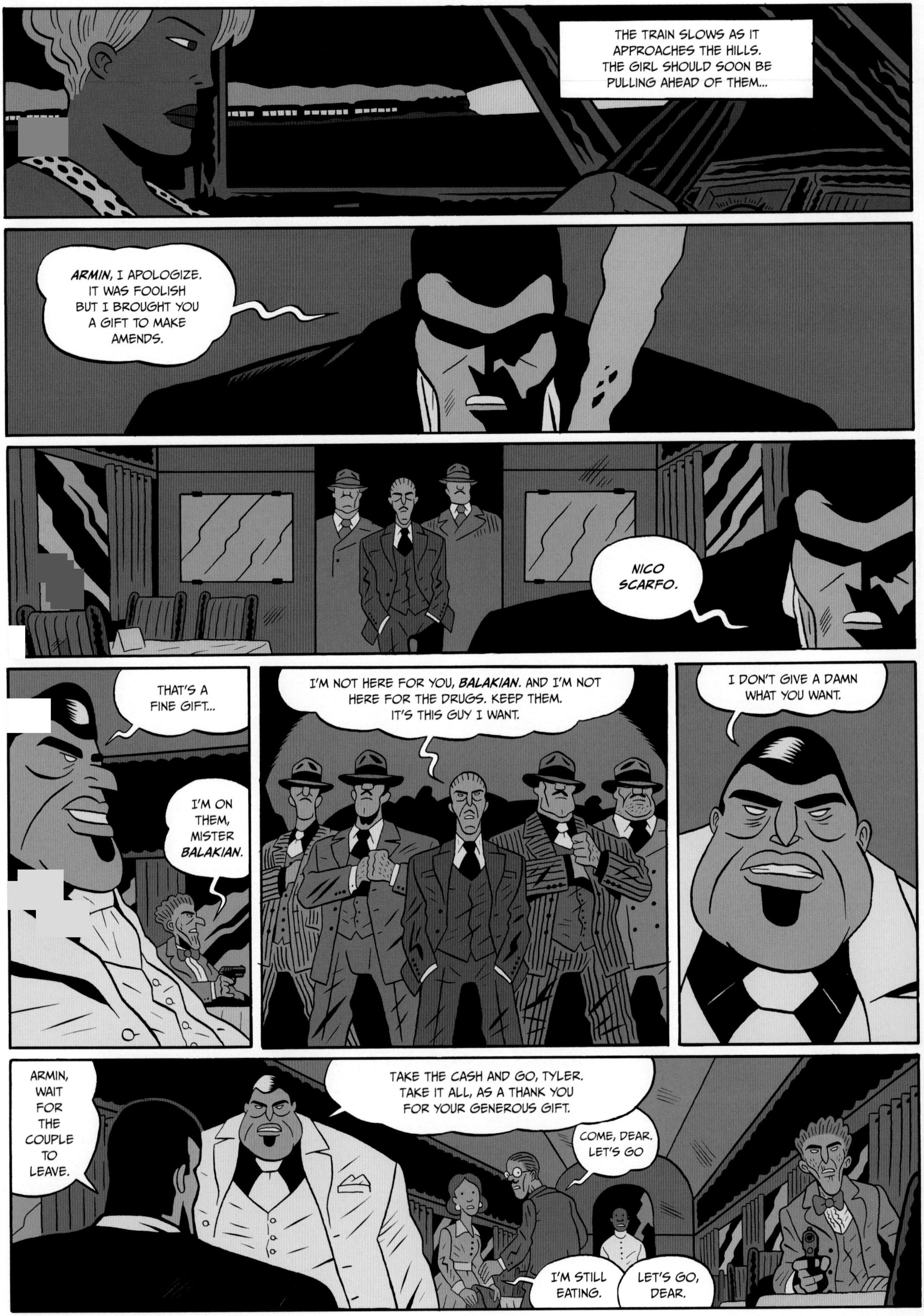
THE TRAIN SLOWS AS IT APPROACHES THE HILLS. THE GIRL SHOULD SOON BE PULLING AHEAD OF THEM...
ARMIN, I APOLOGIZE. IT WAS FOOLISH BUT I BROUGHT YOU A GIFT TO MAKE AMENDS.
NICO SCARFO.
THAT'S A FINE GIFT...
I'M ON THEM, MISTER BALAKIAN.
I'M NOT HERE FOR YOU, BALAKIAN. AND I'M NOT HERE FOR THE DRUGS. KEEP THEM. IT'S THIS GUY I WANT.
I DON'T GIVE A DAMN WHAT YOU WANT.
ARMIN, WAIT FOR THE COUPLE TO LEAVE.
TAKE THE CASH AND GO, TYLER. TAKE IT ALL, AS A THANK YOU FOR YOUR GENEROUS GIFT.
COME, DEAR. LET'S GO
I'M STILL EATING.
LET'S GO, DEAR.

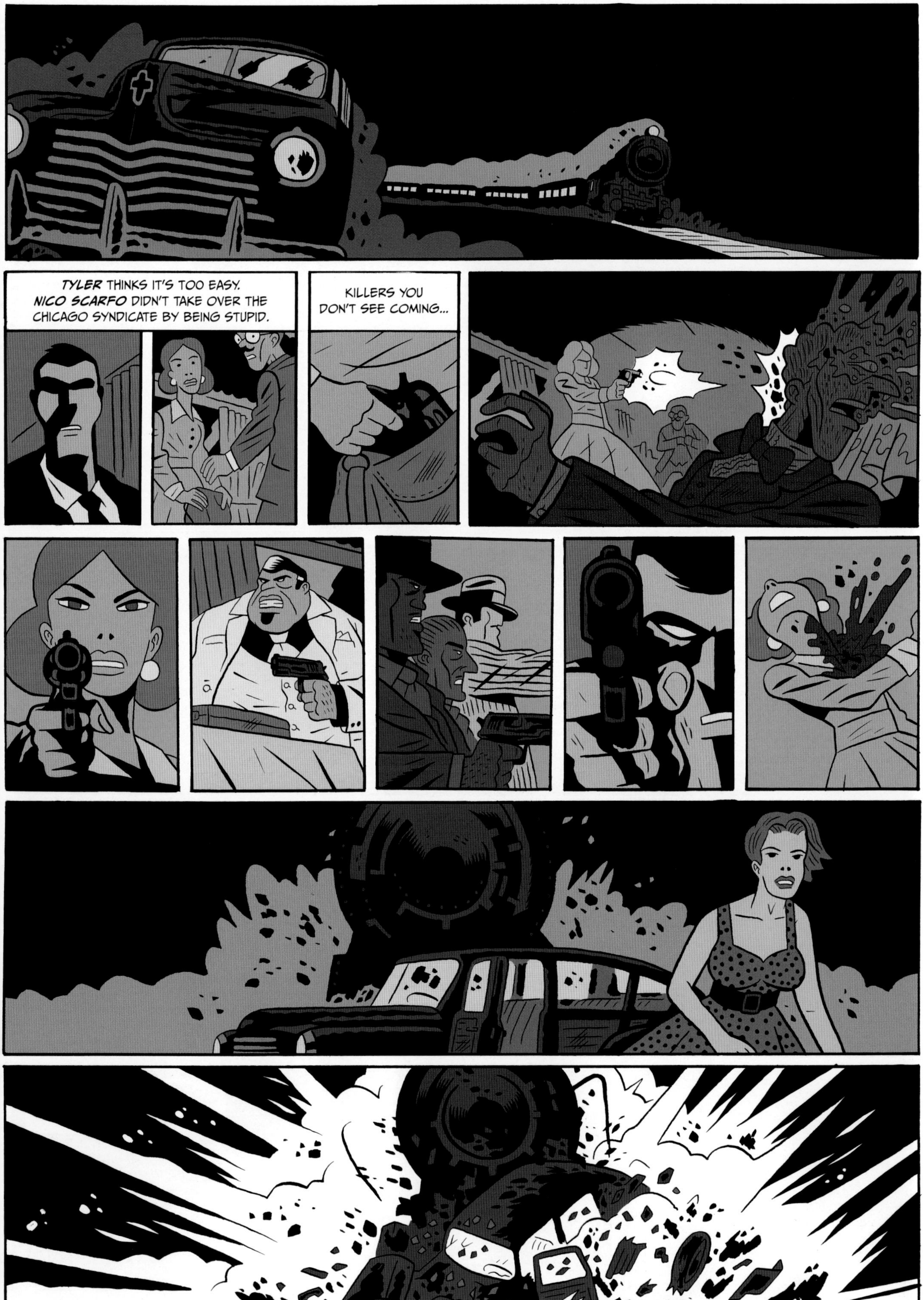

TYLER THINKS IT'S TOO EASY. NICO SCARFO DIDN'T TAKE OVER THE CHICAGO SYNDICATE BY BEING STUPID.
KILLERS YOU DON'T SEE COMING...

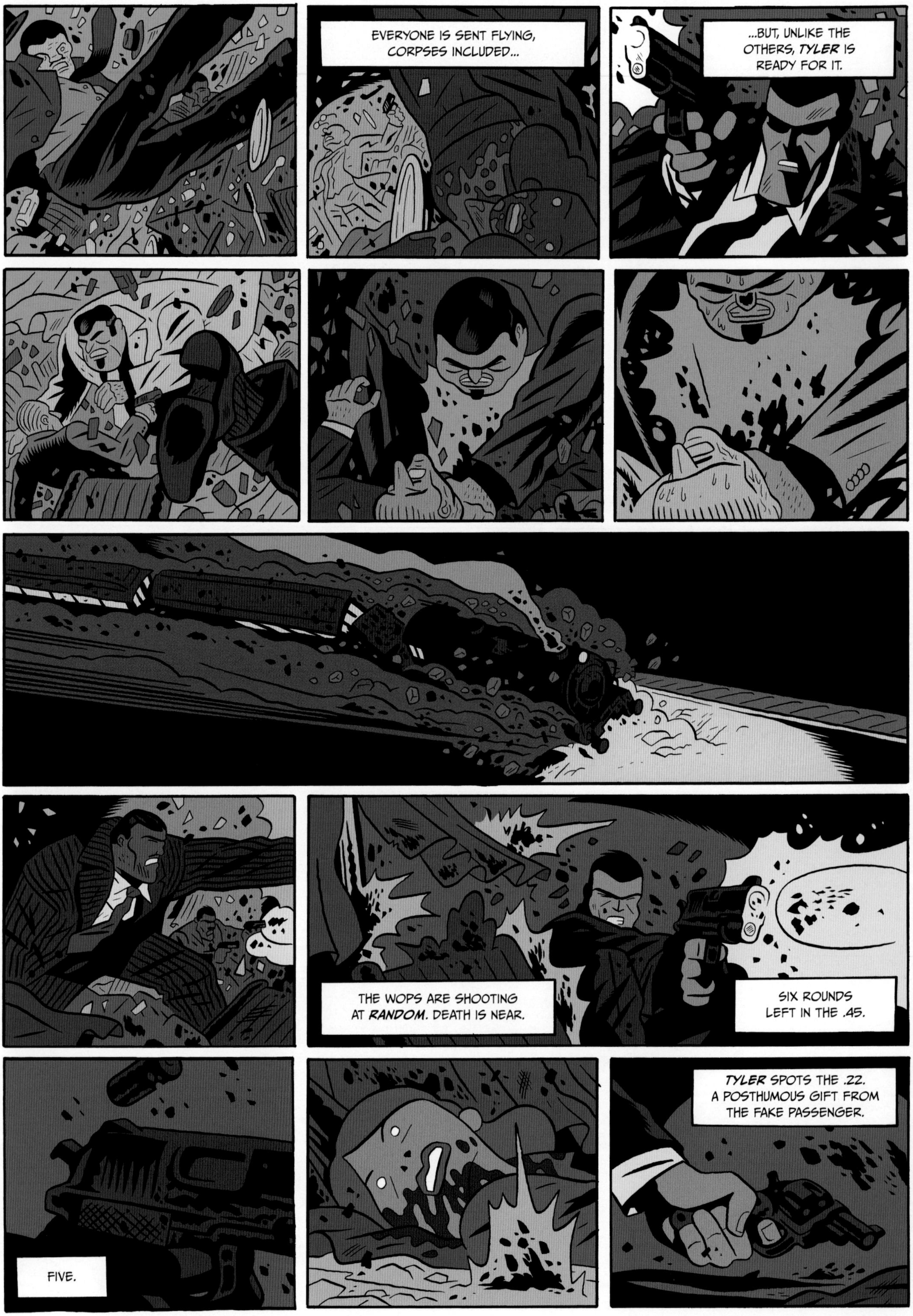
EVERYONE IS SENT FLYING, CORPSES INCLUDED...
...BUT, UNLIKE THE OTHERS, TYLER IS READY FOR IT.
THE WOPS ARE SHOOTING AT RANDOM. DEATH IS NEAR.
SIX ROUNDS LEFT IN THE .45.
FIVE.
TYLER SPOTS THE .22. A POSTHUMOUS GIFT FROM THE FAKE PASSENGER.

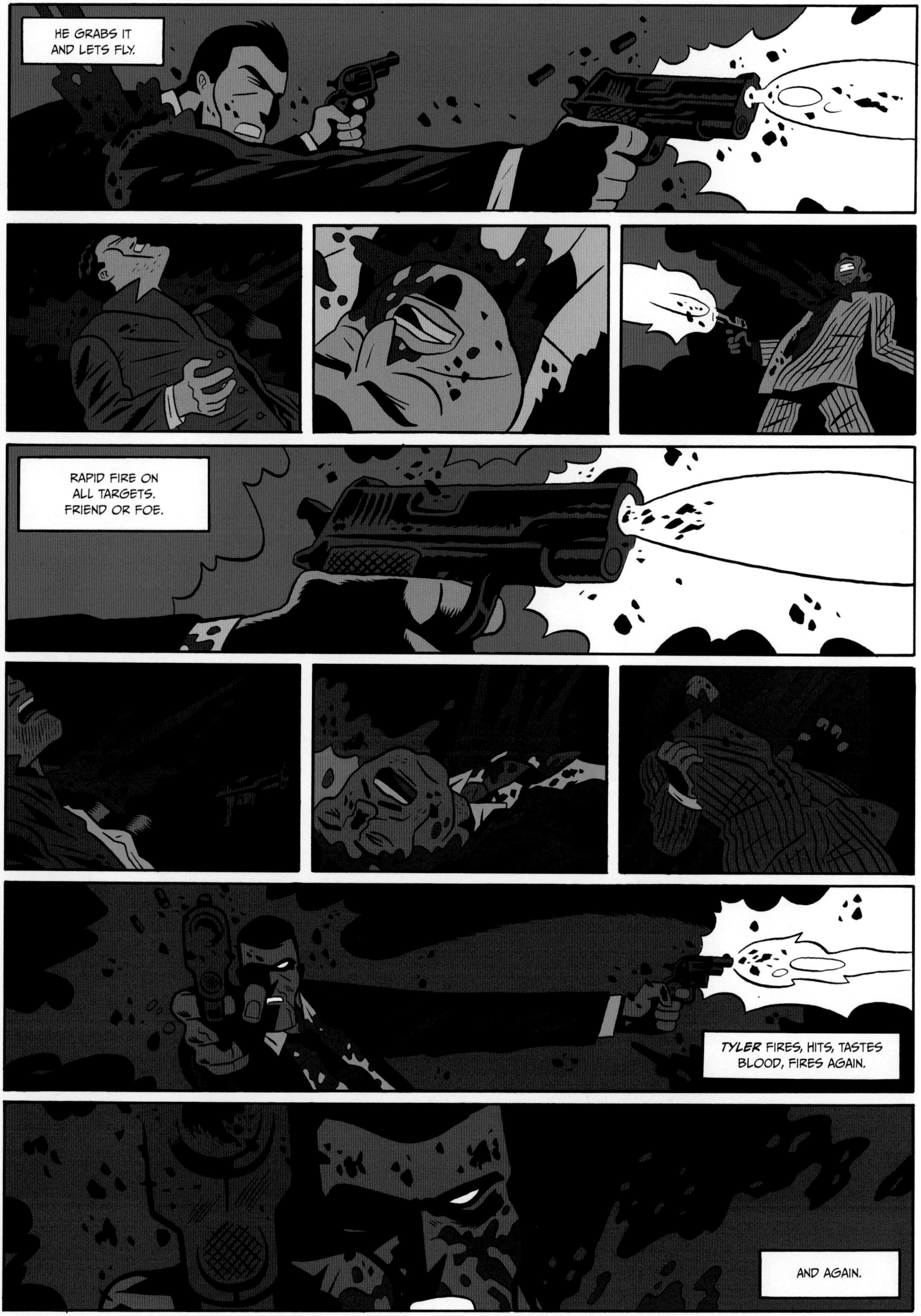
HE GRABS IT AND LETS FLY.
RAPID FIRE ON ALL TARGETS. FRIEND OR FOE.
TYLER FIRES, HITS, TASTES BLOOD, FIRES AGAIN.
AND AGAIN.

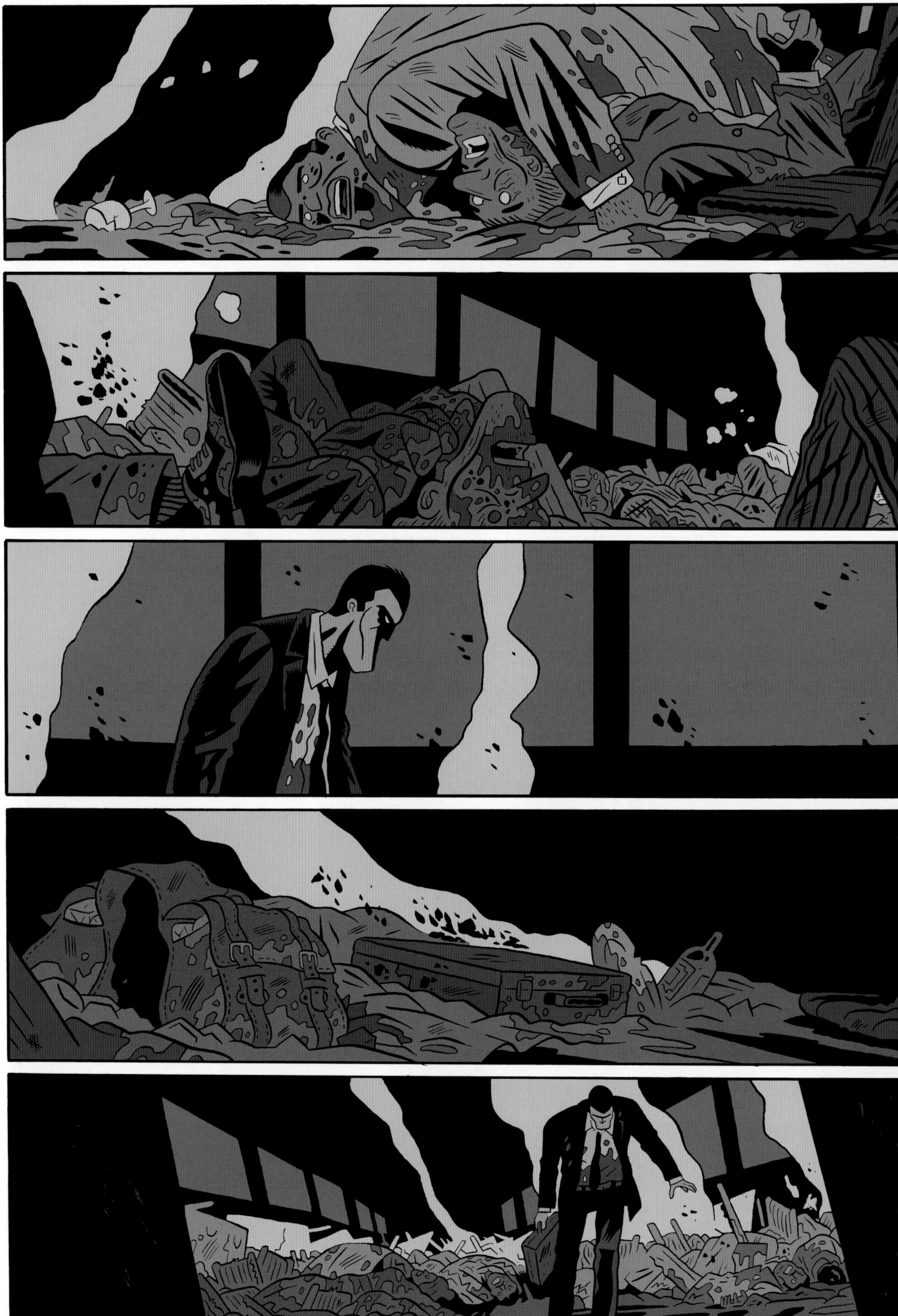

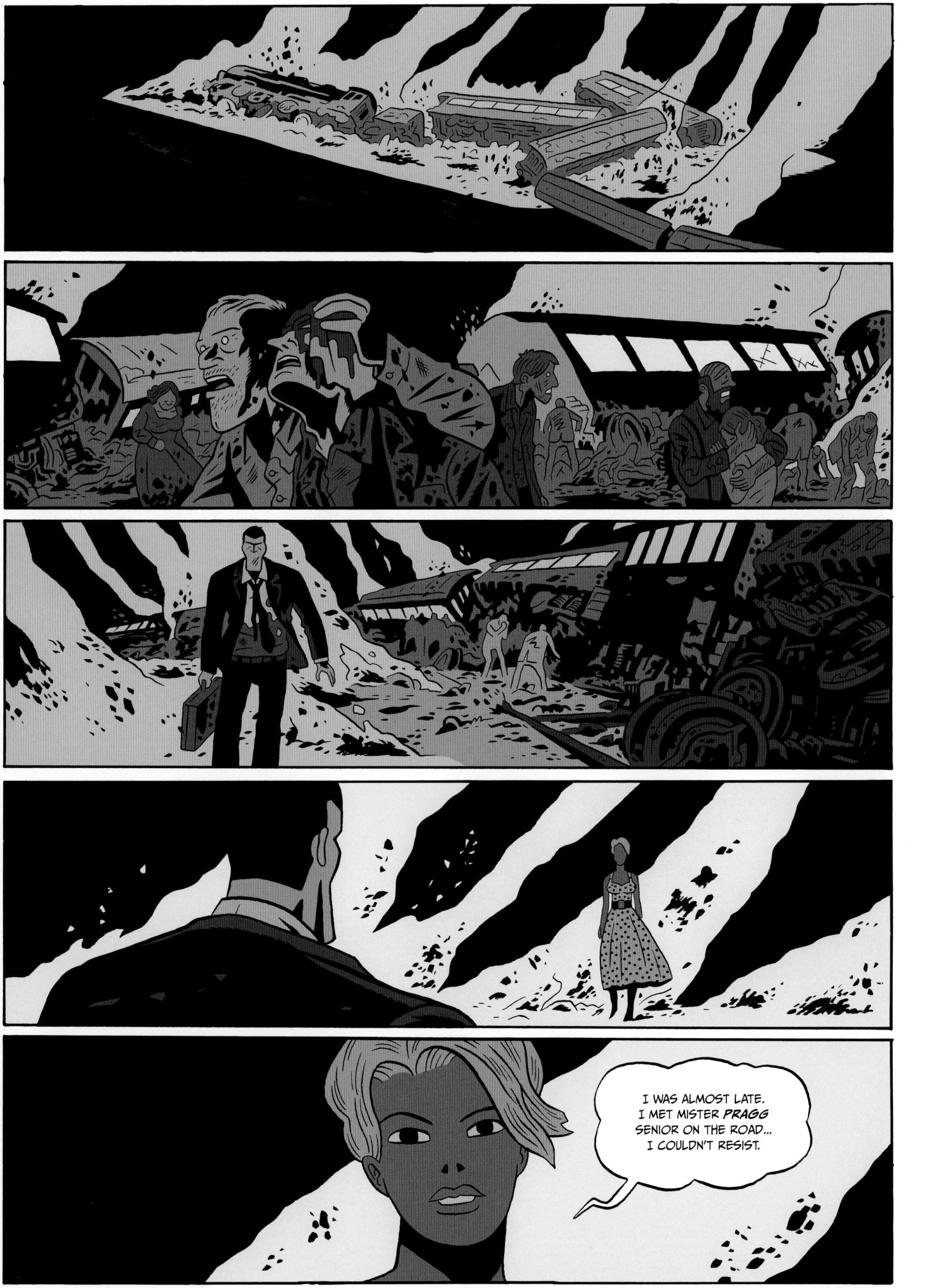
I WAS ALMOST LATE. I MET MISTER PRAGG SENIOR ON THE ROAD... I COULDN'T RESIST.

EPILOGUE

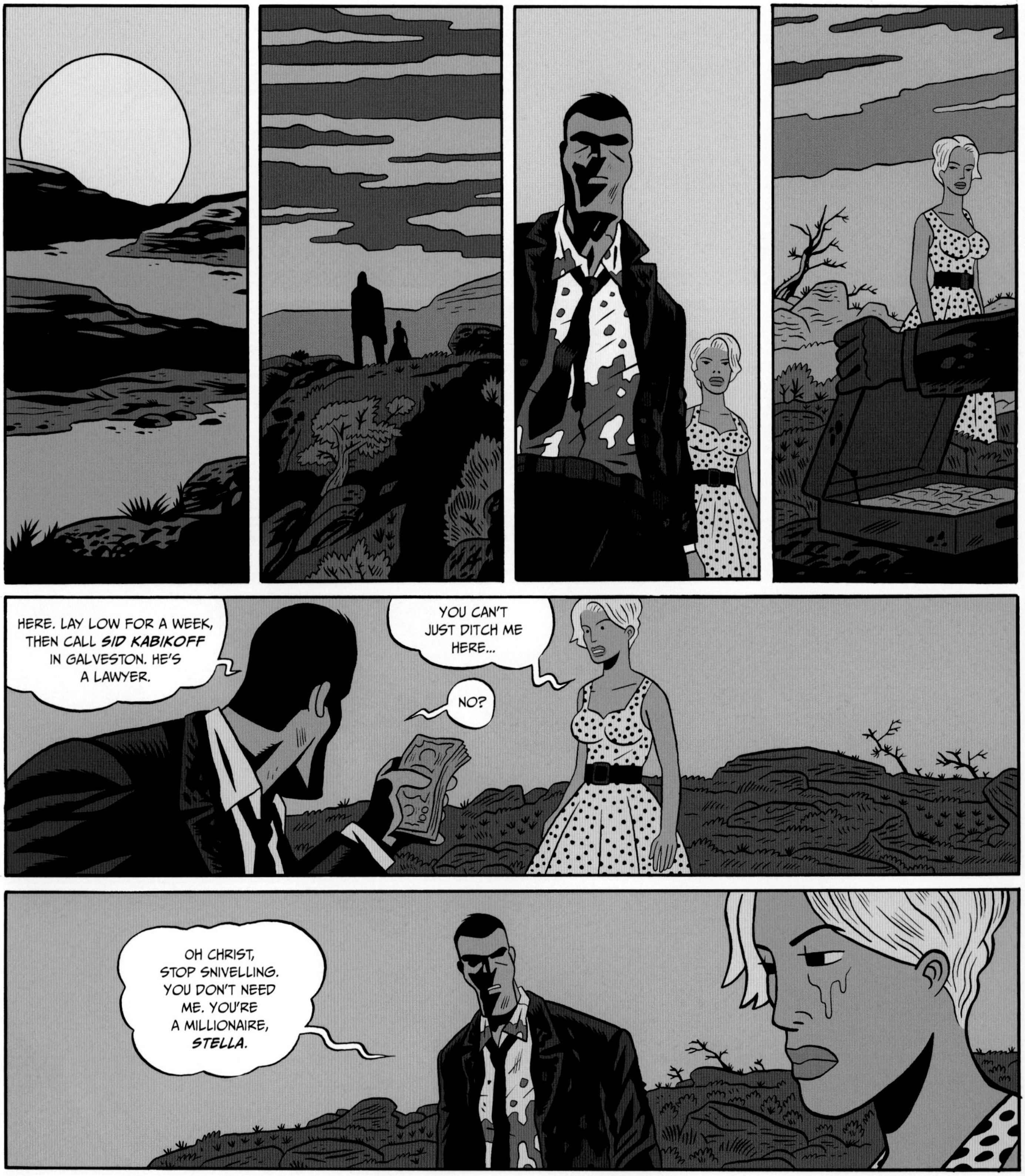
HERE. LAY LOW FOR A WEEK, THEN CALL SID KABIKOFF IN GALVESTON. HE'S A LAWYER.
YOU CAN'T JUST DITCH ME HERE...
NO?
OH CHRIST, STOP SNIVELLING. YOU DON'T NEED ME. YOU'RE A MILLIONAIRE, STELLA.

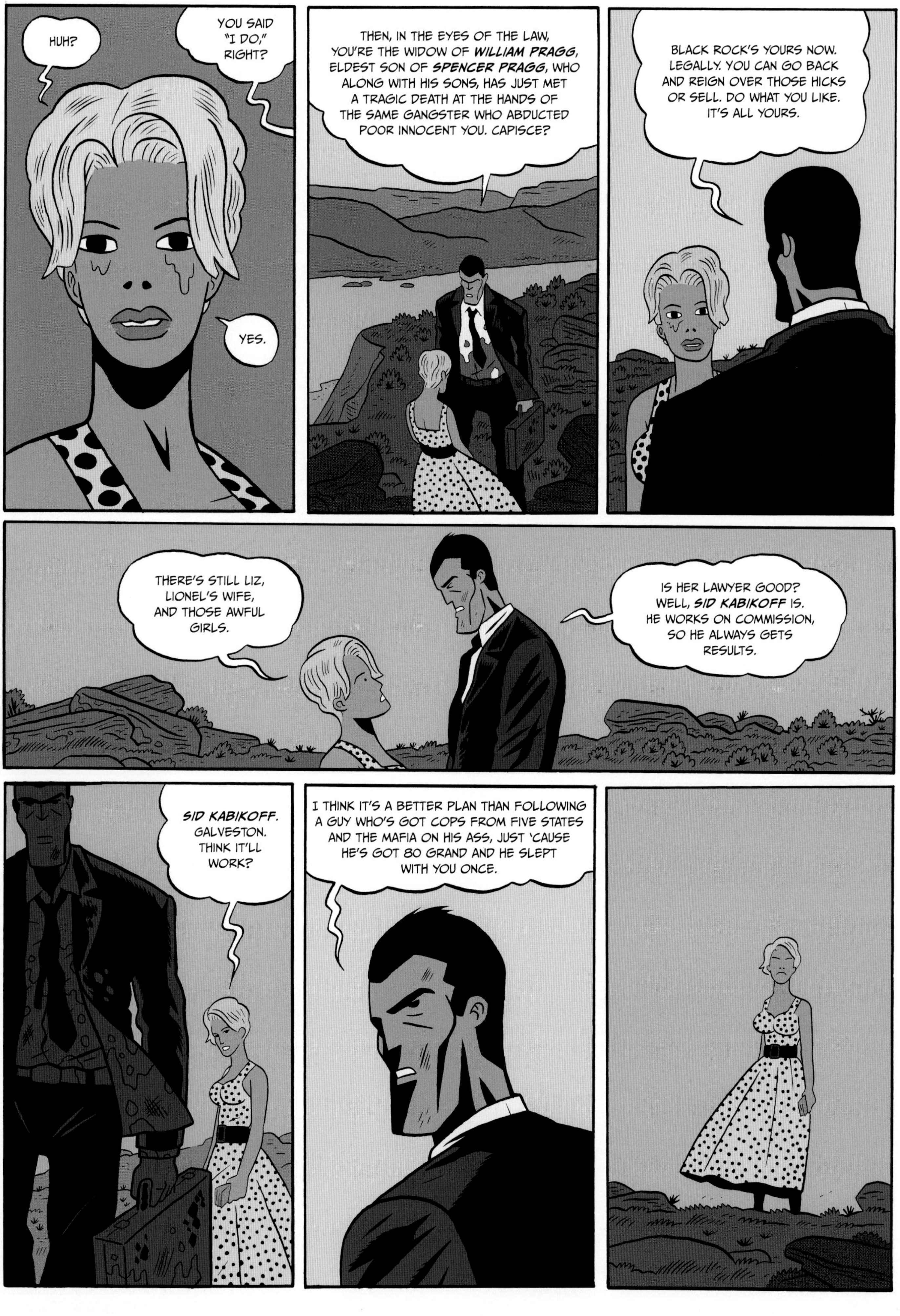
HUH?
YOU SAID "I DO," RIGHT?
YES.
THEN, IN THE EYES OF THE LAW, YOU'RE THE WIDOW OF **WILLIAM PRAGG**, ELDEST SON OF **SPENCER PRAGG**, WHO ALONG WITH HIS SONS, HAS JUST MET A TRAGIC DEATH AT THE HANDS OF THE SAME GANGSTER WHO ABDUCTED POOR INNOCENT YOU. CAPISCE?
BLACK ROCK'S YOURS NOW. LEGALLY. YOU CAN GO BACK AND REIGN OVER THOSE HICKS OR SELL. DO WHAT YOU LIKE. IT'S ALL YOURS.
THERE'S STILL LIZ, LIONEL'S WIFE, AND THOSE AWFUL GIRLS.
IS HER LAWYER GOOD? WELL, **SID KABIKOFF** IS. HE WORKS ON COMMISSION, SO HE ALWAYS GETS RESULTS.
SID KABIKOFF. GALVESTON. THINK IT'LL WORK?
I THINK IT'S A BETTER PLAN THAN FOLLOWING A GUY WHO'S GOT COPS FROM FIVE STATES AND THE MAFIA ON HIS ASS, JUST 'CAUSE HE'S GOT 80 GRAND AND HE SLEPT WITH YOU ONCE.

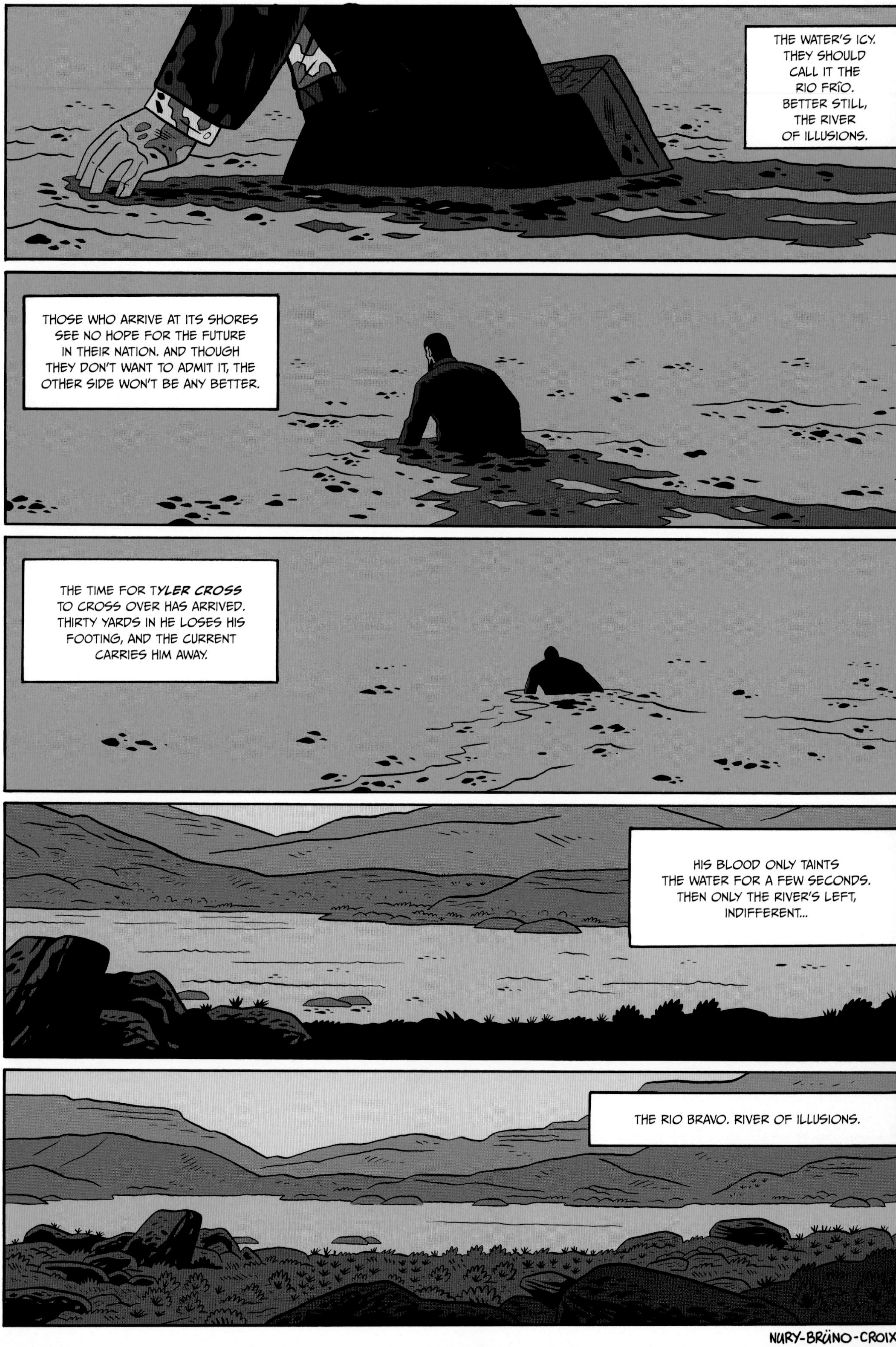
THE WATER'S ICY. THEY SHOULD CALL IT THE RIO FRÎO. BETTER STILL, THE RIVER OF ILLUSIONS.
THOSE WHO ARRIVE AT ITS SHORES SEE NO HOPE FOR THE FUTURE IN THEIR NATION. AND THOUGH THEY DON'T WANT TO ADMIT IT, THE OTHER SIDE WON'T BE ANY BETTER.
THE TIME FOR *TYLER CROSS* TO CROSS OVER HAS ARRIVED. THIRTY YARDS IN HE LOSES HIS FOOTING, AND THE CURRENT CARRIES HIM AWAY.
HIS BLOOD ONLY TAINTS THE WATER FOR A FEW SECONDS. THEN ONLY THE RIVER'S LEFT, INDIFFERENT...
THE RIO BRAVO. RIVER OF ILLUSIONS.
NURY-BRÜNO-CROIX

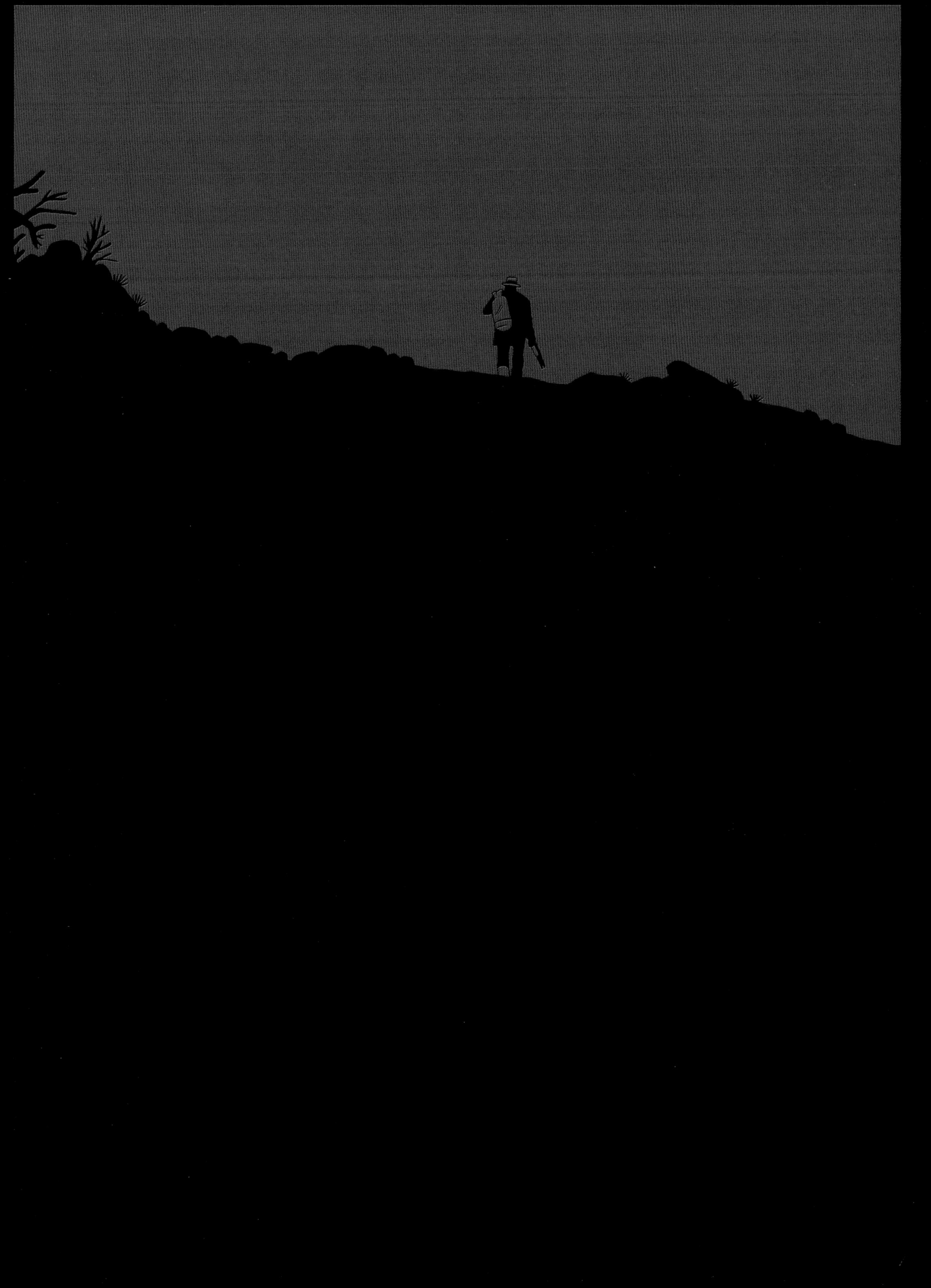

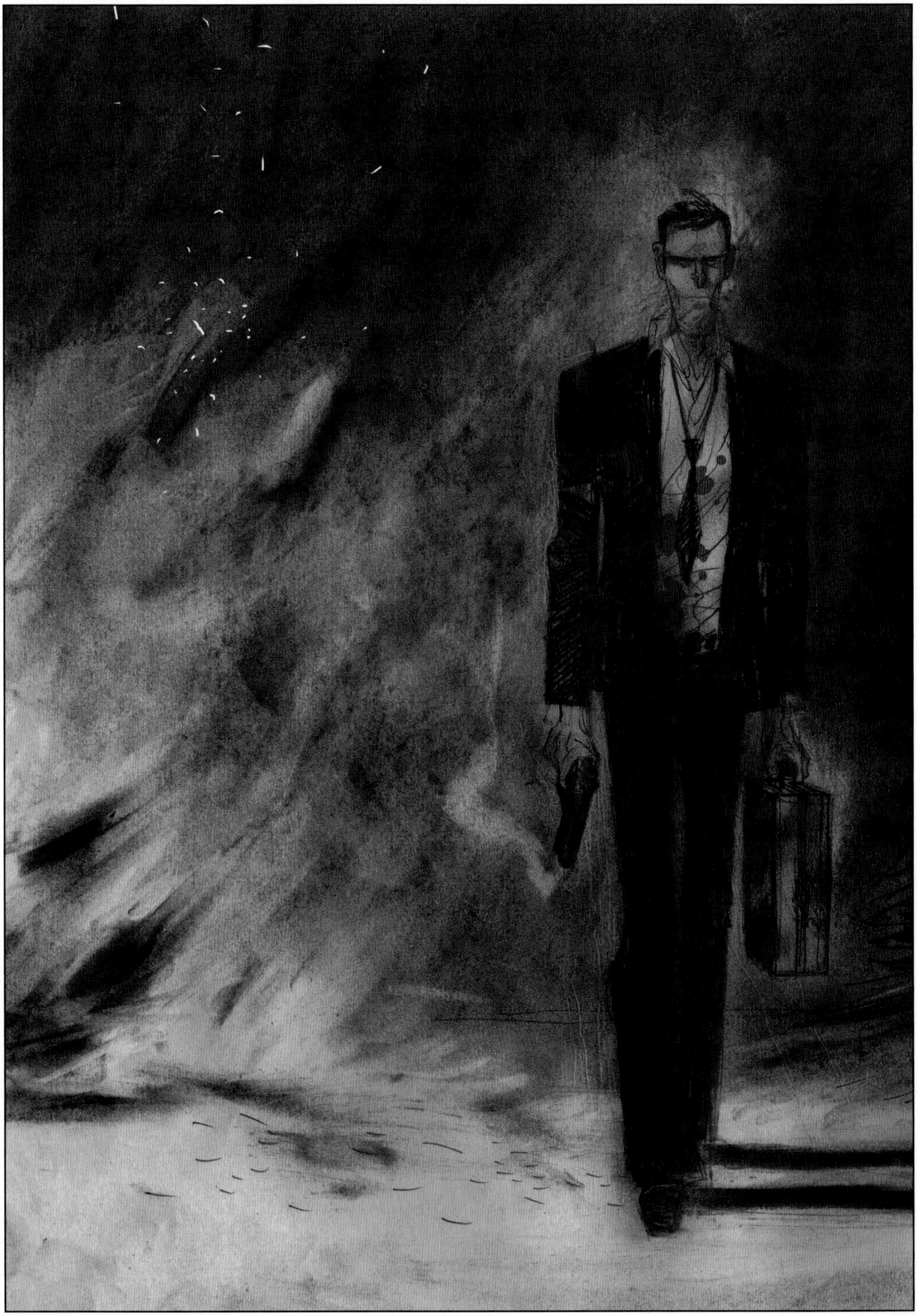

CYRIL PEDROSA

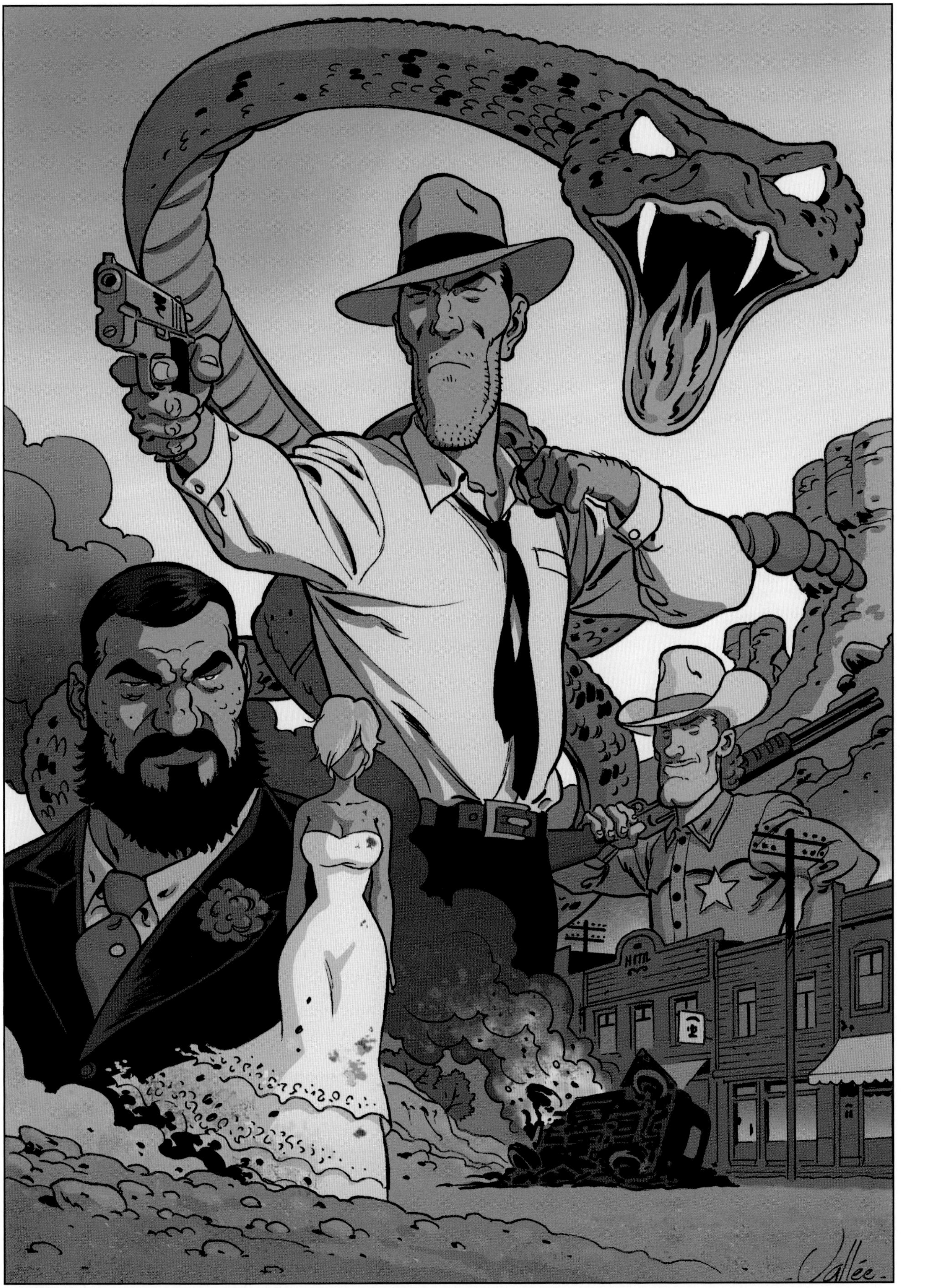

SYLVAIN VALLEE

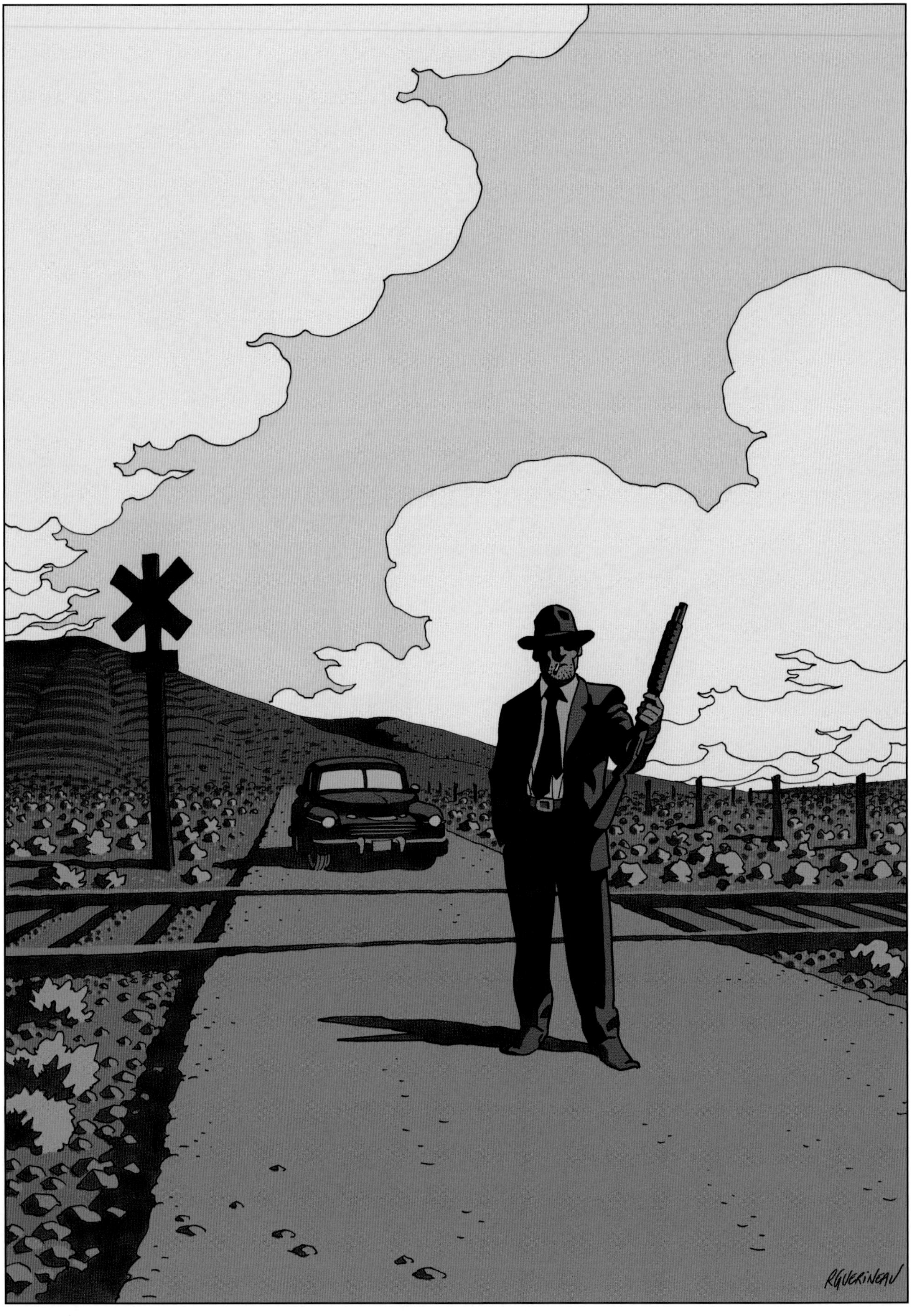
RGUERINEAU

RICHARD GUERINEAU

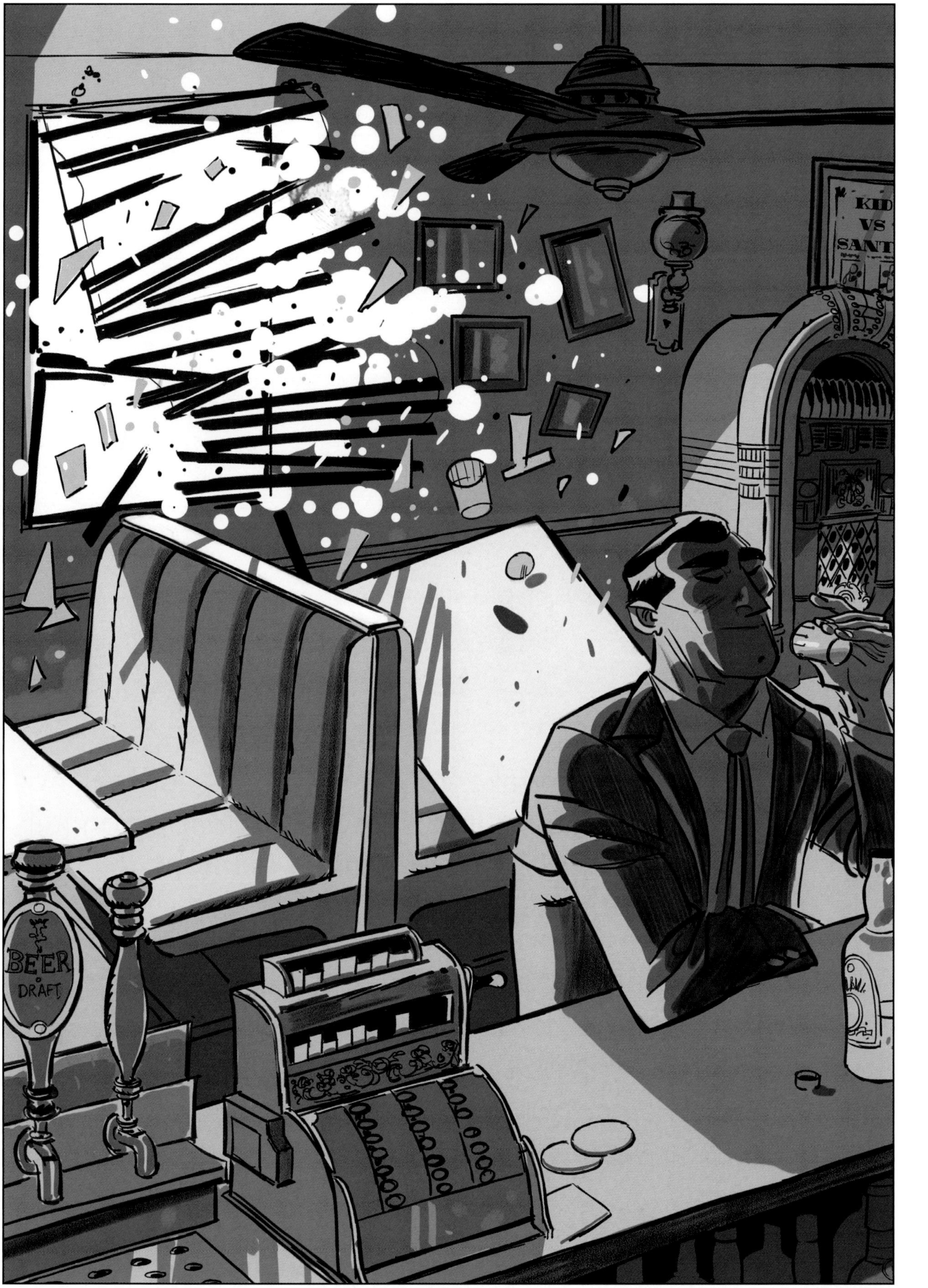
KID
VS
SANT
BEER
DRAFT

PIERRE ALARY

TYLER CROSS

ANGOLA

COMING SOON